# Gyles Brandreth

# WORD
# PLAY

A cornucopia of
puns, anagrams, euphemisms
& other contortions & curiosities
of the English language

# Also by Gyles Brandreth

*Novels*
Who Is Nick Saint?
Venice Midnight

*The Oscar Wilde Murder Mysteries*
Oscar Wilde and the Candlelight Murders
Oscar Wilde and the Ring of Death
Oscar Wilde and the Dead Man's Smile
Oscar Wilde and the Nest of Vipers
Oscar Wilde and the Vatican Murders
Oscar Wilde and the Murders at Reading Gaol

*Biography*
Dan Leno: The Funniest Man on Earth
John Gielgud: An Actor's Life
Brief Encounters: Meetings with Remarkable People
Philip & Elizabeth: Portrait of a Marriage
Charles & Camilla: Portrait of a Love Affair

*Autobiography & Diaries*
Under the Jumper
Breaking the Code: Westminster Diaries
Something Sensational to Read in the Train

*Selected Non-fiction*
Created in Captivity
I Scream for Ice Cream: Pearls from the Pantomime
Yarooh! A Feast of Frank Richards
The Joy of Lex and More Joy of Lex
The 7 Secrets of Happiness
The Lost Art of Having Fun (with Saethryd Brandreth)
Novelty Knits (with Saethryd Brandreth)

*Children's Fiction*
The Ghost at Number Thirteen and sequels
The Slippers That Talked and sequels
Nattie & Nuffin
Max: The Boy Who Made a Million
Maisie: The Girl Who Lost Her Head

*Theatre*
Lewis Carroll Through the Looking-Glass
Dear Ladies (with Hinge & Bracket)
Now We Are Sixty (with Julian Slade)
Zipp! 100 Musicals in 100 Minutes
The Last Photograph (with Susannah Pearse)

Gyles Brandreth

# WORD PLAY

A cornucopia of
puns, anagrams, euphemisms
& other contortions & curiosities
of the English language

CORONET

First published in Great Britain in 2015 by Coronet

An imprint of Hodder & Stoughton

An Hachette UK company

First published in paperback in 2016

1

A CIP catalogue record for this title is available from the British Library

Paperback ISBN: 978 1 473 62029 2
Ebook ISBN: 978 1 473 62031 5

Typeset in Adobe Garamond by Beachstone
www.beachstone.co.uk

Printed and bound by Clays Ltd, St Ives plc

Hodder & Stoughton policy is to use papers that are natural, renewable and recyclable products and made from wood grown in sustainable forests. The logging and manufacturing processes are expected to conform to the environmental regulations of the country of origin.

Hodder & Stoughton Ltd
Carmelite House
50 Victoria Embankment
London EC4Y 0DZ

www.hodder.co.uk

# Contents

'Words, words, words.'

William Shakespeare
*Hamlet*, Act II, Scene 2

# INTRODUCTION

The most frequently used words of introduction among English-speaking people are 'Hi', 'Hello', 'How are you?', 'Good to meet you' and 'How do you do?' in that order. So, 'Hi, hello, how are you, good to meet you, and how do you do?'

I am delighted that you are here. Thank you for opening the book, for a start. And thank you for looking at the introduction: apparently, around 60 per cent of readers don't. I am glad you did. I want to share with you my love of language and my passion for words.

Language is what defines us as human beings. As the philosopher Bertrand Russell remarked, 'No matter how eloquently a dog may bark, he cannot tell you that his parents were poor but honest.' Only words can do that. Words are magic.

In fact, with just one word – *Abracadabra* – you can conjure up a whole world of magic. With three words – *I love you* – you can change your life. Or, with half a dozen, ruin someone else's: *I don't love you after all.* Language is power. Many people reckon that Barack Obama became the forty-fourth president of the United States because of his way with words. Historians will tell you that Winston Churchill helped the Allies win the Second World War with the power of his oratory. In 1588, the English queen, Elizabeth I, delivered a speech to her troops, assembled at Tilbury to defend the country against a Spanish invasion. She told them: 'I know I have the body of a weak and feeble woman, but I have the heart and stomach of a king, and of a king of England too.'

That was almost four and a half centuries ago, but Elizabeth I's words are remembered still. That's the power of language. There's nothing else quite like it.

Elizabeth I, Winston Churchill, Barack Obama and I have a blessing in common: English is our native language and English, happily, is the *lingua franca* of the world. English is the parent tongue of 400 million people across the planet. English is the richest of the world's six thousand and more languages. *The Oxford English Dictionary* lists some 500,000 English words and there are at least half a million English-language technical terms you can add on top of that. Mandarin Chinese may have a vocabulary to rival that of English, but no other language comes near it. The Germans have a vocabulary of 185,000 words. The French have fewer than 100,000 – and that's including *le weekend, le snacque-barre* and *le feel-good*.

I was born in Germany, in a British forces hospital in Wuppertal. The first school I went to was the French Lycée in London. I speak a bit of German and a bit more French, but the English language is the love of my life. I don't mind music; I quite like the ballet; I enjoy painting; but words, to me, are *everything*.

I've been into words all my life. My first words (like most people's) were *Dada* and *Mama*. (Princess Margaret used to say that her son's first word was *chandelier*.) My mother was a gifted teacher; she specialised in working with children who had difficulty with language. She was born and brought up in India and, to the end of her days, peppered her conversation with Indian words and phrases. Quite a few of them feature in the pages that follow. My father was a lawyer, at different times a solicitor and a barrister. (Recently I told a young Australian that my father had been a barrister. 'Where did he work then?' he asked. 'Starbucks? Costa?') My father was born in July 1910. He missed out on being an Edwardian by just six weeks (it was a lifelong disappointment for him) and harked back to the good old days when families entertained themselves in the parlour, playing word games and declaiming popular poetry by the fireside. He knew reams of verse by heart and the Victorian amusements that you will find later in the book are all his favourites.

When I was thirteen, my parents sent me to a boarding school in Hampshire called Bedales. There, my love of language was encouraged by an inspirational English teacher (Harold Gardiner), a remarkable drama teacher (Rachel Field) and by the school's founder (John Badley), who was one hundred years old when I knew him. Mr Badley had been a contemporary of Oscar Wilde, and Oscar's elder son, Cyril, had been a pupil at Bedales. Oscar Wilde, of course, had an amazing way with words. I asked Mr Badley if it was true (as Bernard Shaw said) that Oscar Wilde was the 'greatest talker of his time, perhaps of all time'. Mr Badley told me Wilde's 'secret': 'He could listen as well as talk. He put himself out to be entertaining. He said, "Murder is always a mistake. One should never do anything that one cannot talk about at dinner." He was a delightful person, charming and brilliant, with the most perfect manners of any man I ever met. Because of his imprisonment and disgrace he is seen nowadays as a tragic figure. That should not be his lasting memorial. I knew him quite well. He was such fun.'

Mr Badley was fun, too. For two years, every Wednesday afternoon during term time, I would have tea with him at his cottage in the school grounds and play Scrabble with him. The centenarian won every game we played. I told him he was cheating, using obsolete words. He told me, 'They were current when I learnt them.'

Bedales was a school with a theatrical bent. Laurence Olivier sent his children there. Daniel Day-Lewis went there. When I was about thirteen, the actor Donald Sinden came to look round the school and I was his guide. Over the years, I came to know Sir Donald quite well. He was a great man, very funny, and a wonderful Shakespearean actor. He relished language and taught me the importance of diction. 'Words are no good,' he'd say, 'if people can't hear them.' His rule was: 'Vowels for volume, consonants for clarity.' He taught me his 'vocal warm-up' exercise.

Head up, chest out and repeat after me:
*Hip bath, hip bath, lavatory, lavatory, bidet, bidet, douche!*
*Hip bath, hip bath, lavatory, lavatory, bidet, bidet, douche!*
*Hip bath, hip bath, lavatory, lavatory, bidet, bidet, douche!*

Donald Sinden showed me how to value and enjoy the sound of words. His exact contemporary, Dr Robert Burchfield, showed me how to value and enjoy discovering their meaning. Dr Burchfield was a lexicographer from New Zealand, and for thirty years, until 1986, he was the editor of

*The Oxford English Dictionary.* I met him in 1971 when I founded the
National Scrabble Championships and asked him to be the competition's
official adjudicator. He explained to me that the people who compile
dictionaries are there to record words and their meanings: they are not
there to sit in judgement on them. He also kindly gave me the complete
*OED* – all fourteen volumes of it, including supplements – and, as you
will discover, I have been busy leafing through it while writing *Word Play*.
I love delving into dictionaries. When I play Scrabble (or Bananagrams or
Lexicon), I want to know the meaning of the words I use.

In the same year that I founded the Scrabble Championships, I hosted my
first radio series for the BBC. It was called *A Rhyme in Time* and – guess?
Yes! Bless – it was all about words that rhyme. Or don't. (See the chapter
on Potted Poetry, page 261.) For more than forty years since then I have
been playing word games on radio and TV. I particularly enjoyed *Call My
Bluff*, hosted by Robert Robinson, with Frank Muir and Patrick Campbell
as the team captains. The idea of the game was a simple one. Here's a word
and here's a definition of that word. Is the definition the real one or is it a
bluff? For example:

Yex

*Is it a witches' curse?*
*Is it to belch or hiccup?*
*Is it part of a horse's leg?*

If you don't know the answer, you can dig into your dictionary now or
wait until I reveal it later in the book. And if you want to play *Call My
Bluff* at home you should find a fair few words you can use in wordplay.
I am hoping to introduce you to some interesting ones you may not have
come across before.

Frank Muir introduced me to television and so, in a way, helped shape my
life. Through his good offices, in 1969, while I was still a student, I hosted
my own show for ITV called *Child of the Sixties.* Frank was a funny man –
though Patrick Campbell always thought he talked too much. Once, when
I was appearing on *Call My Bluff*, Frank was telling us – at some length

– how he had recently been made president of his local rifle club. Patrick Campbell murmured, 'Small bore, I imagine.'

Over the years I have appeared in scores of panel games on radio and TV, and even devised a few, but for me one stands way above the crowd: *Just A Minute*. The idea could not be simpler: you are given a subject and invited to talk about it for sixty seconds without hesitating, without repeating any words or phrases and without deviating from the subject. *Just A Minute* is fun to play – and exciting, too, recorded in real time and against the clock.

I have been taking part in *Just A Minute* since 1982 and the only rule I have is not to try to tell jokes: invariably you trip up as you get towards the punch-line. The late Clement Freud holds the record as the game's most frequent winner. He was the master of coming up with a challenge with just three seconds to go and utterly ruthless as a player. If you sat next to him, he would find all sorts of ways of distracting you if he sensed you were about to make a challenge. Once, deliberately, he spilt a glass of water over me just as I was hitting my stride.

In the early years, Kenneth Williams was the undoubted star of the show. Kenneth still holds the record as the player to have achieved the largest number of uninterrupted minutes in *Just A Minute*, ahead of Clement Freud and Derek Nimmo. (I am at number seven, I think, sandwiched between Sue Perkins and Sheila Hancock.)

Some assumed that when Kenneth Williams died the programme would die with him. Not so. A whole new generation of funny folk is now playing the game and it is being produced by bright young things who weren't even alive when the programme was first broadcast in 1967. Over the years there have been around 900 editions and more than 220 players, but just two constants. One is Ian Messiter's simple format. The other is the chairman, Nicholas Parsons, who has not missed a single recording in nearly half a century. Now in his nineties, Parsons is still at the top of his game, encouraging newcomers, disciplining the obstreperous, and getting his own laughs without failing to listen (with remarkable accuracy) to everything that everybody says on the show. Indeed, I reckon he is as sharp as he is thanks to *Just A Minute*. *Word Play* keeps the mind alive.

Nicholas and I are old friends with a fellow-feeling for words. In the 1980s we even shared an entry in *The Guinness Book of Records* as joint holders of the record for making the longest after-dinner speech. In adjacent rooms, at London's Hyde Park Hotel, we talked non-stop for eleven hours. (We were doing it for charity, I hasten to add. We were sponsored. The listeners were, too.)

My favourite television word game has also made it to *The Guinness Book of Records*. In 2015, after thirty-three years, seventy series and six thousand episodes, Channel 4's *Countdown* is now, officially, the most successful game show in television history.

Why? It's a show without razzmatazz, big money prizes or hysterical contestants. What's going on? On the screen, not much. All that happens is that two members of the public are given paper, pencil and thirty seconds in which to arrange nine randomly selected letters of the alphabet into the longest word they can think of. That's it. Oh, yes, there's an arithmetical round as well, involving addition, subtraction, multiplication and division. And an anagram race, where you have to turn PROCEDURE into REPRODUCE against the clock. (Or EDUCATION into AUCTIONED. You get the idea.) That really is it. And if you win the game, you get a teapot. If you win the series, you get a trophy and a leather-bound edition of *The Oxford English Dictionary*.

Each year thousands write in wanting to take part in the programme and millions sit glued to their TV sets watching the show, as though it were a sunrise over Mount Kilimanjaro. What makes this cosy tea-time TV so compelling? As one of the guests who sits in *Countdown*'s Dictionary Corner (in fact the guest who has sat there most often), I have been involved in the show since it began and I can tell you. It's got nothing to do with the charm of the presenters or the hypnotic beat of the *Countdown* clock. It's simply that this is the one show on television that involves viewer participation from start to finish.

As you will discover on page 349, when the crossword puzzle first appeared in the *New York World* in 1913, it quickly became a craze that swept the planet. Today there is hardly a newspaper on earth that does not carry a crossword. The word game on *Countdown* is the TV equivalent of the crossword and the numbers game is the goggle-box Sudoku. For forty-five minutes each afternoon, viewers sit down, paper and pencil in hand, forget the world outside, exercise their little grey cells and play the game. It's a habit, a relaxation and a fix.

The words and numbers puzzles in the show are variations of the sorts of parlour entertainment our Victorian forebears enjoyed. The *Countdown* format itself was invented by a French TV producer, Armand Jammot, in the mid-1960s. It was brought to Britain by a Belgian record producer, Marcel Stellman, whose other claim to fame was writing the English lyrics for the song 'Tulips From Amsterdam'. Stellman sold it to Yorkshire TV in Leeds who initially aired it as a local programme, featuring Yorkshire farmers as contestants, with a celebrity farmer, Ted Moult, sitting in Dictionary Corner.

In November 1982, when Channel 4 took to the airwaves, they picked up the show and broadcast it as their opening programme, with Yorkshire's regional news anchorman, Richard Whiteley, as the host. Until then Richard's only moment of national notoriety had been the time he was attacked in the studio by a ferret. Thanks to *Countdown*, Richard (five foot nine, fourteen and a half stone), with his trademark loud jackets, louder ties, and appalling puns, became one of the nation's unlikeliest cult figures, profiled in a raft of men's magazines (*FHM*, *Maxim*, *Loaded*), honoured by the *Oldie* ('Most Inexplicable Survivor'), given a macho make-over by *Woman's Own* and inducted into the *Lady*'s Hall of Fame.

We were good friends and I loved him for the way he loved his own programme's success. As well as appearing on it, he watched it every day – with a cup of tea and a KitKat. 'Bliss,' he'd say. 'Students watch *Countdown*,' he told me. 'Grannies watch *Countdown*. When I met Princess Margaret she said, "I do believe my sister watches it after the racing." I thought, "Who's her sister?" Then I realised. She meant the Queen.'

Yes, the Queen enjoys *Countdown* – and 'doing the crossword'. Her Majesty enjoys wordplay and, of course, by definition, she speaks the Queen's English. I try to speak the Queen's English, too. I am even patron of the Queen's English Society. We are a group of oddballs who think good English matters. We are not purists: we love the variety and richness of the English language, but it upsets some of us when people say *Febuary* when they mean *February* and *drawring* when they mean *drawing*. We don't like things *done quicker*: we prefer them *done more quickly*. And we like to receive an *invitation* rather than an *invite*.

At the Queen's English Society we love the language, vagaries and all, and in our journal, *Quest*, we dare to ask those difficult linguistic questions to which no one yet seems to have come up with a satisfactory answer. Why is it that writers write, but fingers don't fing, grocers don't groce and hammers don't ham, for example? If the plural of 'tooth' is 'teeth', why isn't 'beeth' the plural of 'booth'? It's odd that you can make amends, but not one amend. And if you get rid of all but one of your odds and ends, what do you call what you are left with?

If teachers taught, why didn't preachers praught? Why is a boxing ring square? Why do people recite at a play and play at a recital? Why do we have noses that run and feet that smell? It's very confusing, isn't it? A slim chance and a fat chance are the same thing, really, but a wise man and a wise guy aren't the same at all, are they? When the stars are out, they are visible. When the lights are out, they are invisible. What's up?

In fact, why do we use the word *up* as much as we do? What are we *up* to? We lock *up* the house, we speak *up* at the meeting, stir *up* trouble and then it's *up* to the secretary to write *up* the report. We work *up* an appetite, we think *up* excuses. We open *up* the shop in the morning and close it *up* at night. When it comes to *up*, we're pretty mixed *up*. Okay, Gyles, we get the idea: time to shut *up*.

If you want to know more about the Queen's English Society, look here: www.queens-english-society.org. If you want to join me on my roller-coaster ride over the ups and downs of the English language, read on. (You will even discover the origin of *okay*. OK?*)* This is an A to Z (and back to A) of my kind of wordplay. Pulling it all together, I have had a lot of fun and I have learnt a great deal, too. For example, I now know that just two words, 'I' and 'you', represent 10 per cent of all informal conversation. The other four dozen words we most often use in spoken English are these:

| | | |
|---|---|---|
| the | will | for |
| he | don't | out |
| it | are | over |
| they | can | about |
| him | go | just |
| them | say | that |
| an | see | is |
| to | tell | was |
| in | a | have |
| with | she | do |
| from | we | want |
| and | me | would |
| now | her | think |
| not | what | be |
| this | on | know |
| get | of | thing |

Surprisingly, *up* isn't in the list. Clearly we need to raise our game. Or *up* it.

We can get by with a very limited range of words – helped out by gestures, grunts, groans and occasional expletives – but to get the best out of life you need words. All the research shows that the more effectively people use the language the more successful and the happier they are.

As far as I'm concerned, when it comes to words, the more the merrier. I want us to use more words: different words, bolder words, better words, old words and new words, surprising and delightful words. Funny and ridiculous words, too. Now and then. The great English actress Dame Sybil Thorndike (who lived to be ninety-three) kept her mind agile by learning a poem by heart every day of her adult life. If you can't find the time to learn a poem a day, try learning a word a day instead. Look it up in the dictionary, memorise it and bring it into your daily conversation – and your wordplay. Playing with words will increase your vocabulary, willy-nilly. And will help you live longer by keeping your wits about you – like Sybil Thorndike and the Queen and Nicholas Parsons.

*Willy-nilly*, by the way, comes from the Old English phrase *Will ye or will ye not?* Did you know that? You didn't? Well, there you go. I've saved you looking it up. (Why do we say that? You're looking down at the dictionary and your eye goes down the page to find the word, so why on earth are you looking it *up*?)

Welcome to my world of *Word Play*. Enjoy. Yolo.

# A

### is for

### ALPHABET SOUP

In 1867, not long after the end of the American Civil War, the *Tri-Weekly Standard* in Raleigh, North Carolina, became the first newspaper in the world to report on a new type of food:

> The latest culinary novelty is alphabetical soup. Instead of the usual cylindric and star shaped morsels of macaroni which have hitherto given body to our broth, the letters of the alphabet have been substituted. These letters of paste preserve their forms in passing through the pot.

In my book words are good enough to eat. I love them, which is why I collect them. And, for starters, let me offer you a tasty selection of a few of my favourites: words that have extraordinary and curious (and, to me, *nourishing*) qualities that have nothing to do with their meaning. Each one, in its own way, is something of a phenomenon.

. . . . . . . . . . . . . . . . . . . . . . . . . . . . . . . . . . . . . . . . .

## THE SHORTEST WORDS

*A* is the first word in the dictionary, one of the shortest words in the language, and the fifth most common word in English literature.

In written English the ten words most used are:

| the | of | and | to | a |
|-----|-----|-----|-----|-----|
| in | that | is | I | it |

The shortest English word that contains all the vowels is *eunoia.* It means 'beautiful thinking', and I think it is a rather beautiful word.

In a recent survey, the word voted the 'most liked' in the language was *lullaby.*

. . . . . . . . . . . . . . . . . . . . . . . . . . . . . . . . . . . . . . . . .

## THE LONGEST WORDS

29 Letters: *floccinaucinihilipilification*
This is the longest non-technical word in *The Oxford English Dictionary*. It means 'the act of estimating as worthless' and dates from 1741.

34 Letters: *supercalifragilisticexpialidocious*
This is a nonsense word invented for the movie *Mary Poppins* (1964). In the whole history of language, no word of more than thirty letters has ever been so widely known.

37 Letters: *praetertranssubstantiationalistically*
An adverb used in Mark McShane's novel *Untimely Ripped* (1963).

45 Letters: *pneumonoultramicroscopicsilicovolcanoconiosis*
The longest word in *The Oxford English Dictionary*. It is the name of a

miner's lung disease and was deliberately coined to be the longest word in the dictionary.

100 Letters: ***babababadalgharaghtakamminarronnkonnbronntonnerronn-tuonnthunntrovarrhu-nawnskawntoohoohoordenenthurnuk***
From the third paragraph of James Joyce's novel *Finnegans Wake* (1939).

1,913 Letters: The full name of the chemical tryptophan synthetase, a protein whose formula is $C_{1289}H_{2051}N_{343}O_{375}S_8$

. . . . . . . . . . . . . . . . . . . . . . . . . . . . . . . . . . . . . . . . . . . . . . .

## LONGEST WORDS WITH DIFFERENT LETTERS

At fifteen letters each, these are the two longest words with unique letters (i.e. no letter is repeated):

*uncopyrightable* and *dermatoglyphics*

. . . . . . . . . . . . . . . . . . . . . . . . . . . . . . . . . . . . . . . . . . . . . . .

## LONGEST ENGLISH WORD CONSISTING ONLY OF VOWELS

*Euouae* is a medieval mnemonic (see page 283) used to recall the musical tones required when chanting the *Gloria Patri*.

It also takes the title as the English word with the most consecutive vowels. Words with five consecutive vowels include *cooeeing* and *queueing*.

. . . . . . . . . . . . . . . . . . . . . . . . . . . . . . . . . . . . . . . . . . . . . . .

## CONSONANT AFTER CONSONANT

*Archchronicler*, *catchphrase*, *eschscholzia* (sea snails of a sort), *latchstring*, *lengthsman* and the medical term *postphthisic* each have six consonants in a row.

*Borschts* has six consonants in a row in just one syllable.

Words with five consecutive consonants include: *angsts*, *birthplace*, *dumbstruck*, *eighths*, *heartthrob*, *lengths*, *postscript*, *strengths*, *thumbscrew*, *twelfths*, *warmths*, *witchcraft*.

. . . . . . . . . . . . . . . . . . . . . . . . . . . . . . . . . . . . . . . . . . . .

## LONGEST WORD WITH STRICTLY ALTERNATING VOWELS AND CONSONANTS

### *honorificabilitudinitatibus*

At twenty-seven letters it means 'with honourableness'. It is also the longest word that appears in *The Complete Works of William Shakespeare*.

The longest everyday word with this unusual property is **unimaginatively**, with fifteen letters.

. . . . . . . . . . . . . . . . . . . . . . . . . . . . . . . . . . . . . . . . . . . .

## LONGEST WORD WITH ONLY ONE VOWEL

*Strengths* is nine letters long. Strengthlessnesses, at eighteen letters, is the longest word in the English language with only one vowel repeated.

. . . . . . . . . . . . . . . . . . . . . . . . . . . . . . . . . . . . . . . . . . . .

## LONGEST WORD WITH LETTERS IN ALPHABETICAL ORDER

*Aegilops*. The word has two distinct meanings: it can be a genus of goat grass or a stye in the inner corner of an eye.

. . . . . . . . . . . . . . . . . . . . . . . . . . . . . . . . . . . . . . . . . . .

## LONGEST WORD WITH LETTERS IN REVERSE ALPHABETICAL ORDER

*spoonfeed*

. . . . . . . . . . . . . . . . . . . . . . . . . . . . . . . . . . . . . . . . . . .

## LONGEST WORD IN WHICH EACH LETTER OCCURS AT LEAST TWICE

*unprosperousness*

. . . . . . . . . . . . . . . . . . . . . . . . . . . . . . . . . . . . . . . . . . .

## LONGEST ENGLISH PALINDROMIC WORD

*tattarrattat*

This palindrome (see page 243) is an authorism (see page 34) coined by the great Irish writer James Joyce. It first appeared in his novel *Ulysses* in 1922.

. . . . . . . . . . . . . . . . . . . . . . . . . . . . . . . . . . . . . . . . . . .

## REPEAT AFTER ME

The *chincherinchee* is a beautiful plant found in South Africa. The word *chincherinchee* is the only known English word that has one letter occurring once, two letters occurring twice, and three letters occurring three times.

*Ultrarevolutionaries* is a word in which each of the five main vowels occurs twice.

. . . . . . . . . . . . . . . . . . . . . . . . . . . . . . . . . . . . . . . . . . . .

## MUSICAL WORDS

*Cabbaged* and *fabaceae*, each with eight letters, are the longest words that can be played on a musical instrument – i.e. using only the letters of the notes, A, B, C, D, E, F and G. Seven-letter words with this property include *acceded*, *baggage*, *cabbage*, *defaced* and *effaced*.

. . . . . . . . . . . . . . . . . . . . . . . . . . . . . . . . . . . . . . . . . . . .

## ALPHABETICALS

*Aegilops*, with eight letters, is the longest word whose letters are arranged in alphabetical order. Seven-letter words with this property include *beefily* and *billowy*. Six-letter words include *abhors*, *accent*, *access*, *almost*, *biopsy*, *bijoux*, *billow*, *chintz* and *effort*.

. . . . . . . . . . . . . . . . . . . . . . . . . . . . . . . . . . . . . . . . . . . .

## VOWEL PLAY

*Caesious* ('having a waxy, bluish-grey coating'), with eight letters, is the shortest word in the English language containing all five main vowels in alphabetical order.

There are not many words in the language that contain all five main vowels in reverse order. The ten-letter *unoriental* is one; the fourteen-letter *subcontinental* is another; *uncomplimentary*, at fifteen letters, is a third. At seven letters, *suoidea* (they are pigs of a sort) is the shortest word in the English language that contains the main five vowels in reverse alphabetical order.

*Facetiously*, eleven letters long, is the shortest word in the English language that contains all six vowels in alphabetical order. *Abstemiously* does the same, but runs to twelve letters. *Adventitiously* at fourteen letters does it, too, but with repeated vowels.

*Twyndyllyngs* (an old word for twins), at twelve letters long, is the longest word in the English language without any of the five main vowels. An eleven-letter word with this property is the singular form, *twyndyllyng*. An eight-letter word with this property is *symphysy*. It's a useful word, too, favoured by the writers of literary erotic fiction. It means the fusion of two bodies – or two parts of the body. And *symphysy* leads us nicely to two seven-letter words that don't feature any of the five main vowels: *nymphly* and *rhythms*.

## WORDS THAT BEAR REPEATING

Linguistic hotshots will recognise immediately that the word *hotshots* consists of the same four letters repeated. There are other eight-letter words that have the same property – all worth looking up, one to beware of and several worth tasting:

> *beriberi, caracara, chowchow, couscous, froufrou, greegree, guitguit, kavakava, lavalava, mahimahi, matamata.*

## A B C , X Y Z

*Crabcake* and *drabcloth* are among the very few everyday English words that contain the letters *abc*. *Hydroxyzine* is the only word in the English language that contains *xyz*.

The longest alphabetic sequences to appear in English words are *mnop* and *rstu*. *Mnop* appears in *gymnophiona* (worm-like sightless amphibians) and *somnopathy* (sleep that is induced sympathetically: what a hypnotist might do for you). *Rstu* appears more frequently, for example in *overstudy*, *overstuff*, *superstud*, and *understudy*.

. . . . . . . . . . . . . . . . . . . . . . . . . . . . . . . . . . . . . . . . . . .

## THE WORD WITH THE MOST MEANINGS

The English word with the most individual meanings is *set*. *The Oxford English Dictionary* lists 430 separate definitions for *set*. And *set* also sets the record for the longest entry in the dictionary at 60,000 words.

. . . . . . . . . . . . . . . . . . . . . . . . . . . . . . . . . . . . . . . . . . .

## SEEING DOUBLE

*Subbookkeeper* is the only English word with four pairs of double letters in a row. *Assessee* and *keelless* are the shortest words with three pairs of double letters.

*Cooee* is the shortest word in the English language with two double letters.

When the playwright Noël Coward was introduced to one of these remarkable word wonders, he murmured appreciatively, 'You live and learn.' After a moment's thought, he added: 'Then, of course, you die and forget it all.'

# B

### is for

### BRAVE NEW WORDS

The English language is rich because it isn't pure. It's a mongrel tongue. Ralph Waldo Emerson called it 'the sea which receives tributaries from every region under heaven'. It has taken almost two thousand years to evolve. The Celts, Jutes, Angles, Saxons, Greeks, Romans, Danes, Normans, Dutch, Germans, French, Spanish, Italians, Indians, Native Americans, Africans, Welsh and Hawaiians – to name just a few – made major contributions. So did some of my favourite authors.

Did you know the original 'Nerd' was a character in Dr Zeuss's 1950 children's book, *If I Ran the Zoo*? Or that the poet, daffodil fancier and hill walker William Wordsworth coined the word 'pedestrians'? The best writers don't just play with words: they invent them.

. . . . . . . . . . . . . . . . . . . . . . . . . . . . . . . . . . . . . . . . . . . . . . . . . . . . .

## CHAUCER'S CHOICE

The granddaddy of English verbal invention is Geoffrey Chaucer, philosopher, alchemist, astronomer, author of *The Canterbury Tales* and the man John Dryden called the 'Father of English Poetry'. Chaucer was born around 1340 and died in 1400. *The Oxford English Dictionary* credits him with the first known use of more English words than any other writer: 2,012 to be precise.

Of course, the trick is to create words that stand the test of time. In the 1920s, in New Orleans, 'muggle' was a slang word for marijuana. In our time, J. K. Rowling, in her Harry Potter books, has turned a 'muggle' into someone who lacks all magical powers. What will 'muggle' mean, if anything, seven hundred years from now?

The genius of Chaucer is that so many of his words from the fourteenth century still count for something. 'Twitter', the onomatopoeic word for birdsong, which has become the byword for modern communication, was one of his. (Feel free to let me know your thoughts on this. You will find me on Twitter @GylesB1.)

Here are some more choice Chaucerisms, words that first appeared in his works but still work for us:

| | | | | |
|---|---|---|---|---|
| agree | sperm | possibility | plumage | future |
| galaxy | praise | laxative | femininity | dismember |
| womanhood | funeral | misery | jolliness | village |
| princess | magician | dung-cart | | |

. . . . . . . . . . . . . . . . . . . . . . . . . . . . . . . . . . . . . . . . . . . . . .

## SHAKESPEARE & CO

William Shakespeare (1564–1616) comes second in terms of the sheer volume of words he is credited with originating: 1,700 of them.

Many of Shakespeare's 'new' words were created by using existing nouns as verbs, verbs as adjectives, reframing their original meanings, adding prefixes, suffixes or simply taking the Latin derivatives and playing around with them to come up with something a little bit different. If you count all the variants of the same word – for example, 'love', 'loves', 'loving', 'loved', 'lovest' – Shakespeare in all his works has a vocabulary of just over 29,000 words. If you discount the grammatical variations, his basic vocab was between 17,000 and 20,000 words.

Of course, like Chaucer before him, Shakespeare gets the credit for words he did not necessarily invent. He might have invented them – or simply have been the guy who first put them down on paper. Here are some of the words first found in Shakespeare and the plays in which we first encounter them:

*addiction*
HENRY V

*advertising*
MEASURE FOR MEASURE

*amazement*
THE TEMPEST

*assassination*
MACBETH

*bandit*
TITUS ANDRONICUS

*barefaced*
HENRY VI, PART 2

*bedroom*
A MIDSUMMER NIGHT'S DREAM

*besmirch*
HAMLET

*birthplace*
CORIOLANUS

*blanket*
KING LEAR

*bloodstained*
HAMLET

*blushing*
HENRY VI, PART 3

*bump*
ROMEO AND JULIET

*champion*
MACBETH

*circumstantial*
AS YOU LIKE IT

*cold-blooded*
KING JOHN

*compromise*
THE MERCHANT OF VENICE

*courtship*
LOVE'S LABOUR'S LOST

*critic*
LOVE'S LABOUR'S LOST

*dawn*
HENRY IV, PART 1

*discontent*
TITUS ANDRONICUS

*dishearten*
HENRY V

*drugged*
KING LEAR

*elbow*
MACBETH

*epileptic*
KING LEAR

*excitement*
HAMLET

*eyeball*
A MIDSUMMER NIGHT'S DREAM

*fashionable*
TROILUS AND CRESSIDA

*frugal*
THE MERRY WIVES OF WINDSOR

*generous*
THE COMEDY OF ERRORS

*gnarled*
LOVE'S LABOUR'S LOST

*gossip*
MEASURE FOR MEASURE

*grovel*
HENRY VI, PART 2

*hobnob*
TWELFTH NIGHT

*hurried*
THE COMEDY OF ERRORS

*label*
TWELFTH NIGHT

*lacklustre*
AS YOU LIKE IT

*laughable*
THE MERCHANT OF VENICE

*luggage*
HENRY IV, PART 1

| | | |
|---|---|---|
| *madcap* | *majestic* | *marketable* |
| LOVE'S LABOUR'S LOST | JULIUS CAESAR | AS YOU LIKE IT |
| *mimic* | *monumental* | *moonbeam* |
| A MIDSUMMER NIGHT'S DREAM | TROILUS AND CRESSIDA | A MIDSUMMER NIGHT'S DREAM |
| *mountaineer* | *negotiate* | *obscene* |
| CYMBELINE | MUCH ADO ABOUT NOTHING | LOVE'S LABOUR'S LOST |
| *obsequiously* | *ode* | *outbreak* |
| RICHARD III | LOVE'S LABOUR'S LOST | HAMLET |
| *pedant* | *puking* | *radiance* |
| THE TAMING OF THE SHREW | AS YOU LIKE IT | ALL'S WELL THAT ENDS WELL |
| *rant* | *remorseless* | *savagery* |
| HAMLET | HENRY VI, PART 2 | KING JOHN |
| *scuffle* | *submerge* | *summit* |
| ANTONY AND CLEOPATRA | ANTONY AND CLEOPATRA | HAMLET |
| *swagger* | *torture* | *tranquil* |
| A MIDSUMMER NIGHT'S DREAM | HENRY VI, PART 2 | OTHELLO |
| *undress* | *unreal* | *varied* |
| THE TAMING OF THE SHREW | MACBETH | TITUS ANDRONICUS |
| *worthless* | *zany* | |
| HENRY VI, PART 1 | TWELFTH NIGHT | |

Yes, before *Hamlet*, ours was a language without excitement. Incredible, isn't it? There is no denying that Shakespeare had a unique way with words. And phrases. When I was a student at Oxford, I met the columnist Bernard Levin, whose admiration of Shakespeare rivalled mine and whose knowledge of the *Complete Works* far exceeded it. Bernard loved to quote Shakespeare and wrote a dazzling piece to prove that we all quote the Bard much more often than we realise. Here it is:

> If you cannot understand my argument, and declare 'It's Greek to me', you are quoting Shakespeare; if you claim to be more sinned against than sinning, you are quoting Shakespeare; if you recall your salad days, you are quoting Shakespeare; if you act more in sorrow than in anger; if your wish is father to the thought; if your lost property has vanished into thin air, you are quoting Shakespeare; if you have ever refused to budge an inch or suffered from green-eyed jealousy, if you have played fast and loose, if you have been tongue-tied, a tower of strength, hoodwinked or in a pickle, if you have knitted your brows, made a virtue of necessity,

insisted on fair play, slept not one wink, stood on ceremony, danced attendance (on your lord and master), laughed yourself into stitches, had short shrift, cold comfort or too much of a good thing, if you have seen better days or lived in a fool's paradise – why, be that as it may, the more fool you, for it is a foregone conclusion that you are (as good luck would have it) quoting Shakespeare; if you think it is early days and clear out bag and baggage, if you think it is high time and that that is the long and short of it, if you believe that the game is up and that truth will out even if it involves your own flesh and blood, if you lie low till the crack of doom because you suspect foul play, if you have your teeth set on edge (at one fell swoop) without rhyme or reason, then – to give the devil his due – if the truth were known (for surely you have a tongue in your head) you are quoting Shakespeare; even if you bid me good riddance and send me packing, if you wish I was dead as a door-nail, if you think I am an eyesore, a laughing stock, the devil incarnate, a stony-hearted villain, bloody-minded or a blinking idiot, then – by Jove! O Lord! Tut tut! For goodness' sake! What the dickens! But me no buts! – it is all one to me, for you are quoting Shakespeare.

. . . . . . . . . . . . . . . . . . . . . . . . . . . . . . . . . . . . . . . . . . . . . . . .

## WHAT THE DICKENS!

Isn't that a surprise? 'What the dickens!' has nothing to do with the great English novelist, author of *Great Expectations*, *David Copperfield* and *Oliver Twist*. 'Dickens' was once a euphemism for the devil and the expression is first found in print in Shakespeare's *Merry Wives of Windsor:* 'I cannot tell what the dickens his name is.'

Happily, Charles Dickens (1812–70) has managed to make his way into the dictionary in his own right:

> Dickensian: adj; of or reminiscent of the novels of Charles Dickens especially in suggesting the poor social conditions or comically repulsive characters they portray.

In *The Oxford English Dictionary*, Dickens is credited with coining 258 new words and has 1,586 first-citations for giving a new sense to a word. Of the 258, my favourite is:

### *Butterfingers*

which first appeared in *The Posthumous Papers of the Pickwick Club*, more commonly known as *The Pickwick Papers*, in 1836:

> At every bad attempt at a catch, and every failure to stop the ball, he launched his personal displeasure at the head of the devoted individual in such denunciations as 'Ah, ah! – stupid' – 'Now, butterfingers' – 'Muff' – 'Humbug' – and so forth.

Dickens did not originate 'muff', an old word with a variety of meanings, or 'humbug', though he popularised the expression 'Bah! Humbug!' by giving it to Ebenezer Scrooge in *A Christmas Carol*.

Words and phrases Dickens did give the language include:

*doormat*
when used to describe someone who gets walked all over by other people;
*the creeps*
as in to give someone the creeps;

| | | | | | |
|---|---|---|---|---|---|
| *boredom* | *cheesiness* | *fluffiness* | *flummox* | *rampage* | *clap eyes* |
| *slow coach* | *dustbin* | *casualty ward* | *fairy story* | *egg box* | *devil may care* |

. . . . . . . . . . . . . . . . . . . . . . . . . . . . . . . . . . . . . . . . . . . .

## WHAT-HO WODEHOUSE!

Can you imagine being British and getting through the day without a cuppa?

Well, you'd have to if it weren't for Sir Pelham Grenville Wodehouse who first used the expression in his 1925 novel, *Sam the Sudden*.

P. G. Wodehouse (1881–1975) is one of the twentieth century's most delightful – and prolific – novelists. His use of vocabulary is highly individual and highly entertaining. Although he is credited with inventing only twenty-two specific words, he picked up all sorts of slang words and vogue expressions and became the first writer to put them into print. A Wodehouse speciality was the substitution of a circumlocution for a well-known word, as in 'gasper' for 'cigarette'. He also commonly converted words and phrases into different parts of speech, for instance 'french cheffing' (what Bertie Wooster's aunt's French chef does) and 'upping with the lark' (from the phrase 'to get up with the lark').

Here are my favourite Wodehouse word wonders:

*to beetle around*
beetle meaning to fly off like a beetle

*crispish*
as in somewhat crisp: 'Aunt Dahlia, having spent most of her youth in the hunting-field, has a crispish way of expressing herself'

*crumpet*
as a term of endearment for a person, usually as in 'old crumpet'

*to have a dash at*
to make an attempt

*came the dawn*
a cliché announcing daybreak: the first known use is by Wodehouse in 1923

*dirty work*
abbreviated from 'dirty work at the crossroads'

*down to earth*
as in back to reality, to come back down to earth

*elbow*
as in 'give someone the elbow'

*even-Stephen*
a rhyming intensified form of even

*up to the eyebrows*
first used in *Carry On, Jeeves*, 1925

*fifty-fifty*
on the basis of 50 per cent, half and half equally

*flesh and blood*
one of Bertie's ways of referring to his aunt

*foggy between the ears*
not very intelligent or perceptive

*gosh-awfulness*
first recorded in *Right Ho, Jeeves*, 1934

*down the hatch*
as in down the throat, when referring to toasting or drinking

*lame-brain*
a stupid person

*niff*
to give a disagreeable smell

*pip pip*
goodbye

*pip squeak*
insignificant person

*plonk*
dull, thudding sound, as of one solid object hitting another

*pottiness*
the state or condition of being potty; silliness, madness, craziness

| | | |
|---|---|---|
| **right ho**<br>to express agreement;<br>to acquiesce | **shimmy**<br>to dance in, as in 'he<br>shimmied into the room' | **smackers**<br>pounds or dollars |
| **snifter**<br>a drink | **sozzled, squiffy, stewed**<br>drunk | **toddle**<br>to go |
| **tut-tut**<br>used as a verb | **twenty-minute egg**<br>a hard-boiled person | **what ho**<br>a greeting or exclamation |

. . . . . . . . . . . . . . . . . . . . . . . . . . . . . . . . . . . . . . . . .

## WORDS FROM WONDERLAND

Novelists like Dickens and Wodehouse earn their place in the *Word Play* Hall of Fame because of the way they use old words in new senses, changing their parts of speech, forming new compounds, adding new affixes or inventing circumlocutions. It is not often that they come up with an entirely new word altogether.

Foremost among the original word inventors stands the Reverend Charles Lutwidge Dodgson (1832–98), who invented his own pen-name, 'Lewis Carroll'. 'Chortle' is one of his words that has stood the test of time. It's a combination of 'chuckle' and 'snort' and Carroll conjured it up for his second book about the adventures of Alice.

Some of Carroll's other inventions are words we might recognise, but probably neither use nor understand. Here are a dozen of his ingenious linguistic creations that make their first appearance in the poem *Jabberwocky* in Chapter 1 of *Through the Looking Glass* – with definitions (sometimes contradictory) supplied by Carroll, Humpty Dumpty and Alice.

> *Jabberwock* is the name of the fabulous monster in the poem and is formed on the verb 'to jabber'
>
> *Brillig*, according to Humpty Dumpty in Chapter 6, means 'four o'clock in the afternoon – the time you begin broiling things for dinner'
>
> *Slithy*: Humpty Dumpty says, '"Slithy" means "lithe and slimy". "Lithe" is the same as "active".' You see it's like a portmanteau,

there are two meanings packed up into one word

*Toves* are 'something like badgers – they are something like lizards – and they are something like corkscrews'

*Gyre*, again according to Humpty Dumpty, means 'to go round and round like a gyroscope'. According to Carroll, it means, 'to scratch like a dog'. Since Carroll invented Humpty Dumpty, which of them was right?

*Gimble* is to make holes like a gimlet

*Wabe*, as Alice rightly guesses, is the grass plot around a sundial frequented by *toves*

*Mimsy* is another portmanteau: flimsy + miserable

*Borogrove* is a thin, shabby-looking bird with its feathers sticking out all round – something like a live mop

*Mome*, lost, missing home or solemn

*Raths*, a sort of green pig; a species of turtle

*Outgrabe*, according to Carroll, 'the past tense of the verb outgribe meaning to shriek or creak'

. . . . . . . . . . . . . . . . . . . . . . . . . . . . . . . . . . . . . . . . . . . .

## AUTHOR! AUTHOR!

Paul Dickson is a world authority on baseball and the English language. He has a particular passion for what he calls 'authorisms': words, phrases or names created by a writer. He spent hours in the Library of Congress in Washington DC researching his *magnum opus* on the subject and concluded that these were his top ten:

### 1. *BANANA REPUBLIC*

A politically unstable, undemocratic and tropical nation, whose economy is largely dependent on the export of a single limited-resource product, such as a fruit or a mineral. The pejorative term was coined by O. Henry (William Sidney Porter) in his 1904 collection of short stories, *Cabbages and Kings*.

## 2. *BEATNIK*

This one was created by *San Francisco Chronicle* columnist Herb Caen in his column of 2 April 1958 about a party for 'fifty beatniks'. Caen was later quoted, 'I coined the word "beatnik" simply because Russia's Sputnik satellite was aloft at the time and the word popped out.'

## 3. *BEDAZZLED*

A word that Shakespeare gives us in *The Taming of the Shrew* when Katharina says: 'Pardon, old father, my mistaking eyes, that have been so bedazzled with the sun that everything I look on seemeth green.'

## 4. *CATCH-22*

The working title for Joseph Heller's modern classic about the mindlessness of war was *Catch-18*, a reference to a military regulation that keeps the pilots in the story flying one suicidal mission after another. The only way to be excused from flying such missions is to be declared insane, but asking to be excused for the reason of insanity is proof of a rational mind and bars being excused. Shortly before the appearance of the book in 1961, Leon Uris's bestselling novel *Mila 18* was published. To avoid numerical confusion, Heller and his editor decided to change *18* to *22*.

## 5. *CYBERSPACE*

Novelist William Gibson invented this word in a 1982 short story, but it became popular after the publication of his sci-fi novel *Neuromancer* in 1984. He described cyberspace as 'a graphic representation of data abstracted from the banks of every computer in the human system'.

## 6. *FREELANCE*

The word is not recorded before Sir Walter Scott introduced it in *Ivanhoe*. Scott's freelancers were mercenaries who pledged their loyalty and arms for a fee. This was its first appearance: 'I offered Richard the service of my Free Lances, and he refused them – I will lead them to Hull, seize on shipping, and embark for Flanders; thanks to the bustling times, a man of action will always find employment.'

## 7. *HARD-BOILED*

Hardened, hard-headed, uncompromising. A term documented as being first used by Mark Twain in 1886 as an adjective meaning 'hardened'. In a speech he alluded to hard-boiled, hide-bound grammar.

## 8. *MALAPROPISM*

An incorrect word in place of a word with a similar sound, resulting in a nonsensical, often humorous utterance (see page 68). This eponym originated from the character Mrs Malaprop, in the 1775 play *The Rivals* by Irish playwright Richard Brinsley Sheridan. The adjective 'malapropian' is first used by George Eliot: 'Mr Lewes is sending what a Malapropian friend once called a "missile" to Sara.'

## 9. *SERENDIPITY*

The writer and politician Horace Walpole invented the word in 1754 as an allusion to Serendip, an old name for Sri Lanka. Walpole was a prolific letter writer, and he explained to one of his correspondents that he had based the word on the title of a fairytale, *The Three Princes of Serendip*. The three princes were always making discoveries, by accidents and sagacity, of things they were not looking for.

## 10. *WHODUNIT*

Book critic Donald Gordon created the term in the July 1930 *American News of Books* when he said of a new mystery novel: '*Half-Mast Murder*, by Milward Kennedy – A satisfactory whodunit.' The term became so popular that by 1939, according to the *Merriam-Webster Dictionary* people, 'at least one language pundit had declared it "already heavily overworked" and predicted it would "soon be dumped into the taboo bin". History has proven that prophecy false, and whodunit is still going strong.'

And I am going to add to the Dickson list, with my own top ten 'authorisms'.

## *BLAH-BLAH-BLAH*

As a slang word for 'meaningless talk', 'blah' has been around since about the time of the 1914–18 war, but I think we can credit the lyricist Ira

Gershwin with popularising one of my favourite phrases: 'Blah-blah-blah'. It's the title of a song, with music by George Gershwin, originally written for a show that never got off the ground, *East Is West*, then 'brought out of the trunk' by the Gershwins for the 1931 film, *Delicious*. The best of the lyrics go like this:

> *Blah, blah, blah, blah moon*
> *Blah, blah, blah, above*
> *Blah, blah, blah, blah croon*
> *Blah, blah, blah, blah love*

## BLURB
A word invented in 1907 by American humorist Gelett Burgess to promote his book, *Are You a Bromide?*. On the back cover of the book Burgess featured a photograph of a 'Miss Belinda Blurb' with her hand to her mouth 'in the act of blurbing' the merits of the book. The book itself has long been forgotten, but the blurb is still with us.

## FEMINIST
It seems that feminist is a man-made word, first coined by Alexandre Dumas, author of *Camille* (better known as *The Lady of the Camellias*), son of Alexandre Dumas, author of *The Three Musketeers* and *The Count of Monte Cristo*. Dumas *fils* used the term in 1873. Here it is in its first translation by G. Vandenhoff:

> The feminists [féministes] (excuse this neologism) say, with perfectly good intentions, too: All the evil rises from the fact that we will not allow that woman is the equal of man.

## HONEY TRAP
First used by John le Carré in his 1974 classic, *Tinker Tailor Soldier Spy*:

> You see, long ago when I was a little boy I made a mistake and walked into a honey-trap.

## OXBRIDGE
This portmanteau was created by William Makepeace Thackeray, in

whose novel *Pendennis* the eponymous character attends Boniface College, Oxbridge.

## PANDEMONIUM

The word was created by John Milton for his epic poem, *Paradise Lost*. Constructed from the Greek *pan* meaning 'all' and *daimon* meaning 'demon', Pandemonium is where the devils and demons reside; it is the 'high Capital of Satan and his peers'. Over the years it has come to describe more mundane locations of chaos and madness, as in 'Ooh, it was pandemonium down at Westfield this afternoon.'

## SCAREDY-CAT

A Dorothy Parker creation, from her short story, *The Waltz*:

> It's so nice to meet a man who isn't scaredy-cat about catching my beri-beri.

## TWEEN

Canadian singer-songwriter Justin Bieber is regularly described as a tween idol. Could J. R. R. Tolkien have created a creature as remarkable as Justin? Tolkien invented the word 'tween' in *The Fellowship of the Ring* and described one as a hobbit in 'the irresponsible twenties between childhood and coming of age at thirty-three'.

## UNPUTDOWNABLE

Raymond Chandler came up with this word in 1947. Before then, people used to describe a good book as '*un-laydownable*'.

## YAHOO

The word 'yahoo' has its origins in *Gulliver's Travels*, Jonathan Swift's 1726 allegorical adventure in which the Yahoos are a race of dangerously brutish human-like creatures. Within a few years of its publication, the term 'yahoo' had been adopted into English to describe a loutish, violent or unsophisticated person. Now it's an internet search engine. Enough said.

*Postscript*

Having mentioned Swift, it's worth adding that some authors, like him, as well as inventing new words, try to get rid of old ones.

In the eighteenth century, Swift and the great dictionary-maker Dr Samuel Johnson wanted to ban a whole raft of words, including these: *sham*, *bully*, *stingy*, *banter*, *clever*, *bamboozle*, *mob*, *fun*.

Happily, they didn't succeed.

# C

**is for**

## COLLECTING COLLECTIVES

I collect collective nouns. Is there a collective noun for collective nouns? There ought to be. My Twitter followers have come up with a few interesting suggestions:

A *confusion* of collectives    A *clutch* of collectives    A *catch* of collectives

A *bunch* of collectives    A *gathering* of collectives    A *cacophony* of collectives

A *whimsy* of collectives    A *soviet* of collectives

I like the last, with its nod to the collective farms of the old Soviet Union, but perhaps a straightforward 'collection of collectives' is all we want. (I suppose 'a soviet of napkins' would be considered non-U. See page 233. 'A fold of napkins' sounds more likely.)

The best-known collective nouns relate to animals and birds. These are my favourites:

a *flock* of camels    a *herd* of antelope    a *colony* of bats

a *colony* of beavers    a *swarm* or hive of bees    a *sounder* of boar

an *obstinacy* of buffalo    a *clowder* of cats    a *clutch* of chicks an *intrusion* of cockroaches

a *band* of coyote

a *smack* of jellyfish

a *route* of wolves

a *cete* of badgers

a *deceit* of lapwings

a *dray* of squirrels

a *hover* of trout

a *mustering* of storks

a *host* of sparrows

a *parliament* of owls

an *army* of caterpillars

a *sloth* of bears

a *dule* of doves

a *school* of fish

a *harras* of horses

a *cast* of hawks

a *string* of ponies

an *ostentation* of peacocks

a *quiver* of cobra

a *float* of crocodiles

a *descent* of woodpeckers

an *unkindness* of ravens

a *shrewdness* of apes

a *pride* of lions

a *knot* of toads

a *flight* of swallows

a *pitying* of turtledoves

a *covey* of partridges

a *gam* of whales

a *peep* of chickens

a *drove* of cattle

a *balding* of ducks

a *skulk* of foxes

a *siege* of herons

a *gaggle* of geese

a *crash* of rhinoceros

an *ambush* of tigers

a *kine* of cows

a *yap* of Chihuahuas

a *kindle* of kittens

a *building* of rooks

an *exaltation* of larks

a *plague* of locusts

a *murmuration* of starlings

a *rafter* of turkeys

a *watch* of nightingales

a *bale* of turtles

a *colony* of ants

a *murder* of crows

a *nest* of rabbits

a *congregation* of plovers

a *leap* of leopards

a *brood* of hens

a *husk* of hares

a *pod* of seals

Don't worry if your list of favourite collective nouns differs from mine. There is no definitive list. A flock of camels when it is on the move becomes a caravan or a train. It can be a dole as much as a dule of doves – or a flight or a plague. If it's turtle-doves we're talking about, it's usually a pitying.

With sparrows you can have a host or a ubiquity or even a quarrel. Storks come in a muster or a phalanx and, with swans, you can have a gaggle or a gargle, a ballet or a bank, a whiteness or even (if they are airborne) a wedge.

Now and then I have tried to add to the established Noah's Ark of animal collectives. My offerings to date have included a picnic of bears, a gobble of turkeys, a coat of doves, a jonah of whales and a tin of sardines.

Of course, there is more room for manoeuvre, and original wordplay, when you extend collectives beyond the animal kingdom. A Welsh friend offered me a couple of controversial possibilities: 'A Wales of Jonahs' and 'a secession of nationalists'. 'A cacophony of mime artists' is nicely counter-intuitive. Here are the rest of my favourites:

a *mine* of egotists

a *wobble* of bicycles

a *riot* of protesters

an *elongation* of anglers

an *expanse* of broads

a *lot* of developers

a *complement* of sycophants

a *dilation* of pupils

a *delivery* of postmen

a *furrow* of brows

a *culture* of bacteria

a *sentence* of judges

a *promise* of politicians

a *ponder* of philosophers

a *flush* of plumbers

a *tenet* of palindromes

a *clutch* of gears

a *box* of pugilists

a *guzzle* of gourmets

a *want* of whisky

a *condescension* of know-it-alls

an *anticipation* of aunts

a *depression* of neurotics

a *nun* of your business

a *lack* of principals

an *emulsion* of painters

a *strike* of workers

a *habit* of nuns

a *hack* of smokers

a *dearth* of servants

a *knot* of Windsors

a *nucleus* of physicists

a *scoop* of journalists

a *procrastination* of tomorrows

a *brace* of orthodontists

a *flash* of paparazzi

a *dampness* of babies

a *wagon* of teetotallers

an *I-told-you-so* of pessimists

a *corps* of apples

a *wince* of dentists

a *peck* of kisses

a *host* of parasites

a *caste* of actors

a *range* of ovens

an *entrance* of actresses

a *shower* of meteorologists

a *Mammon* of bankers

an *annoyance* of neighbours

a *portfolio* of stockbrokers

a *prudence* of vicars

an *aftermath* of deadlines

a *rash* of dermatologists

# D

### is for

### DOUBLE BUBBLE

Double Bubble is the name of a game I play when I need to nod off.

Insomnia is not good for you. According to my doctor, without any sleep you would be dead within a fortnight. According to the same doctor (a good man who knows his stuff), a lack of sufficient sleep can trigger the early onset of dementia. That's not so funny, is it?

So, to help me get to sleep in good order, and to keep those little grey cells active at the same time, I play with words in my head as I lie in my bed. I don't count sheep, but the sound sheep make – *baa* – is where the Double Bubble game usually begins.

There are numerous words that use a particular letter twice. For example, *there* has two *e*s, *numerous* has two *u*s, *particular* has two *a*s and two *r*s, and *letter* has two *e*s and two *t*s. When you play Double Bubble, all you have to do is close your eyes and run through the alphabet from A to Z listing in your head twenty-six words in which the same letter appears twice – for example:

| | | | | |
|---|---|---|---|---|
| *a* baa | *b* ebb | *c* cock | *d* did | *e* bee |
| *f* off | *g* gag | *h* high | *i* iris | *j* jejune |

| *k* kick | *l* all | *m* mum | *n* inn | *o* coo |
| *p* pup | *q* quinquennium | *r* err | *s* ass | *t* tot |
| *u* usual | *v* viva | *w* wow | *x* executrix | *y* yolky |
| *z* jazz | | | | |

A *quinquennium* is a five-year period; *viva* is an interjection of goodwill; and for *x*, *executrix* is allowable (this is only a game, after all) – she is a female executor.

You should have nodded off long before you have completed Double Bubble. If you haven't, you can follow it up with a second game: Treble Trouble. Compiling an A to Z of words in which the same letter appears three times is more difficult, but it can be done:

| *a* banana | *b* bobby | *c* coccyx | *d* daddy | *e* epee |
| *f* fluff | *g* gaggle | *h* heighth | *i* iiwi | *j* Jijjin |
| *k* kakariki | *l* lull | *m* mummy | *n* nanny | *o* ovolo |
| *p* poppy | *q* Qaraqalpaq | *r* error | *s* sass | *t* tatty |
| *u* unusual | *v* viva-voce | *w* powwow | *x* hexahydroxycyclohexane | |
| *y* syzygy | *z* zizz | | | |

*Heighth* is a dialectical spelling of 'height'; *iiwi* is a brightly coloured Hawaiian bird; *Jiffin* is a town in Jordan; *kakariki* is both a parakeet and a lizard from New Zealand; *Qaraqalpaq* is a Turkic people of Central Asia; and *hexahydroxycyclohexane* is a chemical, a member of the vitamin B complex, which is essential for life; and *zizz* is both a whirring sound and what you hope you'll be having before the game is done.

A complete A to Z of words in which the same letter is repeated four times is impossible – and attempting to create the list may promote insomnia, which rather defeats the object of the exercise. With *v* and *x* I failed, but in the wee small hours I have done my best with the rest:

| *a* maharaja | *b* bubbybush | *c* scacchic |
| *d* diddled | *e* teepee | *f* riffraff |
| *g* gagging | *h* high-thoughted | *i* visibility |

| | | |
|---|---|---|
| *j* jejunojejunostomy | *k* kakkak | *l* pellmell |
| *m* mummydom | *n* non-union | *o* voodoo |
| *p* whippersnapper | *q* Qawiqsaqq | *r* recurrer |
| *s* assess | *t* statuette | *u* muumuu |
| *v* ??? | *w* wow-wow | *x* ??? |
| *y* fyyryryn | *z* razzamatazz | |

A *bubbybush* is another name for the strawberry shrub; *scacchic* means 'relating to chess'; *high-thoughted* is merely to have high thoughts; a *jejunojejunostomy* is the operative formation of a passage between two portions of the jejunum, part of the small intestine; a *kakkak* is a small bittern from the island of Guam; *Qawiqsaqq* is the name of a particular bluff in Alaska; a *muumuu* is a loose dress worn mainly in Hawaii; a *wow-wow* is any of several gibbons; *fyyryryn* is a Middle English spelling of 'fire iron'.

You won't be surprised to learn that I couldn't find words containing five *j*s, *q*s, *v*s, or *x*s, but – wide awake and mildly hysterical – I did manage the rest of the alphabet:

| | | |
|---|---|---|
| *a* abracadabra | *b* hubble-bubble | *c* circumcrescence |
| *d* fuddy-duddy | *e* telemetered | *f* fluffy-ruffle |
| *g* wiggle-waggling | *h* High-Championship | *i* illimitability |
| *j* ??? | *k* Kvikkjokk | *l* lillypilly |
| *m* mmm'mm | *n* non-intervention | *o* oronooko |
| *p* pepper-upper | *q* ??? | *r* terror-stirring |
| *s* assesses | *t* totipotentiality | *u* Uburu-uku |
| *v* ??? | *w* M'daywawkawntwawns | *x* ??? |
| *y* gryffygryffygryffs | *z* Zzzzz | |

A *hubble-bubble* is a flurry of activity; a *circumcrescence* is 'growing over'; *fluffy-ruffle* is an adjective meaning 'with fluffy ruffled margins'; *Kvikkjokk* is a town in Sweden; *lillypilly* is an Australian tree with hard, fine-grained wood; *mmm'mm* is a way of describing sex appeal; *oronooko* is a type of tobacco; *totipotentiality* is a biological term, the capability of developing along any of the lines inherently possible; *Uburu-uku* is a place in Nigeria; *M'daywawkawntwawns* are Native Americans of the Dakota people, a name more frequently spelt *Mdewakantons*; *gryffygryffygryffs* comes from James Joyce's *Finnegans Wake*, about two-thirds of the way through Chapter 11; and *Zzzzz* is the name of a wake-up service in Los Angeles. (If you're playing this game, you won't need them.)

. . . . . . . . . . . . . . . . . . . . . . . . . . . . . . . . . . . . . . . . . . . . .

## SEEING DOUBLE

Words in which the same letter appears twice and together are common enough. *Common*, with its double *m*, is one of them. In your head, can you compile a list of twenty-six words in each of which a different letter of the alphabet appears twice and together? *jj*, *qq*, *xx*, and *yy* are the tough ones.

If you are in bed right now, close the book and compile your list in the dark. If not, read on. Here's how I managed it:

| | | |
|---|---|---|
| *a* bazaar | *b* ebb | *c* accord |
| *d* add | *e* fee | *f* off |
| *g* egg | *h* withhold | *i* skiing |
| *j* hajji | *k* trekking | *l* all |
| *m* rummy | *n* inn | *o* boo |
| *p* apple | *q* Zaqqum | *r* err |
| *s* ass | *t* butt | *u* vacuum |
| *v* flivver | *w* powwow | *x* xx-disease |
| *y* gayyou | *z* buzz | |

A *hajji* is a pilgrim going to Mecca; a *Zaqqum* is an infernal tree with bitter fruit; *xx-disease* is a disease of cattle, also called hyperkeratosis; a *gayyou* is a narrow, flat-bottomed boat.

. . . . . . . . . . . . . . . . . . . . . . . . . . . . . . . . . . . . . . . . . . . . .

## THREE'S COMPANY

If sleep does elude you, despite my best endeavours, it may be because

you have a guilty conscience or money worries. I am not speaking
from experience, of course, but I am anxious to help. You need to stop
brooding, turn on the light, get out of bed and start leafing through your
favourite dictionaries. Finding words in which the same letters appear
three, four or more times in a row is a challenge, but it's also a wonderful
distraction and I think you'll find you're equal to it.

Look what I have discovered in the twilight hours.

*Kaawa* is the name of a town on the island of Oahu in Hawaii; and *Faaa*
is the name of a settlement on the west coast of Tahiti.

*The Oxford English Dictionary* contains *weest*, the superlative form of *wee*
in an illustrative quotation dating from 1878. The same dictionary also
features *seeer*, 'one who sees'.

*The American Thesaurus of Slang* contains the three words *pfff*, *pffft*, and
*pffft*, all meaning 'to go to ruin'.

The exclamation *shh*, requesting silence, seems common enough but,
bizarrely, no dictionary I know actually deigns to list it. *Hmm* does appear
in dictionaries of slang and is an expression of pleasure or astonishment.

The straightforward *frillless*, without a frill, is given in *The Oxford English
Dictionary*; and *wallless* is in an earlier edition of the unabridged *Webster's*.

*Brrr* is expressive of shivering with cold or apprehension and appears in
the 1972 supplement of *The Oxford English Dictionary*.

There are several examples of triple-*s* words. *The Oxford English Dictionary*
contains *countessship*, *duchessship*, and *goddessship*, while its 1972
supplement contains *bossship*. An earlier edition of *Webster's* gives both
*headmistressship* and *patronessship*.

The *Oxford* offers two words with three *u*s: *vertuuus*, a fourteenth-century
spelling of *virtuous*, and *uuula*, an early form of *uvula*.

*Bzzzbzzz* is given in *The American Thesaurus of Slang* as a synonym for gossip.

Four *a*s appear in *Aaaahtamad*, the name of an unidentified town in Palestine.

*Eeeeve* is the local name of the Hawaiian bird *iiwi*.

Five *o*s appear in the curious *Cookkooose*, a name given to the tribes of the Kusan Indian family.

Four *s*s appear in the palindromic *esssse*, an old spelling of *ashes*, which is given as a main entry in *The Oxford English Dictionary*. And *zzzz* is given as a verb 'to snore' in *The American Thesaurus of Slang*.

*The American Thesaurus of Slang* also has **OOOOO** as an exclamation of surprise. In the eighteenth century, there was a British racehorse called *Potoooooooo*. This was pronounced *potatoes*, made up from *pot* and eight *o*s.

The most extreme example to appear in print is in Philip Roth's best-selling *Portnoy's Complaint.* On the last page is a howl of anguish, represented by 231 consecutive *a*s, followed by four *h*s – thus:

Aaaaaaaaaaaaaaaaaaaaaaaaaaaaaaaaaaaaaaaaaaaaaaaaaaaaaaaaaaaaaaaaaaaa
aaaaaaaaaaaaaaaaaaaaaaaaaaaaaaaaaaaaaaaaaaaaaaaaaaaaaaaaaaaaaaaaaaaaaaa
aaaaaaaaaaaaaaaaaaaaaaaaaaaaaaaaaaaaaaaaaaaaaaaaaaaaaahhhh!!!!

Beat that!

**E**

**is for**

**ELLIPTICAL KISS**

Whoever first described a kiss as 'elliptical' (*a lip tickle*) was a wordplayer of the first order.

In my book, pun power is at the heart of wordplay. The *Merriam-Webster Dictionary* describes the pun, nicely and concisely, as 'a humorous way of using a word or phrase so that more than one meaning is suggested'. I love puns and I am fascinated by the paradox that lies behind them: the worse they are, the better they are.

> *What do you call a patronising confidence trickster coming down the stairs? A condescending con descending.*

Terrible, isn't it? And beautiful, too.

> *I'd like to share a pun about chemistry with you, but would it get the right reaction?*

Oh, no . . . Oh, yes!

Puns come in all shapes and sizes. There are short, sharp ones:

*Puberty is a hair-raising experience.*

And long, leaden ones:

*Once upon a time there were three Native American squaws. One sat on a leopard skin. One sat on a doe skin. The third sat on a hippopotamus skin. The squaw on the leopard skin had one son, as did the squaw on the doe skin, but the squaw on the hippopotamus skin had twins. This, of course, proves that the squaw on the hippopotamus is equal to the sons of the squaws on the other two hides.*

There are drunken puns:

*Absinthe makes the tart grow fonder.*

And exceedingly drunken ones:

*Orange juice sorry you made me cry? Don't be soda pressed; them's martini bruises.*

There are puns that get to the heart of the matter:

*Better to have loved a short girl, than never to have loved a tall.*

And puns that don't:

*What a friend we have in cheeses.*

There are clever puns, like this one from Richard Hughes's 1938 novel, *In Hazard*:

*Presently she told Dick she had a cat so smart that it first ate cheese and then breathed down the mouse holes – with baited breath – to entice the creatures out.*

And not-so-clever ones:

*'Waiter, this coffee tastes like mud.'*
*'Well, it was only ground this morning.'*
*'And the eggs taste disgusting.'*
*'Don't blame me, I only laid the table.'*

Many literary giants of the past have been master punsters. Shakespeare revelled in puns. 'Ask for me tomorrow,' says Mercutio, as he is about to die, 'and you shall find me a grave man.' Another playwright, Richard Brinsley Sheridan, punned his way into this compliment, addressed to the adorable Miss Payne:

*'Tis true I am ill; but I cannot complain,*
*For he never knew pleasure who never knew Payne.*

Hilaire Belloc wrote his own punning epitaph:

*When I am dead I hope it may be said:*
*'His sins were scarlet, but his books were read.'*

And Ernest Hemingway would probably have enjoyed the literary echo in the headline that announced his death:

*PAPPA PASSES.*

According to the Bible, Jesus was a punster. *Petros* is Greek for 'rock', so when Jesus declared that Peter was to be the rock on which the Church would be built, the play on words must have been intentional.

The great create puns. They also inspire them. Here is Franklin P. Adams on Christopher Columbus:

*Oh, I should like to see Columbus's birthplace.*
*And then I'd write a fine, authentic poem.*
*And critics, none of who would read it through,*
*Would say, 'At least we have the Genoan article.'*

Of all the dreadfully good and wonderfully bad puns I have come across, my favourite is the payoff in Bennett Cerf's story about the private detective hired to trace a missing person named Rhee, who used to work for *Life* magazine in New York. Eventually the detective ran his man to ground and exclaimed:

*'Ah, sweet Mr Rhee of Life, at last I've found you.'*

It could hardly be better. Or worse.

. . . . . . . . . . . . . . . . . . . . . . . . . . . . . . . . . . . . . . . . . . . . . .

## SUPERPUNS

Because I love puns, I cultivate the company of punsters. Last night I happened to be recording an edition of the BBC Radio 4 panel game *Just A Minute*, and a fellow panellist was the comedian Marcus Brigstocke. Before the show, Marcus came up with this gem:

Did you hear about the inflatable school? It had an inflatable headmaster and inflatable pupils. One day an inflatable schoolboy came to school with a pin. The headmaster said to the schoolboy: 'Do you realise that you've let me down, you've let yourself down and, worst of all, you've let the whole school down?'

Another of my favourite comedians is the great Milton Jones. He is a regular on the BBC Radio 4 word game I host called *Wordaholics* and almost every line he utters is a punning play on words:

*Militant feminists – I take my hat off to them. They don't like that.*
*Years ago I used to supply Filofaxes for the Mafia. Yes, I was involved in very organised crime.*
*My wife – it's difficult to say what she does. She sells sea shells on the sea shore.*

Marcus, Milton and I have each taken a number of shows to the Edinburgh Festival Fringe. Scotland is a good place to meet fellow pun-lovers. (It was in Edinburgh that I encountered a cuddly estate manager – he was known as the Feelgood Factor. He was having an affair with a girl from the Orkneys – it was a proper island highland fling. Oh, yes.) In Edinburgh my shows are presented by a company with a suitably punning name: Bound & Gagged Comedy. Bound & Gagged also produce the comedian Tim Vine, brother of the broadcaster Jeremy Vine, and arguably the world's most prolific and inspired professional punster. He delivers his puns not in punnets but in puntechnicons. Here are twenty-one I have picked at random from the Vine. Twenty-one? I suppose you'd call it a puntoon.

*A friend of mine always wanted to be run over by a steam train. When it happened, he was chuffed to bits.*

*So I was getting into my car and this bloke says to me: 'Can you give me a lift?' I said: 'Sure, you look great, the world's your oyster, go for it.'*

*So this bloke said to me, 'Tim, do you know Marie Osmond is about to appear in the world's worst film?' I said 'Warner Brothers?' He said, 'I already have!'*

*So I went to the doctor. He said, 'Say aaah.' I said, 'Why?' He said, 'My dog's died.'*

*Black Beauty. Now there's a dark horse!*

*I took part in the sun-tanning Olympics. I got bronze.*

*This bloke said to me, 'I'm going to chop off the bottom of one of your trouser legs and put it in a library.' I thought, That's a turn-up for the books.*

*I phoned the local gym and I asked if they could teach me how to do the splits. He said, 'How flexible are you?' I said, 'I can't make Tuesdays.'*

*conjunctivitis.com – that's a site for sore eyes.*

*I saw this bloke chatting up a cheetah. I thought, He's trying to pull a fast one.*

*This policeman came up to me with a pencil and a piece of very thin paper. He said, 'I want you to trace someone for me!'*

*I had a dream last night. This voice said, 'On your marks, get set, go!' and I woke up with a start.*

*This bloke said to me, 'I'm going to attack you with the neck of a guitar.' I said, 'Is that a fret?'*

*So I was working in a health-food shop. This bloke walked in and said,
'Evening primrose oil.' I said, 'Mr Vine to you!' He said, 'Soya chunks?'
I said, 'You shouldn't have been looking.'*

*Last night I dreamt I was the author of Lord of the Rings. I was Tolkien in
my sleep.*

*I saw Schindler's List, and the bloke behind me started wailing. I got hit
on the back of the head with a harpoon.*

*I've decided to sell my Hoover. Well, it was just collecting dust.*

*Exit signs. They're on the way out, aren't they?*

*Advent calendars – their days are numbered!*

*The advantage of easy origami is twofold...*

*Velcro, what a rip-off!*

Another of my favourite punsters is my friend Alan F. G. Lewis. Creating
puns has been his life's work. 'The pun is mightier than the sword' is his
family motto. *A Pun My Soul* is the title of his autobiography. Of the
thousands that have poured out of him, here are some of my favourites:

*Baldness is a kind of failure. Wish I'd made the greyed.*

*Chalet or shanty? It's a decision he should dwell on.*

*He's a theatre buff with a tendency to fawn.*

*Schnapps and hock are my favourite Teutonics.*

*He was like a bull in a china shop until she cowed him.*

*Slimmer's motto: here today, gaunt tomorrow.*

*The guru refused to let his dentist freeze his jaw because he wanted to
transcend dental medication.*

*When I'm stoned I get a little boulder.*

*The hard part of being broke is watching the rest of the world go buy.*

*Atrophy is a reward for a long political service.*

*A pessimist is a person who looks at the world through morose-coloured
glasses.*

*Only a fool would milk his company of expenses when none has been in
curd.*

*Pity the poor man who has a big load of debt and doesn't know how to
budge it.*

*The old Christmas spirit is like artificial holly: dead and buried.*

*I was neutral till a live wire promised me the earth.*
*The system of decimal notation has its points but fractions are often vulgar.*
*A Puritan is a man who noes what he likes.*

. . . . . . . . . . . . . . . . . . . . . . . . . . . . . . . . . . . . . . . . . . .

## PICK A PUN

You can see how it's done, but can you do it? As a modest training exercise, cast your eye over each of these ten sentences and, where you can, fill in the gap with a pun of your own.

In a church, it's an accepted custom never to talk above a . . . . .

A married man who wants to conceal his drunken infidelities can easily wake up in the morning wondering who he's . . . . . next to.

Two cheerleaders ended up at the altar. They met by . . . . .

You can see by her light touch that she has a . . . . . for the piano.

'Shall we have salad?' 'Yes, . . . . . '

Some thought Edgar Allan Poe was a . . . . . lunatic.

Bad news about the two lighthouse keepers – their marriage is on the . . . . .

When the fencing team tried to wrap up the tournament, they kept getting . . . . .

In Chicago, the Windy City, every prospect . . . . .

There once was a . . . . . about a girl named Pearl who was so . . . . . -headed, she didn't have anything to . . . . .

In case you need them, here are some possible answers: 1. vesper 2. lying 3. chants 4. flare 5. lettuce 6. raven 7. rocks 8. foiled, 9. breezes 10. yarn . . . woolly . . . nitwit

Were your answers wittier than mine? Of course they were. I am not surprised. In the 1970s I supplied riddles for the Tom Smith Christmas Cracker Company. My contract was not renewed.

**is for**

**FRANGLAIS SPOKEN HERE**

Imagine the Lord talking French! Aside from a few odd words in Hebrew, I took it completely for granted that God had never spoken anything but the most dignified English.

Clarence Day was right. God speaks English – always has done, always will. And it's probably because they want to keep on the right side of the Almighty that the French have started to bring English words into their vocabulary.

The language of *haute cuisine* was once exclusively French, but nowadays at almost any Paris restaurant you can order *le fast food*, *le banana split*, *le biftek* and *les chips* – which is what the British call chips and the Americans call French fries.

In the world of sport Frenchmen now speak of *le fair-play*, *le score* and *les jockeys.* Sometimes their thinking does get a little muddled ... *un jerk* is a good dancer, *un scratcher* is a great golfer, and *un egghead* is an imbecile ... but on the whole they are on *le right track*.

These days, these are now French phrases:

| *le weekend* | *le shopping* | *le chewing gum* |
| *le check-in* | *le check-out* | *les baked beans* |
| *le jogging* | *le baby-foot* (table football) | *le blockbuster* |
| *supercool* | | |

In the English-speaking world, we tweet, we Google and we Skype. The French equivalents? *Tweeter*, *Googeliser* and *Skyper*.

And the French for walkie-talkie? *Le talkie-walkie*.

While the French are speaking English ever more so, English-speaking people do give French a go – but only a *morceau*.

'Franglais' is the term for the unique language produced when English speakers pepper their conversation with French words and phrases. The late Miles Kington, who coined the term, said, 'Its rules are simple. Insert as many French words as you know into the sentence, fill in the rest with English, then speak it with absolute conviction.' *Par exemple*:

*Je suis tired*     *Je ne care pas*     *J'agree*

And for 'long time, no see': *Longtemps, pas voir*.

Gems from the Kington Franglais phrasebook include a man accused of driving his car '*avec toute la finesse d'un Rangers fan*' and a door-to-door salesman, who assures his customers: '*Je ne suis pas un nutter religieux.*'

Kington popularised Franglais in books like *Let's Parler Franglais One More Temps* and *The Franglais Lieutenant's Woman and Other Literary Masterpieces*, but he did not invent the phenomenon. In the fourteenth century Geoffrey Chaucer had the Prioress in *The Canterbury Tales* speak a kind of medieval Franglais, and 150 years ago Mark Twain, in *The Innocents Abroad*, featured this letter written to a Parisian landlord:

*PARIS, le 7 Juillet. Monsieur le Landlord – Sir: Pourquoi don't you mettez some savon in your bed-chambers? Est-ce que vous pensez I will steal it? La nuit passée you charged me pour deux chandelles when I only had one; hier vous avez charged me avec glace when I had none at all; tout les jours you are coming some fresh game or other on me, mais vous ne pouvez pas play this savon dodge on me twice. Savon is a necessary de la vie to any body but a Frenchman, et je l'aurai hors de cet hotel or make trouble. You hear me. Allons. BLUCHER.*

Famously, in the 1940s, a frustrated Winston Churchill complained to an obdurate Charles de Gaulle during the French general's enforced exile in wartime London: 'Si vous m'opposerez, je vous get riderai!'

And in 1981, the sometime Rolling Stone, Bill Wyman, found himself at the top of the charts with 'Je Suis Un Rock Star'. Around the same time, the actor Kenneth Williams made his mark with an unusual love song that was more French than Franglais. In the song, a young man tells the story of his love for 'ma crêpe Suzette' and does so entirely with French names, words and phrases that have found their way into the English language. Kenneth sang the song to the tune of 'Auld Lang Syne'.

*Honi soit qui mal y pense*
*Faites vos jeux, reconnaissance*
*Hammersmith Palais de danses*
*Badinage, ma crêpe Suzette.*

*Double entendre, restaurant*
*Jacques Cousteau, Yves St Laurent*
*Ou est la plume de ma tante?*
*C'est la vie, ma crêpe Suzette.*

*Corsage, massage, Frere Jacques*
*Salon, par avion, Petula Clark*
*Fiancée, ensemble, lorgnette*
*Lingerie, eau de toilette*
*A Gauloises cigarette*
*Entourage, ma crêpe Suzette.*

*Citroen, Mirage, Caravelle,*
*Hors d'oeuvre, Brut et Chanel*
*Chaise longue, Sacha Distel*
*Fusillage, ma crêpe Suzette.*

*Pince-nez, bidet, commissionaire*
*Mon repos, Brigitte Bardot,*
*Jeux sans frontières*

*Faux pas, Grand Prix, espionage,*
*Brie et Camembert fromage,*
*Mayonnaise, all-night garage*
*RSVP ma crêpe Suzette.*

When I had a go at performing Kenneth's song in my *Word Power!* show in Edinburgh in 2015, I decided that some of the lyrics needed updating:

*Corsage, massage, triage, brioche,*
*Pain au chocolat, à la carte, Juliette Binoche.*
*Baguette, banquette, vinaigrette,*
*Quelle horreur, agent provocateur, brunette,*

*Au pair, pas de deux, tête-a-tête*
*Au revoir, ma crêpe Suzette!*
*François Hollande, Valerie Trierweiler, Julie Gayet,*
*Ménage à trois, crème fraîche, crème brulée*

*Faux pas, Grand Prix, espionage,*
*Gruyère, Camembert, fromage,*
*Mayonnaise, Nigel Farage,*
*RSVP, ma crêpe Suzette.*

. . . . . . . . . . . . . . . . . . . . . . . . . . . . . . . . . . . . . . . . . . . .

## VINGT-ET-UN

*Oui, mes amis*, while the French are speaking more and more English, we continue to speak a great deal of French, sometimes without knowing it. For a full account of Anglo-Franco linguistic relations I recommend Mark Daniel's *très amusant* and informative tome *French Letters and the English Canon*. Meanwhile, here are twenty-one words that bridge the Channel: they are French – and English, too.

### *BRASSERIE*
The fascinating thing about this term, which has come to refer to a restaurant or dining establishment with a French bent, is that its origins lie in that most British of drinks, beer. The *brasserie* was where beer was both made and drunk and comes from the French verb *brasser*, 'to brew'.

### *CACHET*
Nowadays we refer to something having a certain cachet when we want to suggest it has something special about it. The literal translation of *cachet* is 'stamp' or 'seal' and, like our 'seal of approval', is a reference to the noblemen who once used them on their correspondence.

### *CASSETTE*
I know I am showing my age here, but I still hold a fondness for cassette tapes and boxes full of them. The word comes from the French for 'little case': *case-ette*.

### *CLICHÉ*
In nineteenth-century France a *cliché* was the repetitive sound made by a certain type of printing plate, also known as a 'stereotype'. (The verb *clicher*'s previous meaning is 'to strike'.) It has since come to mean an overused, too-often-repeated turn of phrase or metaphor.

### *DÉBUT*
Simply translated as 'beginning', debut is now used to refer to a first

of some kind, such as 'her debut album, his debut performance' – and is even occasionally to be found working as a verb: 'He debuted at the Carnegie Hall.'

## DISCO

I'm not often to be found in the discotheque these days – you'd be far more likely to spot me in the *bibliothèque.* The two aren't as dissimilar as you might think, at least not etymologically speaking. Just as a *bibliothèque* is a library where books are kept, so the original *discothèque* was a place where records were kept.

## DUVET

The hospital corners, starched sheets and stiff blankets of my youth are mostly a distant memory in modern Britain. Now most of us sleep under a 'duvet', the word coming from the French 'down' or 'fuzz', a reference to the goosedown originally used to fill these cosy comforters.

## ÉCLAIR

I love the British entertainer, Jenny Eclair, but I am less partial to the edible confection of the same name. The eclair made of choux pastry, cream and chocolate is a little too rich for my liking. The French word *éclair* means 'lightning' and I have come across different suggestions as to why this particular pastry has inspired this particular name. Mark Daniel suggests it is because 'the cream bursts from its dark case like lightning'. Others suggest that the chocolate on the surface shines like lightning. My favourite explanation is because the eclair is eaten in a flash.

## ÉLITE

The French word dates from the late eighteenth century and comes from *élire* 'to elect'. The elite were the elected, the chosen ones, and therefore special. Of course, whether that's how we would view our elected representatives these days is another matter.

## ENTOURAGE

*Entourer* means 'to circle or surround', and your entourage is the group of people you surround yourself with. In P. Diddy's entourage he has a specified umbrella holder; Mariah Carey's includes a lady whose only job it is is to lift Mariah's teacup to her lips; and in my entourage . . . Well, I'd like to have someone to carry my dictionaries.

## GAFFE

A gaffe is a social blunder or clumsy remark. It comes from the French word *gaffe*, which means 'boat hook'. Neither Mark Daniel nor the internet, nor even the several dictionaries I have consulted, can enlighten me as to why. (A *faux-pas*, which is like a gaffe, is much easier to disassemble: a *faux-pas* in translation is 'false step'.)

## GAUCHE

The translation of *gauche* is 'left'. It also translates as 'awkward, clumsy'. Why? It is because we are mainly, as people, right-handed, so when we attempt to do things with our left hands they tend to be clumsily done.

## MAÎTRE D'

The *maître d'* is the all-powerful person who decides whether you get the best table in the house or are destined to be seated next to the toilet. (I would, of course, normally refer to the toilet as the lavatory – see page 233: U and Non-U – but when in the Franglais chapter . . . ) *Maître d'* translates as 'master of' and is shortened from *maître d'hôtel*.

## NICHE

I like to think words are my niche – my nook: the little space in this big bad world that I have hollowed out for my own, as the starling hollows out his home in the sapling tree. Which is, indeed, where the word comes from, as *nicher* is the French verb for 'to nest'.

## PIÈCE DE RÉSISTANCE

The *pièce de résistance* is the best, the ultimate, the most sublime expression of someone's work. Will history be referring to *Word Play* as mine? Only time will tell because *pièce de résistance* translates as the piece of work that has staying power. It was traditionally the main course of a meal.

## PIED-À-TERRE
A pied-à-terre is a small place where one can lay one's head. From the French 'a foot on the earth', it often refers to a second home in the city, a little bolthole that you keep for your visits to town from your larger, primary residence located elsewhere.

## RENDEZVOUS
A rendezvous is what I am having with my wife later at the local brasserie. It translates as 'present yourself', using the polite form of 'you'. My wife and I probably know each other well enough to have a rendez-tu but I'm a stickler for good manners and I remember that great Frenchman, Charles de Gaulle, leader of the Free French during the Second World War and president of the French Republic, 1959–69, always called Madame de Gaulle, his wife of almost fifty years, '*vous*' to show her the respect that was her due.

## RSVP
In the late eighteenth century it was *de rigueur* for the upper echelons of British society to adopt the *etiquette* of the French, which was when the French term '*Répondez s'il vous plaît*' began appearing at the bottom of the finest British invitations. The literal translation of the phrase is 'Respond if you please' causing pedants to mutter ungraciously, 'Quel tautology!' when an invitation falls through their letterbox bearing the words 'Please RSVP'.

## SABOTAGE
An act of sabotage is when my wife deliberately spills coffee on my new laptop, forcing me to stop work on my *pièce de résistance* so that we're on time for our rendezvous at the brasserie.

A *sabot* is a wooden shoe or clog, traditionally worn by French peasants and workers. 'Sabotage' is the word that came into being when peasants wearing *sabots* set about kicking things and workers threw their shoes into machinery to sabotage it and preserve their jobs.

## *TOUCHÉ*

Originally a fencing term from the French ***toucher***, 'to touch', it indicates when you or your opponent have made contact. Now it refers to scoring a conversational 'hit', when your opponent acknowledges you have made a clever, witty or particularly apt point.

## *VINGT-ET-UN*

***Vingt-et-un*** is another name for the card game Black Jack, also known as Twenty-one because that is the maximum pip value you can hold in one hand before you go bust. It is also the number of words and phrases in this list.

• • • • • • • • • • • • • • • • • • • • • • • • • • • • • • • • • • • • • • • • • • • • • •

## AND FINALLY

While it's clear that English has a certain *je ne sais quoi*, what's going on here? Is this French? It looks French. Or is this English? It sounds English. Read it out loud and then decide.

> *Reine, reine, gueux éveille,*
> *Gomme à gaine, en horreur, taie.*

# G

## is for

## GOLDWYNISMS

You will find spoonerisms, Bushisms and malapropisms here, too. And I am giving Winifred's Bloomers an airing as well. This is the chapter where we celebrate the linguistic blooper – intentional or not.

We are beginning with Samuel Goldfish (1882–1974) who had a wonderfully winning way with words. Polish by birth, he became an American citizen, changed his name to Samuel Goldwyn and grew to be one of the legendary Hollywood movie moguls. In my book, as memorable as the great MGM pictures he produced were the great verbal clangers he created.

An agent once tried to sell Goldwyn a prominent actor. Goldwyn replied that he was not interested in established stars. He wanted to build his own stars instead. 'Look how I developed Jon Hall,' said Goldwyn. 'He's a better leading man than Robert Taylor will ever be – some day.'

Goldwynisms are unique because they are turns of phrase that manage to make some sense and no sense at all at one and the same time. In my Goldwyn Book of Quotations these are the gems that have pride of place:

Every director bites the hand that lays the golden egg.

A verbal contract isn't worth the paper it's written on.

You ought to take the bull between the teeth.

We're overpaying him, but he's worth it.

Why should people go out and pay good money to see bad films when they can stay at home and watch television for nothing?

We've all passed a lot of water since then.

How'm I gonna do decent pictures when all my good writers are in jail? Don't misunderstand me, they all ought to be hung.

Chaplin is no businessman – all he knows is he can't take anything less.

We want a story that starts with an earthquake and works its way up to a climax.

My Toujours Lautrec!

Tell me, how did you love my picture?

Yes, my wife's hands are very beautiful. I'm going to have a bust made of them.

Anybody who goes to see a psychiatrist ought to have his head examined.

When working on a movie about the life of Christ: Why only twelve disciples? Go and get thousands.

Gentlemen, I want you to know that I am not always right, but I am never wrong.

If Roosevelt were alive, he'd turn over in his grave.

I'll give you a definite maybe.

It's more than magnificent – it's mediocre.

If you cannot give me your word of honour, will you give me your promise?

When told that a story was rather caustic, he replied: I don't care what it costs. If it's good, we'll make it.

Of a book: I read part of it all the way through.

Of a piece of dialogue: Let's have some new clichés.

A bachelor's life is no life for a single man.

A wide screen just makes a bad film twice as bad.

Going to call him 'William'? What kind of name is that? Every Tom, Dick and Harry's called William. Why don't you call him Bill?

In two words: im-possible.

. . . . . . . . . . . . . . . . . . . . . . . . . . . . . . . . . . . . . . . . . . . .

## SPOONERISMS

I was lucky enough to be a scholar at New College, Oxford, from 1967 to 1970, so, inevitably, I have a soft spot for spoonerisms. They take their name from the Reverend William Spooner, warden of New College, from 1903 to 1924.

A spoonerism is the accidental transposition of the initial letters of the words in a phrase so as to change the phrase's meaning or make nonsense of it:

'You have tasted a whole worm.'
'You have hissed all my mystery lectures.'
'You were fighting a liar in the quadrangle.'
'You will leave by the town drain.'
'I have received a blushing crow.'
'Is the bean dizzy?'
'Let us toast the queer old dean!'

These are classic spoonerisms, no doubt, but please take it from a Mew College nan, not one of them fell from the lips of the great man himself.

Spooner is supposed to have created the original spoonerism by getting up in the New College chapel one day and announcing the next hymn as 'Kinquering Kongs Their Titles Take'. All the research suggests he did no such thing. Neither, it seems, was he responsible for the other spoonerisms now attributed to him. Yes, he was an absent-minded professor ('In the sermon I have just preached, wherever I said Aristotle I meant St Paul'), a short-sighted albino with a knack for getting things muddled ('I remember your name, I just can't think of your face'), but apart from once admitting to looking in a 'dark glassly', he was not a regular perpetrator of spoonerisms.

'Give me a well-boiled icycle'; 'It's roaring with pain outside', 'May I sew you to another sheet?' are spine foonerisms by any standard, but take it from me: they are probably making the wood garden gurn in his trave.

## MALAPROPISMS

If there was any justice in the world of words, malapropisms would have been named after Shakespeare's Constable Dogberry rather than Sheridan's Mrs Malaprop. Malapropisms are ludicrous misuses of words, especially by confusion with similar words, and Shakespeare got there first. Dogberry, in *Much Ado About Nothing*, indulges in them with abandon. Here he is instructing the watch:

> You are thought here to be the most senseless and fit man for the constable of the watch, therefore bear you the lantern. This is your charge: you shall comprehend all vagrom men: you are to bid any man stand, in the prince's name.

As Dogberry observes, 'comparisons are odorous', so that any 'caparison', as Mrs Malaprop has it, of the quality of malapropisms used by these two great comic creations can only be of academic interest – and so can safely be left to the academics. It is more than two hundred years since Mrs Malaprop first walked the stage in Richard Brinsley Sheridan's comedy *The Rivals*, but the passage of time has not dulled the sparkle of the great lady's malapropisms:

> 'No caparisons, miss, if you please. Caparisons don't become a young woman.'
> 'She's as headstrong as an allegory on the banks of the Nile.'
> 'Illiterate him, I say, quite from your memory.'
> 'I own the soft impeachment.'
> 'He is the very pine-apple of politeness!'
> 'An aspersion upon my parts of speech! Was ever such a brute! Sure, if I reprehend anything in this world, it is the use of my oracular tongue, and a nice derangement of epitaphs!'

. . . . . . . . . . . . . . . . . . . . . . . . . . . . . . . . . . . . . . . . . . . . .

## MALAPROP *DE NOS JOURS*

Shakespeare and Sheridan made up their malapropisms. I didn't make up these. I have simply collected them over the years.

'He had to use a fire distinguisher.'
'My sister has extra-century perceptions.'
'She really gyrates on my nerves.'
'He was lapping up the tension.'
'I was so surprised you could have knocked me over with a fender.'
'He works in an incinerator where they burn the refuge.'
'He had to use biceps to deliver the baby.'
'He communicates to work.'
'My husband is a marvellous lover. He knows all my erroneous zones.'
'My sister uses massacre on her eyes.'
'He's a wealthy typhoo.'
'No phonographic pictures allowed.'
'Don't trust him. He's a wolf in cheap clothing.'

That last one I happened to overhear on the 0900 train from London King's Cross to Edinburgh earlier this week. These next few are attributable, too.

'Republicans understand the importance of bondage between a mother and a child.' Dan Quayle, 44th vice president of the United States
'Well that was a cliff-dweller.' Wes Westrum, sports commentator, about a close baseball game
'The police are not here to create disorder, they are here to preserve disorder.' Richard Daley, former mayor of Chicago
Daley is also reported to have said a friend was attending 'Alcoholics Unanimous' and that he had ridden a 'tantrum bicycle'.
Bertie Ahern, the former Irish taoiseach, is said to have given a warning to his country against 'upsetting the apple tart' of his country's economic success.

'He's going up and down like a metronome.' Ron Pickering, sports
   commentator
'Create a little dysentery among the ranks.' Christopher Moltisanti,
   from *The Sopranos*
The *New Scientist* magazine reported one of its employees calling a
   colleague 'a suppository of knowledge'. The magazine went on
   to say that the worker in question later apologised for his 'Miss
   Marple-ism'.

## RADIO MALAPROP

If you're a serious collector of bloomers, bloopers and malapropisms you
should listen to the radio – especially late at night when the insomniacs in
search of company give the radio station a call:

'You are out of your rocker.'
'Too many people have been sold down the drain.'
'If the circumstances were on the other foot.'
'I don't pull any bones about it.'
'You're talking around the bush.'

One late-night talk-show host of my acquaintance boggled a caller with
this reproof: 'You have just used two words that set my hair on edge.'

It's all too easily done:

'I think we need to let down to the brass roots of the problem.'
'The nutshell of it is...'
'If he had actually broken a crime and could be accused of breaking a
   crime...'

Sometimes the slips are scripted. I heard a news report that described the
victim of a traffic accident as 'killed fatally' and another that spoke of
fatigue as 'a major cause of automobile safety'.

And then there are the ads:

'It's Christmas, and you're socked under with bills . . . '
'It's your money, your decision. Discuss this with your loving ones in
the confidence of your home.'

· · · · · · · · · · · · · · · · · · · · · · · · · · · · · · · · · · · · · · · · · · · · · · · · · · ·

## MILHOUS MALAPROP

To err is human, and lest one be deluded into thinking that the mighty,
if fallen, are immune, out of the past comes Richard M. Nixon, 37th
president of the United States, before the distractions of Watergate,
commenting on the death of his political rival, Adlai Stevenson: 'In
eloquence of expression, he had no peers and very few equals.'

· · · · · · · · · · · · · · · · · · · · · · · · · · · · · · · · · · · · · · · · · · · · · · · · · · ·

## BUSHISMS

'The trouble with the French is that they don't have a word for
entrepreneur.' So said George W. Bush, 43rd president of the United
States.

Bush became so famous for his malapropisms that in the United States
malapropisms have come to be known as 'Bushisms'. Here are twenty
of the best, courtesy of Jacob Weinsberg, editor of the Slate Group and
distinguished author of *The Bush Tragedy*:

1. 'Our enemies are innovative and resourceful, and so are we. They never
   stop thinking about new ways to harm our country and our people,
   and neither do we.' Washington, DC, 5 August 2004
2. 'I know how hard it is for you to put food on your family.' Greater
   Nashua, New Hampshire, Chamber of Commerce, 27 January 2000
3. 'Rarely is the question asked: Is our children learning?' Florence, South
   Carolina, 11 January 2000

4. 'Neither in French nor in English nor in Mexican.' Declining to answer reporters' questions at the Summit of the Americas, Québec City, Canada, 21 April 2001

5. 'You teach a child to read, and he or her will be able to pass a literacy test.' Townsend, Tennessee, 21 February 2001

6. 'I've heard he's been called Bush's poodle. He's bigger than that.' Discussing former British prime minister Tony Blair, as quoted by the *Sun* newspaper, 27 June 2007

7. 'And so, General, I want to thank you for your service. And I appreciate the fact that you really snatched defeat out of the jaws of those who are trying to defeat us in Iraq.' Meeting with Army General Ray Odierno, Washington, DC, 3 March 2008

8. 'There's an old saying in Tennessee I know it's in Texas, probably in Tennessee that says, "Fool me once, shame on shame on you. Fool me you can't get fooled again".' Nashville, Tennessee, 17 September 2002

9. 'And there is distrust in Washington. I am surprised, frankly, at the amount of distrust that exists in this town. And I'm sorry it's the case, and I'll work hard to try to elevate it.' Speaking on National Public Radio, 29 January 2007

10. 'We'll let our friends be the peacekeepers and the great country called America will be the pacemakers.' Houston, Texas, 6 September, 2000

11. 'It's important for us to explain to our nation that life is important. It's not only life of babies, but it's life of children living in, you know, the dark dungeons of the internet.' Arlington Heights, Illinois, 24 October 2000

12. 'One of the great things about books is sometimes there are some fantastic pictures.' *U.S. News & World Report*, 3 January 2000

13. 'People say, "How can I help on this war against terror? How can I fight evil?" You can do so by mentoring a child; by going into a shut-in's house and say I love you".' Washington, DC, 19 September 2002

14. 'Well, I think if you say you're going to do something and don't do it, that's trustworthiness.' CNN online chat, 30 August 2000

15. 'I'm looking forward to a good night's sleep on the soil of a friend.' On the prospect of visiting Denmark, Washington, DC, 29 June 2005

16. 'I think it's really important for this great state of baseball to reach out

to people of all walks of life to make sure that the sport is inclusive. The best way to do it is to convince little kids how to the beauty of playing baseball.' Washington, DC, 13 February 2006

17. 'Families is where our nation finds hope, where wings take dream.' LaCrosse, Wisconsin, 18 October 2000

18. 'You know, when I campaigned here in 2000, I said, "I want to be a war president." No president wants to be a war president, but I am one.' Des Moines, Iowa, 26 October 2006

19. 'There's a huge trust. I see it all the time when people come up to me and say, "I don't want you to let me down again".' Boston, Massachusetts, 3 October 2000

20. 'They misunderestimated me.' Bentonville, Arkansas, 6 November 2000

. . . . . . . . . . . . . . . . . . . . . . . . . . . . . . . . . . . . . . . . . . . .

## WINIFRED'S BLOOMERS

Bush, Spooner, Malaprop – they are famous. But nobody seems to know much about Winifred and her bloomers. Well, read on. I am about to reveal all.

Who was Winifred and what were her bloomers?

Winifred Ashton was a novelist and playwright better known as Clemence Dane (1888–1965). Her bloomers were her matchless verbal slips. Miss Dane was known as Winifred to her friends, the closest of whom included the playwright Noël Coward, the actress Joyce Carey, and the designer Gladys Calthrop. They revelled in her facility for uttering innocently outrageous double entendres. In his biography of Coward, Cole Lesley records a few of the choicest of Winifred's bloomers:

> The first I can remember was when poor Gladys was made by Noël to explain to Winifred that she simply could not say in her latest novel, 'He stretched out and grasped the other's gnarled, stumpy tool.' The bloomers poured innocently from her like an ever-rolling stream. 'Olwen's got crabs!' she cried as you arrived for dinner, or, 'We're

having roast cock tonight!' At the Old Vic, in the crowded foyer, she argued in ringing tones, 'But Joyce, it's well known that Shakespeare sucked Bacon dry.' It was Joyce too who anxiously enquired after some goldfish last seen in a pool in the blazing sun and was reassured: 'Oh they're all right now! They've got a vast erection covered with everlasting pea!' 'Oh the pleasure of waking up to see a row of tits outside your window,' she said ... Schoolgirl slang sometimes came into it, for she was in fact the original from whom Noël created Madame Arcati: 'Do you remember the night we all had Dick on toast?' she enquired in front of the Governor of Jamaica and Lady Foot. Then there was her ghost story: 'Night after night for weeks she tried to make him come ...'

# H

**is for**

**HERITAGE**

Words are like people: when you are playing with them, it's good to know a bit about their background.

The English language has a long history, and traditionally scholars divide it into three:

> Old English (or Anglo-Saxon) dating from the earliest written records, around 740, to the time of the Norman conquest

> Middle English, running from 1066 to around 1500, when the development of printing introduced a degree of standardisation

> Modern English, from 1500 to the present day

While much of Old English has disappeared, some has survived. Here are some words that haven't changed much in more than a thousand years:

| OLD ENGLISH | MODERN ENGLISH |
|---|---|
| freond | friend |
| god | good |
| hand, hond | hand |
| ned | need |
| read | red |
| scip | ship |
| springan | to spring |
| swete | sweet |
| wegan | to weigh |

During the Middle English period, words poured into the language from French. Many were connected with the Church and Christian beliefs and practices: *cardinal, sermon, abbey, baptism, crucifix, confession, redemption, temptation.* Many were legal: *justice, prison, quit, assault, evidence, felon, plaintiff, slander, fraud, perjury, punishment.* Some were words to do with public affairs: *council, authority, bailiff, govern, majesty, mayor, parliament, treason.* And because the ruling classes were French speaking for a long time, the vocabulary of fashion, food and social life also became permeated with words of French origin: *beef, mutton, pork, venison, spice, orange, lemon, peach, coat, boot, buckle, frock, gown, mittens.*

Except in pronunciation, most of the main features of present-day English can be found as early as 1500. The main additions to the vocabulary during the early Modern English period are words derived from Latin and Greek. Here is a random selection, with the language of origin and first recorded date (according to *The Oxford English Dictionary*):

*abdomen* (Latin), 1541
*anonymous* (Greek), 1601
*apparatus* (Latin), 1628
*atmosphere* (Greek through Latin), 1638
*botanic* (Greek through Latin), 1656
*catastrophe* (Greek), 1579
*complication* (Latin), 1611

*excursion* (Latin), 1579
*fabulous* (Latin), 1546
*gesticulate* (Latin), 1601
*humiliate* (Latin), 1533–4
*meditate* (Latin), 1625
*radiate* (Latin), 1649
*syndrome* (Greek through Latin), 1541
*thermometer* (Greek), 1633
*torpedo* (Latin), *c.* 1520
*typical* (Latin), 1598
*vacuum* (Latin), 1550
*zoology* (Latin and Greek), 1650

Yes, 'torpedo' is five hundred years old. That surprised me, too.

. . . . . . . . . . . . . . . . . . . . . . . . . . . . . . . . . . . . . . . . . . .

## HAVEN'T A PRAYER?

How good is your Anglo-Saxon?

It may be better than you think. Even if the words don't seem to make any sense to you, read the next nine lines out loud:

> *Faeder ure thu the art on heofenum*
> *si thin nama gehalgod*
> *to becume thin rice*
> *gewirthe thin will on earothan swa swa on heofenum*
> *urne daeghwaemlice hlaf syle us todaeg*
> *and forgyf us sure gyltas*
> *swa swa we forgyfath urum gyltendum*
> *and ne gelaed thu us on costnunge*
> *ac alys us of yfele. Sothlice.*

You may not have been familiar with most of the words, but I trust you were suitably surprised – and impressed – by the way in which you nonetheless understood the gist of what was being said. You have just read the Lord's Prayer in Anglo-Saxon.

It's reckoned that the English words most frequently *sung* in the world today are 'Happy birthday to you'. In the history of the world to date, there is no doubt that the most frequently spoken set of words is the Lord's Prayer – the best known version of which is the one featured in the Book of Common Prayer (1611), beginning:

> *Our Father which art in Heaven*
> *Hallowed be thy name...*

At church, as a small boy, I thought we were praying for the local priest, the Reverend Harold Wishart, who had recently passed away:

> *Our Father Wishart in Heaven, Harold be thy name...*

. . . . . . . . . . . . . . . . . . . . . . . . . . . . . . . . . . . . . . . . . . . . . . .

## BASIC INSTINCT

English is an old language that has evolved organically. It works because it has roots. A number of would-be 'universal' non-English languages have been invented, among them Novial, Valapük, Interlingual, Interglossa, and, the best known, Esperanto, but they haven't taken the world by storm. Languages that don't have roots don't seem to prosper.

Basic English was devised as an English-based 'universal' language in 1929 and some people still believe it has merit. 'Basic' is an acronym for British, American Scientific, International and Commercial. The language has a vocabulary of just 850 English words: 600 things (nouns), 150 qualities (adjectives) and 100 operators (verbs and structural words, prepositions and conjunctions).

The inventors of Basic English maintained that, with their easy-to-learn language, every kind of communication was possible. Despite the endorsement of world leaders like Franklin D. Roosevelt and Winston Churchill, Basic English has never fired anyone's imagination. When you read the Lord's Prayer translated into Basic, you will understand why:

*Father of all up in the sky.*
*You get our deepest respect.*
*We hope your nation with you*
*asking for ruler will come*
*down to us.*
*We hope you have your own way*
*in the place we live as on high.*
*Give us food for now, and*
*overlook wrongdoing as we*
*overlook wrongdoing by persons to us.*
*Please guide us from courses of*
*desire, and keep us from badness.*

Now here is the same prayer in a real language based on English: Pidgin. It developed in the sixteenth century in South America and Africa, but is still widely spoken in parts of West Africa and New Guinea:

*Papa belong me-fella, you stop long heaven*
*All 'e sanctu 'im name belong you.*
*Kingdom belong you 'e come.*
*All 'e hear 'im talk belong you long ground*
*all same long heaven.*
*Today give kaikai belong day long me-fella.*
*Forgive 'im wrong belong me-fella,*
*all-same me-fella forgive 'im wrong all*
*'e makem long me-fella.*
*You no bring-em me-fell long try 'im.*
*Take 'way some t'ing no-nogood long me-fella.*

# I

### is for

## INCOMPREHENSIBLE PROBLEM IN CHINESE

*Incomprehensible* is an anagram of *problem in Chinese*. An anagram is a rearrangement of the letters in a word or phrase to form another word or phrase. It's the way you turn *scythe* into *chesty*, *roast mules* into *somersault* and *voices rant on* into *conversation*.

It is easier described than done. Can you rearrange the letters in *Monday* to form another everyday English word?

• • • • • • • • • • • • • • • • • • • • • • • • • • • • • • • • • • • • • • • • • • • • • • • • •

### A N A G R E A T E S T

With anagrams the ingenuity lies in changing a word into a word or phrase that is spectacularly apt – or amusingly not. Here is my top team:

> *dictionary = indicatory*
> *mummy = my mum*
> *desperation = a rope ends it*
> *punishment = nine thumps*
> *endearments = tender names*
> *prosecutors = court posers*

*twinges = we sting*
*softheartedness = often sheds tear*
*therapeutics = apt is the cure*
*degradedness = greed's sad end*
*panties = a step-in*
*astronomers = moon starers = no more stars*
*postmaster = stamp store*
*waitress = a stew, sir?*
*semolina = is no meal*
*software = swear oft*
*dormitory = dirty room*
*schoolmaster = the classroom*
*butterfly = flutter by*
*listen = silent*

The ingenuity becomes even greater when a whole phrase is turned into a different phrase with much the same meaning. I reckon *eleven plus two = twelve plus one* is unbeatable. Here are some more that come pretty close:

*the United States of America = attaineth its cause: freedom!*
*a decimal point = I'm a dot in place*
*the countryside = no city dust here*
*the nudist colony = no untidy clothes*
*the detectives = detect thieves*
*a shoplifter = has to pilfer*
*one hug = enough*
*gold and silver = grand old evils*
*circumstantial evidence = can ruin a selected victim*
*one good turn deserves another = do rogues endorse that? No, never!*
*the centenarians = I can hear ten 'tens'*
*I run to escape = a persecution*
*The Morse Code = here come dots*
*The Meaning of Life = the fine game of nil*
*a domesticated animal = docile, as a man tamed it*
*a telescope = to see place*
*the eyes = they see*

*the ears = hear set*
*the cockroach = cook, catch her*
*a sentence of death = faces one at the end*

. . . . . . . . . . . . . . . . . . . . . . . . . . . . . . . . . . . . . . . . . . . . .

## ANABAPTISTS

The names of the great and famous sometimes make telling anagrams.
*I ask me, has Will a peer?* and *I'll make a wise phrase* are two apt
rearrangements of William Shakespeare. *Willie makes a phrase* is a third.
Take Wolfgang Amadeus Mozart, rearrange his name and look what you
get: *a famous German waltz god.* I know Mozart was Austrian, but it's
still quite neat, isn't it? I like *I lace words* from Oscar Wilde and you must
agree that *Sit, write me a lullaby* is a charming message to unravel from
William Butler Yeats. *Flit on, cheering angel* was Lewis Carroll's anagram
for Florence Nightingale and other Victorian anagrammarians concocted
*greatest born idealist* out of Dante Gabriel Rossetti and the apt Latin
phrase *honor est a nilo* out of Horatio Nelson.

Somehow there is a particular pleasure in rearranging political figures
anagrammatically. With Margaret Thatcher you could get *Meg the arch
Tartar* or *that great charmer*, depending on your point of view. Tony Blair
gives you *Libyan rot*, and not much besides. Tony Blair MP, however,
provides *I'm Tory plan B*.

In the 1960s, during my gap year before going to university, I taught at the
Park School in Maryland. At the time, the governor of Maryland was one
Spiro Agnew and I recall much giggling in the classroom when someone
offered up an anagram of his name – *grow a spine* – and we all registered at
the same moment that within 'spine' there lurks another anatomical anagram.

US presidents have proved fertile ground for anagrammarians over the years:

*Thomas Jefferson = O, short name's Jeff*
*Grover Cleveland = govern, clever lad*

*Theodore Roosevelt = hero told to oversee*
*President Franklin Delano Roosevelt = Lo! Real keen person voted first in land*
*Dwight D. Eisenhower = Wow! He's right indeed!*
*Ronald Reagan = an oral danger = a darn long era*
*George Bush = he bugs Gore*
*William Clinton = I'm it, an ill clown*
*William Jefferson Clinton = Firm clean fellow. Joint? Sin!*
*= Jail Mrs Clinton: Felon wife*

Once upon a time conjuring up anagrams was a very satisfying form of wordplay. I reckon the advent of the internet has taken much of the fun out of the sport. Gone are the days of slaving over a name, HB pencil in hand, arranging and rearranging the letters, waiting for the wittiest, most apt of anagrams to emerge. Now all you have to do is get onto your computer, find one of the myriad anagram sites available online and they will do the job for you. You just enter the name of your celebrity of choice and all the possibilities (some brilliant, some lame, many actionable) spring instantly into view. There are apps you can buy to do the job, too. I like these anagrams, but I did not devise them. Somewhere, somehow, an anonymous computer did.

*Elvis Aaron Presley = seen alive, sorry pal*
*Madonna Louise Ciccone = occasional nude income*
*Bradley William Pitt = a partially liable dimwit*
*Jennifer Aniston = fine in torn jeans*
*Clint Eastwood = old west action*
*Woody Allen = a lewd loony*
*Gillian Anderson = no aliens darling*
*Ursula Andress = a rude lass runs*
*Kim Basinger = semi barking*
*Justin Timberlake = I'm a jerk, but listen*
*Britney Spears = Presbyterians*
*Christopher Walken = crank the lower hips*
*Vin Diesel = I end lives*
*Ian Botham = Oh man I bat*
*Frankie Dettori = taken it for ride*

*Alec Guinness = genuine class*
*Dame Agatha Christie = I am a right death case*
*Oliver Reed = erode liver*
*Wayne Sleep = yes new leap*
*Patrick Stewart = cap Star Trek wit*
*Rod Stewart = worst dater*
*Daniel Day-Lewis = ideal sinewy lad*
*Christopher Evans = he's a rich TV person*
*Germaine Greer = emerge angrier*
*Rowan Sebastian Atkinson = I, an artist, so known as Bean*
*Nigel Havers = girls' heaven*
*Felicity Kendal = fine tickle lady*
*Luciano Pavarotti = put on a ravioli act*
*Harry Potter = try hero part*

And how does 'Gyles Brandreth' fare in the anagram machine? I can offer you either ***rashly bred gent*** or ***Bland get sherry***. I agree: let's move on.

. . . . . . . . . . . . . . . . . . . . . . . . . . . . . . . . . . . . . . . . . . . .

## ARS MAGNA

Despite the ease with which one can now turn to the internet in search of a quick anagrammatic fix, there are those who still see anagrams as a great art – or ***ars magna***. My friend Paul Williams is one such. He will take a word or a phrase and from it extrapolate a second word or phrase that somehow manages to add an extra dimension to the first – like so:

| | |
|---|---|
| *Trapped nerve* | *Prevented rap* |
| *Wears an armed thong?* | *Answer: a grandmother* |
| *Main light gone* | *In the gloaming* |
| *The sailor no one knew* | *Horatio Nelson, we ken* |
| *I toast musical* | *It's calamitous!* |
| *Insurance policy* | *I can copy rules* |
| *Spanish galleons die* | *Alongside ship lanes* |
| *Person restrains* | *Senior partners* |

| | |
|---|---|
| *Enid Blyton, authoress* | *So enthused Tony Blair* |
| *No African oil silo* | *On Californian soil* |
| *Thrifty ferret hadn't paid* | *Third party, fire and theft* |
| *Journeying to West Ham United?* | *Enjoy touring the new stadium* |

Creating an arresting anagrammatic phrase is one thing. Coming up with a complete story is another. This eccentric piece of Victorian prose earns its place in *Word Play* because it contains the same nine letters served up in fourteen different ways:

How much there is in a word – monastery, says I; why, that makes nasty Rome; and when I looked at it again, it was evidently more nasty – a very vile place or mean sty. Ay, monster, says I, you are found out. What monster? said the Pope. What monster, said I. Why, your own image there, stone Mary. That, he replied is my one star, my Stella Maris, my treasure, my guide! No, said I, you should rather say, my treason. Yet no arms, said he. No, quoth I, quiet may suit best, as long as you have no mastery, I mean money arts. No, said he again, those are Tory means; and Dan, my senator, will baffle them. I don't know that, said I, but I think one might make no mean story out of this one word – monastery.

- - - - - - - - - - - - - - - - - - - - - - - - - - - - - - - - - - - - - - - -

## ANTIGRAMS

Antigrams aren't negative weights or cables you send to your father's sister, but anagrams with a difference: the new word or words created out of the original word or words have the opposite instead of a similar meaning. Thus *real fun* is what you don't have at a *funeral* and *fluster* is far from *restful*. Here are some more of the best:

*Misfortune = it's more fun*
*Santa = Satan*
*enormity = more tiny*
*infection = fine tonic*

*militarism = I limit arms*
*filled = ill fed*
*violence = nice love*
*marital = martial*
*anarchists = arch-saints*
*commendation = aim to condemn*
*evangelists = evil's agents*
*discretion = is no credit*
*protectionism = nice to imports*
*a picture of health = oft pale, I ache, hurt*
*the man who laughs = he's glum, won't ha-ha*

· · · · · · · · · · · · · · · · · · · · · · · · · · · · · · · · · · · · · · · · · · · · · · · · · · · · ·

## DYNAMO

And did you manage to rearrange the letters in *Monday* to form another everyday English word?

# J

### is for

### JUMBO

Oscar Wilde reckoned that if you wanted to join the ranks of the great immortals you needed to start off with a name of five letters – like Oscar. Or Wilde. Or Jesus. Or Plato. Or Gyles.

Or Jumbo.

Nowadays a jumbo is a jet, but once he was an African elephant – and Oscar Wilde met him and declared it was an encounter he was sure that neither he nor the elephant would ever forget. In 1865 the original Jumbo was London Zoo's first African elephant. In 1881 Phineas T. Barnum bought him (for ten thousand dollars) for his circus. Jumbo was a gigantic animal, eleven and a half feet in height, six and a half tons in weight, an accomplished performer and something of a star on both sides of the Atlantic. When he was struck by a train and killed on the night of 15 September 1885, the news of his death was reported around the world. His skeleton is now in the Museum of Natural History in New York.

Jumbo was a legend in his own time. His name is still a household word, because he was an eponymist, one of a select band who have given their very names to the language. Here is my jumbo list of words we all use without, on the whole, realising who deserves the credit.

## AMP

The amp is an electrical unit named after Andre Ampère (1775–1836), the French mathematician and physicist who undertook pioneering work in electricity.

## BARMY

Not everyone agrees with me on this one, but I say there is evidence to suggest that 'barmy' is a corruption of Bartholomew – and St Bartholomew was once known as 'the patron saint of the feeble-minded'.

## BATTY

The term 'batty' is used to describe someone who is thought of as harmlessly eccentric, a little bit on the loopy side. Surprisingly the derivation has nothing to do with nocturnal flying creatures (those bats in the belfry), but comes from the name of a nineteenth-century barrister, Fitzherbert Batty, who lived in Spanish Town, Jamaica, and, unhappily, had mental-health issues. When he was certified in 1839, the news was reported in the press back home and the term slipped into the language.

## BLANKET

The first blankets in England were made out of a fabric called *blanquette* that was the creation of a Flemish weaver, Thomas Blanquette, who lived and wove in Bristol, in the mid-fourteenth century.

## BOWDLERISE

Thomas Bowdler (1754–1825) was a London doctor, who took it upon himself to edit the works of Shakespeare with respectability in mind. In all ten volumes of his edition, 'those words and expressions are omitted which cannot with propriety be read aloud in a family'. Dr Bowdler did the same with Gibbon's *Decline and Fall of the Roman Empire*.

## BOYCOTT

Charles Boycott (1832–97) was an English land agent in Ireland, who was one of the first to be socially excommunicated by followers of the Irish nationalist leader, Charles Stewart Parnell.

## BUNSEN BURNER
Robert Wilhelm Bunsen (1811–99) was a German chemist who invented several scientific instruments, most famous of which was the gas burner that bears his name.

## BRAILLE
Louis Braille, a Frenchman, created the reading system that is named after him. He was blinded in a childhood accident at the age of three. At the age of ten he was sent to study at the Institute for the Blind in Paris. By the age of sixteen he had developed his system, inspired by the wartime 'night' writing of Charles Barbier. In 1829, he published his first book detailing it, and by the end of the nineteenth century it had been adopted by most of the world as the primary reading/writing system for the blind.

## CAESAREAN
The name 'Caesar' comes from the Latin word *caedere*, which means to cut. Legend has it that Julius Caesar (100 BC–44 BC) was given this name after he was cut from the womb of his mother in the ninth month of pregnancy. There is much about this tale that is doubtful, not least that such a procedure would have been fatal and history shows that Caesar's mother, Aurelia, was alive and well for much of her son's life and even acted as his adviser.

It is more likely the term 'Caesarean' derives directly from *caedere*, but it is a good story and Julius Caesar deserves his place here, come what may, because he is responsible for our 365-day Julian calendar and the month of July is named after him. The month of August is named after his great-nephew, Augustus Caesar (63 BC–AD 14), the first of the Roman emperors.

## CHAUVINISM
Though the term has come to be more commonly associated with male chauvinism, it originally meant extreme patriotism. (A male chauvinist is one who adheres strongly to the male cause, poor misguided thing.) The word made its way into the language via a play written by two French brothers, celebrated in the mid-nineteenth century. In the Cogniard brothers' *La Cocarde Tricolore*, a character is inspired by a real-life figure,

Nicolas Chauvin, a French soldier in Napoleon's army. Chauvin was wounded seventeen times, only to be retired on a paltry pension. In spite of this, his devotion to the emperor remained undimmed and he worshipped him uncritically.

## DIESEL
Rudolf Diesel (1858–1913) was a German engineer at the Krupp factory who, in 1897, invented the first practical compression-ignition engine, which ran on cheap crude oil. The diesel engine is named after him.

## DRACONIAN
The adjective 'draconian' refers to Draco, a law-maker who lived in Athens in the seventh century BC. He was the first person to write down the laws of Athens and was renowned for his harsh punishments. Stealing an apple? Death sentence. Urinating in public? Death sentence. Lazy at work? Death sentence. 'Draconian' is now used to describe any regime that seems unduly severe.

## FALLOPIAN TUBE
The fallopian tubes, which connect the ovaries to the uterus, were named after Italian anatomy professor Gabriel Fallopius (1523–62). Fallopius was one of the most outstanding and versatile of the sixteenth-century anatomists. He taught at the universities of Pisa and Padua. He was a less competent surgeon, however, and had to give up surgery after a number of deaths on his operating table.

## GAGA
Here is a possible etymology of the early twentieth-century word 'gaga': from *gateur* (French), 'bedwetter', to *gateux* (French), hospital slang for a bedwetter, to *gaga* (French), slang for a senile old person, to *gaga* (English), the condition we know, often associated with old age. The eponymous etymology is that it is a shortened form of Gauguin, after the Impressionist painter Paul Gauguin (1848–1903), who showed signs of mental disturbance in both his work and life. No one knows for certain how the word came into being, so feel free to take your pick.

### GALVANISE

Luigi Galvani (1737–98) was an Italian physiologist who made frogs' legs twitch by 'galvanising' them through connecting the leg muscles to their corresponding nerves. The modern meaning 'to stimulate strongly' reflects this original experiment.

### GIBBERISH

An onomatopoeic word that has its origins in eighth-century Persia. The celebrated alchemist Jabir Ibn Hayyan wrote tomes on his craft that were so technical and dense they were impossible to follow. The Latin version of his name was Geber, and language that was hard to decipher became known as Geber-ish.

### MAVERICK

Samuel Maverick (1803–70) was an early Texan settler of an independent disposition. His cattle ventures ended with large numbers of unbranded livestock wandering the range freely. Neighbours called all the unbranded cattle 'mavericks' and somehow the name stuck. Over time, it spread beyond the Texas cowboys.

### MESMERISE

Franz Anton Mesmer (1734–1815) was an Austrian doctor, who founded the hypnotic treatment known as mesmerism.

### PASTEURISE

One of the better-known eponyms, the word comes from the name Louis Pasteur (1822–95), French chemist and father of modern bacteriology. Pasteur, among many other things, developed the process of pasteurisation, which heats milk long enough to kill germs but not so long as to ruin the taste.

### SAXOPHONE

Antoine-Joseph Sax (1814–94) was a Belgian musician who invented several brass wind instruments, the most successful of which was the saxophone, patented in 1845.

## SHRAPNEL

Henry Shrapnel (1761–1842) was an English artillery officer and inventor of the exploding shell.

. . . . . . . . . . . . . . . . . . . . . . . . . . . . . . . . . . . . . . . . . . . . . . . . . . . . . . . .

## FASHIONISTAS

Hats off now to the women and men whose names are good enough to wear.

## BLOOMERS

Bloomers were once considered a symbol of women's rights. The term originally referred to a complete outfit, previously called 'Turkish Dress'. The name 'bloomers' originated in America in 1851 when a Miss Elizabeth Smith Miller wore the outfit to the house of her friend, Mrs Amelia Jenks Bloomer (1818–94). Mrs Bloomer was very taken with the new fashion, which had been developed as a less restrictive style of ladies' dress. As the editor of the journal called the *Lily*, Bloomer held a certain amount of influence. As well as printing a description of the outfit with instructions on how to make it in her magazine, she also organised a ball in July 1851 at which all the ladies were under instruction to come sporting the new style of dress. The garment, which allowed more freedom of movement for the women who wore it, became a physical and metaphorical representation of feminist reform.

## CARDIGAN

The cardigan is named after James Thomas Brudenell, the 7th Earl of Cardigan. It was a knitted sleeveless garment worn by Cardigan's soldiers during the Crimean War to protect them from the bitterly cold conditions. That same campaign gave us another classic piece of cold-weather fashion: the balaclava. This face-covering garment was worn by soldiers during the charge of Balaclava in 1854, led by Cardigan.

## LEOTARD

The leotard is named after nineteenth-century French trapeze artist Jules Léotard (1839–70). The stretchy one-piece is worn today by sports enthusiasts, gymnasts and dancers alike and is designed to give freedom of movement and to allow the form of the body to be seen. In Léotard's day, the garment was known as a ***maillot*** and was worn almost solely by circus performers and acrobats. It was only after his death that the garment came to be more widely worn and began to be known generally as a leotard. Viewers of *Countdown* on Channel 4 will be aware that 'leotard' is the most frequently played eponym in the thirty-five-year history of the game.

## PANTALOONS

Pantaloons are named after Pantalone, a sixteenth-century Italian *commedia dell'arte* character, traditionally portrayed as a foolish old man who is outwitted by the young lovers of the piece. Pantalone's costume included slippers, glasses and a peculiar combination of tight stockings and baggy trousers. The modern American term 'pants', for trousers, is a shortened form of the word. The etymology of 'underpants' is self-explanatory, I hope.

## PLIMSOLLS

The plimsoll shoe, the sports shoe of some of our schooldays, is so named because the distinctive rubber line that runs along the edge of the shoe resembles the Plimsoll line on a ship. It indicates how much cargo a ship can safely carry and is named after the man who introduced it in 1824: Samuel Plimsoll of Bristol.

## POMPADOUR

The pompadour hairstyle is named after the fourth mistress of Louis XV of France, Madame de Pompadour (1721–64). Beautiful and influential, she gave her name to a number of fashions, most famously this hairstyle, which involves the hair being swept up and rolled high above the forehead. There have been many versions over the years. Elvis Presley's quiff is an example of a more modern masculine take on the pompadour. US President Ronald Reagan sported one, too, in his prime.

## SIDEBURN

Sideburns are named after the American general Ambrose Burnside (1824–81), who fought in the Union Army during the Civil War. He was a popular figure, though not a very skilled general. After the war, he became a politician and was known around Washington for his unusual facial hair, with prominent mutton-chop whiskers, which came to be known as Burnsides. At some point later generations switched his name around and the sideburn was born.

## STETSON
The cowboys' favourite was originally manufactured by John B. Stetson in 1866. Known as the 'Hat of the West', it has been a perennial American favourite ever since.

## TAM O' SHANTER
A tam o' shanter is a traditional nineteenth-century Scottish bonnet. Originally brown or black, they now come in a variety of colours, as well as a variety of tartans. They have strong associations with the Scottish regiments and are affectionately known in the military as 'tams'. They are named after the poem *Tam O' Shanter* (1789) by Robert Burns.

## TRILBY
The trilby hat made its first appearance in the play of the same name, a stage adaptation of George du Maurier's 1894 novel, *Trilby*. The novel is the story of Trilby O'Ferrall, an artist's model, who inspires the love of many of the students who paint her. The author was the grandfather of novelist Daphne du Maurier and the novel gave us another eponymous word, Svengali, the name of the character in the novel under whose powerful influence Trilby falls.

## WELLINGTON
Rivalling 'sandwich' (see page 330) as perhaps the best-known eponym, the wellington boot is named after Arthur Wellesley, 1st Duke of Wellington (1769–1852). He was said to have instructed his boot-maker to produce leather boots to his own design, cut tight to the calf, hard-wearing yet comfortable. They became all the rage in English society among men keen to emulate their hero. The rubber version we associate with the term today was developed by Charles Goodyear (1800–60), the man in whose honour the tyre company was named.

. . . . . . . . . . . . . . . . . . . . . . . . . . . . . . . . . . . . . . . . .

# FLOWER POWER

Rose, Daisy, Honeysuckle, Pansy... Many people are named after flowers
– and some flowers are named after people.

## CAMELLIA

The camellia is a flowering plant commonly found in eastern and
southern Asia. Swedish botanist Carl Linnaeus (1707–78) named it after
the Moravian Jesuit Georg Josef Kamel (1661–1706), also known as
Camellus, who was both a botanist and a missionary in the Philippines.

## DAHLIA

The dahlia is the national flower of Mexico. It was unknown in Europe
till the late eighteenth century when seed plants were sent to Professor
Cavanilles, director of the Royal Gardens of Madrid. He named the plant
in honour of Swedish botanist Anders Dahl (1751–89), who had died two
years previously. The plant was subsequently introduced to the British Isles
by the Marchioness of Bute. In Britain, everybody pronounces the name
of the flower incorrectly: it's not a short *a* (as in 'alien'), it's a long *a* (as in
'dal', the Asian lentil dish, or Roald Dahl, the author).

## FUCHSIA

These pretty bright pink flowers, which are often said to resemble
ballerinas, are named after the German writer and botanist, Leonard
Fuchs (1501–66) – so here's another flower whose name we routinely
mispronounce. (And, yes, the colour fuchsia is named after the flower.)

## GARDENIA

This evergreen shrub, native to Asia and Africa, was named 'gardenia'
by Linnaeus (see Camellia, above) to honour the American physician
and botanist with the wonderfully appropriate name Alexander Garden
(1730–91). Oscar Wilde, who liked to wear a gardenia in his buttonhole
in season, observed: 'A really well-made buttonhole is the only link
between Art and Nature.'

## *WISTERIA*

The climbing shrub was named after Dr Casper Wistar (1761–1818). A prominent Quaker and professor of chemistry and physiology at the University of Philadelphia, Wistar is also celebrated for writing the first ever American textbook on anatomy.

## *ZINNIA*

The zinnia is named after German botanist Johann Gottfried Zinn. Zinn died young but had already made his mark in the world of botany. Carl Linnaeus decided to name this particular plant after him because the way in which it blooms brightly, then falls at the first frost, echoed the life of the young botanist.

. . . . . . . . . . . . . . . . . . . . . . . . . . . . . . . . . . . . . . . . . . .

## DISCLAIMER

By the way, I am not an eponymist. 'Brandreth' is a word in the dictionary, but we Brandreths are named after it, not the other way round. Disconcertingly, *The Oxford English Dictionary* defines a brandreth as 'a substructure of piles'. I prefer the *Collins English Dictionary* definition: 'a gridiron, trivet or tripod; a wooden frame used to support an object or a structure'. There is a triangular-shaped fell in the Lake District called Brandreth and it is from the place-name that the family name has come.

# K

**is for**

**KNAPSACK STRAP**

'Knapsack strap' is not something I say too often. In fact, it's something I try not to say at all. I have nothing against knapsack straps, so essential to knapsack owners. It's just that I can't get my tongue around the words without getting it into a terrible twist.

Some words and phrases are not easy to say. When I started out as an actor, more than forty years ago, one of the first parts I played professionally was in a radio play that was broadcast live. My role was that of the young detective. As I recall, I had only one line – and this was the line I had:

*That was the chair Schmidt sat in when he was shot.*

When the moment came, I stepped up to the microphone and spoke my line. Somehow it didn't come out quite right.

Since then I have been working on my diction, using these tongue-twisters as linguistic press-ups. All you have to do is repeat each one five times without faltering. Good luck.

# THE WORLD'S FIFTY WORST TONGUE TWISTERS

Knapsack strap

Cuthbert's custard

The rat ran by the river with a lump of raw liver

Three free thugs set three thugs free

Freddy Thrush flies through thick fog

Tuesday is stew day. Stew day is Tuesday

Gig whip

Bubble-bowls

That bloke's back brake-block broke

A big blue bucket of blue blueberries

Black bugs' blood

Crime cuts cut crime

The two-toed tree toad tried to tread where the three-toed tree toad
  trod

She sells seashells by the seashore

Dressed in drip-dry drawers

Do drop in at the Dewdrop Inn

Double bubble gum bubbles double

Diligence dismisseth despondency

There are thirty thousand feathers on that thrush's throat

Ted threw Fred three free throws

Freckled-faced Florence

Pure food for four pure mules

The gum glue grew glum

Groovy gravy, baby!

He's literally literary

Lame lambs limp

Mumbling bumblings. Bumbling mumblings

The new nuns knew the true nuns knew the new nuns too

Tiny orangutang tongues

Is there a pleasant peasant present?

A regal rural ruler
Six thick thistle sticks
Three thrice-freed thieves
The sick sixth sheik's sixth sheep's sick
Greek grapes
Which wristwatches are Swiss wristwatches?
Truly plural
The big black-backed bumblebee
A lump of red leather, a red-leather lump
Critical cricket critics
Thin sticks, thick bricks
Toy boat
He ran from the Indies to the Andes in his undies
Unique New York
The Leith police dismisseth us
Cheap ship trips
Peggy Babcock
Sister Suzie says she shall shortly sew a sheet
This thistle seems like that thistle
Lemon liniment

. . . . . . . . . . . . . . . . . . . . . . . . . . . . . . . . . . . . . . . . . . .

## FOREIGN TONGUES

'Peter Piper picked a peck of pickled peppers. Where's the peck of pickled peppers Peter Piper picked?' is one of the best-known English tongue twisters. In South Africa this is one of their favourites:

*Iqaqa Iaziqikaqika kwaze kwaqhawaka uqhoqhoqha*

In the English translation it reads: 'The skunk rolled and ruptured its larynx.'

There is an equally challenging sentence in Czech, with similar anatomical references:

*Strch prst skrz krk*

That means, 'Stick a finger in the throat.' As a tongue-twister, it certainly sticks in the throat: not a vowel in sight.

Or try this one from Indonesia:

*Kuku kaki kakak kakak ku kayak kuku kaki kakek kakek ku*

Translation: 'My brother's sister's toenails look like my grandfather's toenails.'

Naturally, the French have tongue twisters of a philosophical bent:

*Je suis ce que je suis et si je suis ce que je suis, qu'est-ce que je suis?*

'I am what I am and if I am what I am, what am I?'

Incidentally, in sign language, tongue twisters are known as finger fumblers.

. . . . . . . . . . . . . . . . . . . . . . . . . . . . . . . . . . . . . . . . . . .

## WORLD'S LONGEST TONGUE TWISTER

'If a Hottentot tot taught a Hottentot tot to talk e'er the tot could totter, ought the Hottentot tot be taught to say aught, or naught, or what ought to be taught her? If to hoot and to toot a Hottentot tot be taught by a Hottentot tutor, should the tutor get hot if the Hottentot tot hoot and toot at the Hottentot tutor?'

If you thought that was a mouthful, try this, the tongue twister that just won't give up. It is the world's longest, most terrible tongue twister: 'The Saga of Shrewd Simon Short'. Try to read it out loud without making a single slip. I couldn't do it. Can you?

Shrewd Simon Short sewed shoes. Seventeen summers, speeding storms, spreading sunshine successively, saw Simon's small, shabby shop, still standing staunch, saw Simon's selfsame squeaking sign still swinging silently specifying:

Simon Short, Smithfield's sole surviving shoemaker. Shoes sewed soled super finely.

Simon's spry, sedulous spouse, Sally Short, sewed shirts, stitched sheets, stuffed sofas. Simon's six stout sons – Seth, Samuel, Stephen, Saul, Silas, Shadrach – sold sundries. Sober Seth sold sugar, spices; simple Sam sold saddles, stirrups, screws; sagacious Stephen sold silks, satins, shawls; sceptical Saul sold silver salvers; selfish Shadrach sold salves, shoestrings, stops, saws, skates; slack Silas sold Sally Short's stuffed sofas.

Some seven summers since, Simon's second son Samuel saw Sophia Sophronia Spriggs somewhere. Sweet, smart, sensible Sophia Sophronia Spriggs. Sam soon showed strong symptoms. Sam seldom stayed storing, selling saddles. Sam sighed sorrowfully, sought Sophia Sophronia's society, sang several serenades slyly. Simon stormed, scolded severely, said Sam seemed so silly singing such shameful, senseless songs. 'Strange Sam should slight such splendid sales! Strutting spendthrift! Shattered-brained simpleton.'

'Softly, softly, sire,' said Sally. 'Sam's smitten; Sam's spied some sweetheart.'

'Sentimental schoolboy!' snarled Simon. 'Smitten! Stop such stuff.' Simon sent Sally's snuffbox spinning, seized Sally's scissors, smashed Sally's spectacles, scattering several spools. 'Sneaking scoundrel! Sam's shocking silliness shall surcease!' Scowling, Simon stopped speaking, started swiftly shopward.

Sally sighed sadly. Summoning Sam, she spoke sweet sympathy. 'Sam,' said she, 'Sire seems singularly snappy; so, solicit, sue, secure Sophronia speedily, Sam.'

'So soon? So soon?' said Sam, standing stock-still.

'So soon, surely,' said Sally, smiling, 'specially since Sire shows such spirits.'

So Sam, somewhat scared, sauntered slowly. Shaking stupendously, Sam soliloquised: 'Sophia Sophronia Spriggs, Spriggs – Short – Sophia Sophronia Short-Samuel Short's spouse – sounds splendid! Suppose she should say – she shan't – she shan't!'

Soon Sam spied Sophia starching shirts, singing softly. Seeing Sam she stopped starching, saluting Sam smilingly. Sam stammered shockingly. 'Spl-spl-splendid summer season, Sophia.'

'Selling saddles still, Sam?'

'Sar-sar-tin,' said Sam, starting suddenly. 'Season's somewhat sudorific,' said Sam, steadily, staunching streaming sweat, shaking sensibly.

'Sartin,' said Sophia, smiling significantly. 'Sip some sweet sherbet, Sam.' (Silence: sixty seconds.) 'Sire shot sixty sheldrakes, Saturday,' said Sophia.

'Sixty? Shot!' said Sam. (Silence: seventy-seven seconds.)

'See sister Susan's sunflowers,' said Sophia, socially, silencing such stiff silence.

Sophia's sprightly sauciness stimulated Sam strangely; so Sam suddenly spoke sentimentally: 'Sophia, Susan's sunflowers seem saying Samuel Short, Sophia Sophronia Spriggs stroll serenely, seek some sequestered spot, some sylvan shade. Sparkling springs shall sing soul stirring strains; sweet songsters shall silence secret sighings; super-angelic sylphs shall – '

Sophia snickered; so Sam stopped.

'Sophia,' said Sam, solemnly.

'Sam,' said Sophia.

'Sophia, stop smiling; Sam Short's sincere. Sam's seeking some sweet spouse, Sophia.'

Sophia stood silent.

'Speak, Sophia, speak; such suspense speculates sorrow.'

'Seek, sire, Sam, seek sire.'

So Sam sought sire Spriggs.

Sire Spriggs said, 'Sartin.'

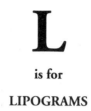

**is for**

## LIPOGRAMS

. . . . . . . . . . . . . . . . . . . . . . . . . . . . . . . . . . . . . . . . .

### ABSENT FRIENDS

Here is a paragraph from a novel, *Gadsby*. The author, a Californian musician named Ernest Vincent Wright, dedicated it 'to Youth' with the hope that *Gadsby* would be 'a valuable aid to schoolchildren in English composition'. The novel sold only fifty copies, so evidently did not take the educational world by storm, but for those of us interested in wordplay it is a remarkable work all the same. Read on:

> Upon this basis I am going to show you how a bunch of bright young folks did find a champion; a man with boys and girls of his own; a man of so dominating and happy individuality that youth is drawn to him as a fly to a sugar bowl. It is not a gossipy yarn; nor is it a dry monotonous account. It is a practical discarding of that worn-out notion that 'a child don't know anything'.

If you are familiar with lipograms, you will probably have noticed that the paragraph you have just read does not contain the letter *e*. In fact the most commonly used vowel in English does not appear in *any* of *Gadsby's* fifty thousand words. According to the author's introduction, the book was composed 'with the *e* type-bar of the type writer tied down'!

If you've never come across one before, welcome to the 'lipogram', a written work composed of words chosen to avoid the use of a particular letter.

Lipograms have been teasing and testing the ingenuity of writers since ancient times. The word has its roots in Greek and a fifth-century Greek poet called Triphiodorus became something of an early master of the lipogram. His greatest feat was an epic poem about the wanderings of Ulysses. This ran to twenty-four books, each named after a letter of the alphabet. The first was called *Alpha*, as you might expect. What the reader would not expect, however, is that Triphiodorus gave it that name because there wasn't a single alpha in the whole book. Book two was called *Beta* because there was no beta, and so on right through the alphabet to Omega. It has been suggested that the *Odyssey* of Triphiodorus might have been improved if the poet had left out all the other letters too, but that seems a little harsh.

Down the centuries others tried their hands at the lipogram. There was Peter Riga, a canon of Notre Dame at Rheims at the end of the twelfth century. He set about writing a summary of the Old and New Testaments in twenty-three chapters. In the first chapter he avoided the letter *a*. The letter *b* was omitted from chapter two. Chapter three had to make do without *c*. Letter by letter the biblical summary lurched to its conclusion. As the author of *A History of Christian-Latin Poetry* commented, 'Misplaced ingenuity could go no further.'

In the sixteenth century, the Spanish poet and dramatist Lope de Vega produced five novels excluding, in turn, the five vowels *a, e, i, o* and *u*, finding time to do this alongside writing in excess of fifteen hundred plays.

In 1816 Parisian theatregoers were treated to *Pièce Sans A (Play Without A)*, which promised an evening's entertainment without the assistance of the first letter of the alphabet. Apparently, the evening got off to an unfortunate start. The first actor to speak got his first line wrong. '*Ah,*

*Monsieur,*' he declared, '*vous voilà.*' The audience loved this and their laughter subsided just long enough for the prompter to put the actor right: '*Eh, Monsieur, vous voici!*'

More recently, the Frenchman Georges Perec caused a limited stir with his 300-page novel *La disparition* (1969), which was written without the letter *e*. It was translated into English as *A Void* (1994). According to one critic, 'The silent disappearance of the letter might be considered a metaphor for the Jewish experience during the Second World War.' More than that, since the name 'Georges Perec' is rich in *e*s, the disappearance of the letter also ensured the author's own 'disappearance'.

In the English language in our time, A. Ross Eckler has probably achieved the most conspicuous lipogrammatic success with his reworking of the nursery rhyme 'Mary Had a Little Lamb'. Here is the verse, recast by Mr Eckler, without an *s*:

> *Mary had a little lamb,*
> *With fleece a pale white hue,*
> *And everywhere that Mary went*
> *The lamb kept her in view.*
> *To academe he went with her,*
> *Illegal, and quite rare;*
> *It made the children laugh and play*
> *To view a lamb in there.*

And here's how he does it without any *a*s:

> *Polly owned one little sheep,*
> *Its fleece shone white like snow,*
> *Every region where Polly went*
> *The sheep did surely go.*
> *He followed her to school one time,*
> *Which broke the rigid rule;*
> *The children frolicked in their room*
> *To see the sheep in school.*

A. Ross Eckler lipogrammatises nursery rhymes. I do the same for Shakespeare. Just as the famous Dr Bowdler sought to improve the works of Shakespeare by cutting out or altering all indelicacies (turning 'bed' into 'bridal chariot', for example) I seek to improve his plays by dropping a different letter from each one. I began with *Hamlet*, from which I scrupulously excluded the letter **i**. Here's how the most famous of all soliloquies turned out:

> *To be, or not to be; that's the query:*
> *Whether you would be nobler to suffer mentally*
> *The stones and arrows of outrageous fortune,*
> *Or take arms to oppose a sea of troubles,*
> *And through combat end them? To pass, to sleep.*

Five acts later, with not a dry *i* in the house, *Hamlet* dies, sorry, fades away, with the haunting line:

> *The rest be hush-hush.*

From *Macbeth* I dropped **a** and **e**. Here is the hero, Mcb'th, having one of his hallucinations:

> *Is it thy tiny sword in front I'm glimpsing,*
> *With its blunt bit pointing to my wrist? I wish to touch it:*
> *I find I'm no good doing it, but I spy it still...*

From the whole of *Twelfth Night* I excluded **l**, the twelfth letter from the beginning of the alphabet, and **o**, the twelfth letter from the end of the alphabet. In my version of the play, Awseeneau launches the proceedings with these lyrical lines:

> *If music be desire's sustenance, make music yet;*
> *Give me excessive music, that, surfeiting,*
> *The appetite may sicken, and thus die...*

Currently I'm working on *Othello* without the *o*s. It isn't easy, but what is art without suffering?

· · · · · · · · · · · · · · · · · · · · · · · · · · · · · · · · · · · · · · · ·

## UNIVOCALICS UNITE

While a lipogram concentrates on omitting a particular vowel, a univocalic is the exact opposite: restricting itself to the sole use of a particular vowel. For this reason univocalic verse presents a remarkable, if somewhat contrived, cohesion.

This Victorian univocal about the Russo-Turkish war relies on *a* as its only vowel:

> *War harms all ranks, all arts, all crafts appal;*
> *At Mars' harsh blast, arch, rampant, altar fall!*
> *Ah! hard as adamant a braggart Czar*
> *Arms vassal-swarms, and fans a fatal war!*
> *Rampant at that bad call, a Vandal band*
> *Harass, and harm, and ransack Wallach-land.*
> *A Tarta phalanx Balkan's scarp hath past,*
> *And Allah's standard galls, alas! at last.*

A few years later Charles C. Tombaugh, composed univocalics for each vowel. Here is *The Approach of Evening*, which he wrote for the letter *i*:

> *Idling, I sit in this mild twilight dim,*
> *Whilst birds, in wild, swift vigils, circling skim.*
> *Light winds in sighing sink, till, rising bright,*
> *Night's Virgin Pilgrim swims in vivid light!*

The univocal is by no means the preserve of the nineteenth century. Georges Perec's 1972 novella *Les revenentes* complemented his earlier lipogrammatic work by being a univocalic piece in which the letter *e* is the only vowel used.

And England's answer to Georges Perec, George Marvill, composed this for a competition in the *New Statesman*. Look carefully and you'll see that

he succeeds on two counts: not only is *o* the only vowel employed, his
exchange between the owls is a palindrome.

   'Too hot to hoot!'
   'Too hot to woo!'
   'Too wot?'
   'Too hot to hoot!'
   'To woo!'
   'Too wot?'
   'To hoot! Too hot to hoot!'

## MONOSYLLABICS

'Monosyllabics' are another challenge wordsmiths like to set for
themselves.

Many of the words we use contain just one syllable. Many more contain
more. The monosyllabist does his or her best to use only words of one
syllable. It isn't easy.

As an exercise, try to write a sensible sentence consisting entirely of
monosyllabics.

If you do it with ease, try to write a poem in the same way. Here is a
near-monosyllabic verse from the seventeenth-century lyric poet Robert
Herrick:

   **To Daffodils**
   *We have short time to stay, as you,*
   *We have as short a spring;*
   *As quick a growth to meet decay,*
   *As you, or anything.*
   *We die*
   *As your hours do, and dry*

*Away,*
*Like to the summer's rain;*
*Or as the pearls of morning's dew,*
*Ne'er to be found again.*

Herrick slips up once or twice. In this pithy poem, I am proud to say I
don't slip up at all. What follows is a perfect example of monosyllabic verse.
I wrote it a few years ago to mark the passing of Spot, the family goldfish.

Spot, unfortunately, was eaten by Oscar, one of our cats. (It wasn't
entirely Oscar's fault. He was in a state, having been teased by one of the
dogs – the mongrel that thinks his name is Down Boy. The other dog
is better behaved: he's a sophisticated French poodle called Phydeaux.)
When pets die in our household, we like to bury them in the garden,
but because there was nothing left of poor old Spot, we could not have a
proper interment: we had to settle for a memorial gathering. It was on this
occasion that I first recited my unique monosyllabic verse. I am proud to
say it has featured on Roger McGough's radio programme, *Poetry Please*,
and it lays claim to being the shortest poem on record.

**Ode to a Goldfish**
*O*
*Wet*
*Pet!*

# M

### is for

### MIX ME A METAPHOR

We all mix metaphors. Even the best of us. The most famous passage in world literature contains a beauty of a mixed metaphor in the fourth line:

> *To be, or not to be: that is the question:*
> *Whether 'tis nobler in the mind to suffer*
> *The slings and arrows of outrageous fortune,*
> *Or take arms against a sea of troubles,*
> *And by opposing end them?*

A mixed metaphor combines two or more inconsistent metaphors, and if Shakespeare can use one in *Hamlet*'s great soliloquy, why shouldn't the rest of us join the fun?

The most notorious mixed metaphor is probably one attributed to Boyle Roche (1743–1807), an Irish politician who seems to have French-kissed the Blarney Stone:

> *Mr Speaker, I smell a rat; I see him forming in the air and darkening the sky: but I'll nip him in the bud.*

(Roche had quite a way with words. On another occasion he thundered: 'Half the lies our opponents tell about us are not true.')

Bureaucrats, it seems, have a special gift for mixing metaphors. Here are some choice examples:

> *The recovery of the house-building programme will require action in a number of fields.*
> *We now have 137 and a half pairs of surgical boots on our hands.*
> *Instead of supersonic aircraft standing on their own feet by charging slightly increased fares, subsonic aircraft are required to cross-subsidise.*
> *Flexibility is one of the cornerstones of programme budgeting.*

Here are four gems reported from Capitol Hill, Washington DC:

> *The problem started small, but it is baseballing.*
> *He threw a cold shoulder on that idea.*
> *I'm not going to bail out his chestnuts.*
> *I support Mr Arbuzov and the other Soviet diffidents.*

And here's a magnificent seven, courtesy of John Rentoul and Anthony Polson in the *Independent*:

1. 'Ahmadinejad wields axe to cement his position' – *Independent* headline, 14 December 2010
2. 'It would open up a can of worms and a legal minefield about freedom, religion and equalities legislation . . . It may open up old wounds and put people into the trenches; no one wants that' – David Burrowes, Conservative MP, on gay marriage, 17 January 2012
3. 'Labour are fighting like rats in a barrel' – Charlie Elphicke, Conservative MP, 16 February 2014
4. 'I'm kick-starting a drive to get employee ownership into the bloodstream' – Nick Clegg, 17 January 2012
5. 'They've put all their eggs in one basket and it's misfired' – Paul Merson, Sky football pundit, of West Ham's purchase of Andy Carroll
6. 'Out of the hat on Monday night the home secretary produced the

rabbit, the Temporary Provisions Bill, as her fig leaf to cover her major U-turn' – Simon Hughes, Liberal Democrat MP, 2008
7. 'We're like the canary down the mine. We're the first people who pick up what's going on out there and what we're seeing at the moment is a boiling pot whose lid is coming off' – Markos Chrysostomou, Haringey Citizens Advice Bureau, 19 November 2012

Among the classic mixed metaphors of yesteryear, I am particularly fond of this, from Ernest Bevin, the Labour government's foreign secretary in 1948. This was his response to the idea of a Council of Europe:

*I don't like it. When you open that Pandora's box, you will find it full of Trojan horses.*

A novelist, not a politician, is responsible for my all-time favourite. This is a line from the great Ian Fleming:

*Bond's knees, the Achilles' heel of all skiers, were beginning to ache.*

I reckon Ian Fleming knew what he was doing when he wrote that. I am not so sure about John Prescott, sometime MP, deputy prime minister and amateur pugilist. He once declared, 'The Green Belt is a Labour idea and we're determined to build on it.' Lord Prescott, as he now is, has a special way with words. He has the gift of treating the English language like a Rubik's Cube. Coming in to land at Heathrow Airport after a turbulent flight, he expressed his relief in a memorable turn of phrase: 'Thank God I'm back on *terra cotta*.'

. . . . . . . . . . . . . . . . . . . . . . . . . . . . . . . . . . . . . . . . . . . .

## METAPHORS AND MALAPHORS

Malaphors aren't quite malapropisms and aren't quite mixed metaphors but the best are as memorable as either. Whatever you want to call these, I hope you'll agree: each one is a pearl worth its weight in gold.

I can read him like the back of my book.

The sacred cows have come home to roost with a vengeance.

We could stand here and talk until the cows turn blue.

We will get there by hook or ladder.

There is no head of steam to which one can harness oneself.

It's time to grab the bull by the tail and look him in the eye.

All these whited sepulchres are tarred with the same brush.

We're not out of the wood yet by a long chalk.

The skeleton at the feast was a mare's nest.

He was watching me like I was a hawk.

He's a wolf in cheap clothing.

They're diabolically opposed.

From now on, I'm watching everything you do with a fine-tuned comb.

It's as easy as falling off a piece of cake.

He's like a duck out of water.

These haemorrhoids are a real pain in the neck.

It's time to step up to the plate and lay your cards on the table.

He's burning the midnight oil from both ends.

It sticks out like a sore throat.

It's like looking for a needle in a hayride.

People are dying like hot cakes.

He's a little green behind the ears.

We have to get all our ducks on the same page.

He's a rough diamond with a heart of gold.

The fan is going to hit the roof.

I have a lot of black sheep in my closet.

I'm sweating like a bullet.

Wild horses on their bended knees would not make me do it.

I know some of these sound as if I have made them up. I haven't. People do say the strangest things. Only today on the radio, in response to the news that Zayn Malik had decided to leave the group One Direction, I heard the young pop hero described as 'sporting facial hair and looking like a rabbit caught in the headlines'. You couldn't make it up.

# N

### is for

### NOSTALGIA (AND NOVELTY)

. . . . . . . . . . . . . . . . . . . . . . . . . . . . . . . . . . . . . . . . . . . .

## FROM ACCLUMSID TO ZUCHE

They say nostalgia isn't what it used to be – but that's up to us, surely?
Some of the oldest words in the language are some of the most delightful.
We don't use them much, not because we don't want to but simply because
we are not familiar with them. Here, with definitions and a loose guide
to pronunciation where appropriate, are some of my favourite lost words.
Unless you are a hoddypeak, you'll glop them down with adlubescence –
and start slipping them casually into your conversation.

> *acclumsid* numbed, paralysed, clumsy. From the Old English *clumsen*,
>   'to be stiff, numb'
> *acersecomic* one whose hair has never been cut
> *adlubescence* pleasure, delight (accent on the *bes*)
> *agathokakological* with a mingling of good and evil (accent on *log*)
> *agruw* horrify, cause shuddering (accent on *gruw*)

*atabales* kettledrums

*barlafumble* call for a truce by a person who has fallen in play or
wrestling; request for time out

*bawdreaing* bawdy misbehaviour

*beek* bask in the sun or before a fire

*bellibone* lovely maiden, pretty lass. An anglicisation of the French
*belle et bonne*, fair and good

*bronstrops* prostitute

*brool* low, deep humming; a murmur

*croodle* a faint humming

*dilling* child born when the parents are old; possibly a corruption of
darling or dillingpig, the weakling in a litter

*eldnyng* jealous, suspicion

*fadoodle* nonsense, something foolish. Apparently now it is urban slang
for the penis

*flapdragon* sport of catching raisins in bowls of flaming brandy or
drinking the brandy without getting burned as a tribute to one's
mistress

*flosh* swamp or stagnant pool overgrown with weeds

*glop* swallow greedily; stare at in wonder or alarm

*gundygut* glutton

*gwenders* disagreeable tingling from the cold

*hoddypeak* simpleton, blockhead

*killbuck* fierce-looking fellow

*lennow* flabby, limp

*loverdrury* keepsake, love token

*magsman* swindler

*malshave* caterpillar

*nyle* fog, mist

*okselle* armpit

*pingle* eat with little appetite

*poop-noddy* fool or simpleton; the game of love

*popolly* little darling (from the French *poupelet*); a female favourite,
special loved one or mistress

*porknell* one as fat as a pig

*quetch* moan and twitch in pain; shake

*quop* throb, palpitate
*ribble* wrinkle, furrow
*ringo* treat; a sweet made from the root of the sea holly, supposed to be
    an aphrodisiac
*spuddle* assume airs of importance without reason; make trifles seem
    important
*squiddle* waste time with idle talk
*turngiddy* dizzy
*ug* fear, dread
*vellication* twitching or convulsive movement
*wallydraigle* worthless slovenly woman
*wheeple* ineffectual attempt of a man to whistle loudly; an
    onomatopoeic term, from the low cheep of a bird
*xenodochial* hospitable to strangers
*yurky* itchy (pronounced *yooky*)
*zuche* tree stump

. . . . . . . . . . . . . . . . . . . . . . . . . . . . . . . . . . . . . . . . . . . . . . . . . . . . . .

## HUM DIDDLE DOO DAH

I was introduced to the world of lost words in the 1970s by a remarkable
American author, Susan Kelz Sperling. She hunts for lost words as a pig
hunts for truffles and her marvellous book, *Poplollies and Bellibones*, is one
of my bedside favourites.

Not only does Susan collect lost words, she has fun with them. Here is one
of the delicious round games she plays with her rich vocabulary of words
gone-but-not-quite-forgotten:

## A ROUND OF HUM

What is *hum*?
*Hum* is a strong liquor made by combining ale or beer with spirits. Too
    much hum can make one's head *quop*.

What is *quop*?

*Quop* means to throb. A man's heart may *quop* with longing to hold his loved one's *feat*.

What is *feat*?

A *feat* is a dangling curl of hair. A *woup* with the *feat* of an elephant inside is considered lucky to wear.

What is a *woup*?

A *woup* is a simple metal hoop or ring not set with stones. Large *woups* to anchor one's feet could have been used at the base of a *gofe*.

What is a *gofe*?

A *gofe* is the pillory that was usually erected on the *wong*, where the greatest number of people could stroll by and see it.

What is a *wong*?

A *wong* is the meadowland that people used as their common, where they would meet to take their cows to graze. Nowadays a public *wong* is covered with *nesh* plantings and lush trees.

What is *nesh*?

Nesh means fresh, delicate or soft, as vegetables, foliage or fruit should be. Braiding one's hair with *nesh* flowers makes a beautiful *kell*.

What is a *kell*?

A *kell* is a woman's headdress, be it as close set as a net or a cap or as fancy as a wig to don for a party. A lady's *kell* is more elaborate if she is going to a ball where *hum* is served.

· · · · · · · · · · · · · · · · · · · · · · · · · · · · · · · · · · · · · · · · · · ·

## ENDANGERED WORDS

Some of our oldest, finest words are gone for good. Others are with us still – just – but sorely neglected. Here are two dozen splendid words that are in danger of disappearing.

You score a point for every word you recognise. If you score 5 that isn't bad; 10 is impressive; and if you score 15 or more you're either Susan Sperling or my friend Susie Dent, from *Countdown*'s Dictionary Corner, or you cheated by looking at the answers.

1. A *biggonet* is (a) a primitive form of bra, (b) a form of female dress, (c) a type of automatic rifle, (d) a divorced bigamist.
2. A *cracknel* is (a) a head injury, (b) a seventeenth-century epithet applied to a prostitute, (c) a crayfish, (d) a biscuit.
3. A *dziggetai* is (a) a Mongolian mule, (b) an Egyptian mummy, (c) an Indian spirit, (d) a Greek coin.
4. *Epistaxis* is (a) a fleet of large taxis, (b) a letter demanding money with menaces, (c) bleeding from the nose, (d) an evergreen shrub.
5. A *factotum* is (a) an unreliable piece of information, (b) a pagan symbol, (c) an intestinal complaint caused by excessive eating, (d) a servant.
6. A *grackle* is (a) a bird, (b) a rope, (c) a tree, (d) the noise made by feet walking on gravel.
7. A *heder* is (a) a male sheep, (b) a female snail, (c) an executioner, (d) a kind of acid.
8. *Imparidigitate* is (a) having a disease which makes it impossible to stay still, (b) suffering from the after-effects of syphilis, (c) being able to speak five or more foreign languages, (d) having an odd number of fingers or toes on each limb.
9. *Jargonelle* is (a) slang used by women, (b) a kind of pear, (c) a primitive form of trumpet, (d) a pewter drinking vessel.
10. To *kittle* is (a) to tickle, (b) to burn wood, (c) to tell lies, (d) to make saddles.
11. A *lachrymist* is (a) someone who turns metal into gold, (b) someone who collects precious stones, (c) someone who weeps, (d) a pearl diver.
12. *Mulierosity* is (a) being fond of women, (b) being simple-minded, (c) being generous with other people's money, (d) talking very fast while remaining comprehensible.
13. An *ogdoad* is (a) a species of frog, (b) a Roman altar, (c) a vegetable, (d) a bone in the foot.
14. A *pennon* is (a) a small flag, (b) a writing implement, (c) a vegetable, (d) a bone in the foot.
15. A *quat* is (a) a liquid measure, (b) a small boil, (c) a flat-bottomed boat, (d) a bat that is *not* nocturnal.
16. A *kosarian* is (a) someone who grows roses, (b) a craftsman specialising in wood carving, (c) a biblical scholar, (d) a member of the Confraternity of the Rosary.

17. A *sapodilla* is (a) a South American insect, (b) a large evergreen tree, (c) an intoxicating drink made from red berries, (d) the punctuation mark added to a *c* to make it soft.

18. A *tirrit* is (a) a small ferret, (b) a fit of temper, (c) a false moustache, (d) an unkind epithet for a girl of easy virtue.

19. A *uvarovite* is (a) a nomadic tribesman, (b) a kind of long-lasting glue or adhesive, (c) a medieval court jester, (d) an emerald-green garnet.

20. *Venenose* refers to (a) something poisonous, (b) a claret wine in perfect condition, (c) a fabric, (d) a disgusting smell.

21. A *whim-wham* is (a) a Native American hideaway, (b) a trinket or trifle, (c) a drink made with eggs, milk and brandy, (d) a spell uttered by a white witch.

22. A *xyster* is (a) a female relative by marriage, (b) a plant with leaves that sting, (c) an instrument for scraping bones, (d) part of a ship's rudder.

23. A *yex* is (a) an armadillo, (b) a pincushion, (c) approximately seven miles, (d) a belch or hiccup.

24. A *zopilote* is (a) a camel herdsman, (b) the middle tier of a trireme, (c) the transparent cell wall of the mammalian ovum, (d) a vulture.

ANSWERS

1 (b). 2 (d). 3 (a). 4 (c). 5 (d). 6 (a). 7 (a). 8 (d). 9 (b). 10 (a). 11 (c). 12 (a). 13 (c). 14 (a). 15 (b). 16 (a) and (d). 17 (b). 18 (b). 19 (d). 20 (a). 21 (b). 22 (c). 23 (d). 24 (d).

• • • • • • • • • • • • • • • • • • • • • • • • • • • • • • • • • • • • • • • • • • • • • • • •

# NEW WORDS

N is for 'novelty' as well as 'nostalgia', so off with the old and on with the new.

As old words disappear, so new ones arrive. I can tell you what words have arrived on the scene in your lifetime – and in which year their use was first recorded. (I am assuming you weren't born before 1930. You certainly don't look it.)

| | | |
|---|---|---|
| 1930 *teenager* | 1931 *microwave* | 1932 *malnourishment* |
| 1933 *doodle* | 1934 *agitprop* | 1935 *audition (v.)* |
| 1936 *Muzak* | 1937 *autobahn* | 1938 *weenybopper* |
| 1939 *loud-hailer* | 1940 *Mae West (life jacket)* | 1941 *majorette* |
| 1942 *astronavigation* | 1943 *acronym* | 1944 *aerosol* |
| 1945 *microsleep* | 1946 *microdot* | 1947 *apartheid* |
| 1948 *automation* | 1949 *male menopause* | 1950 *aqualung* |
| 1951 *discotheque* | 1952 *to take the mickey out of (someone)* | 1953 *adventure playground* |
| 1954 *non-U* | 1955 *admass (the part of society easily influenced by advertising and mass media)* | 1956 *brinkmanship* |
| 1957 *sexploitation* | 1958 *aerospace* | 1959 *microbus* |
| 1960 *biorhythm* | 1961 *mini* | 1962 *non-event* |
| 1963 *Mandrax (a sedative)* | 1964 *monokini* | 1965 *metrication* |

. . . . . . . . . . . . . . . . . . . . . . . . . . . . . . . . . . . . . . . . . . .

## NOW WORDS

From the 1990s:

| | | |
|---|---|---|
| *all that (as in I'm...)* | *as if!* | *bad hair day* |
| *bling bling* | *bootylicious* | *Brit pop* |
| *bromance* | *chick flick* | *chick lit* |
| *diss* | *fashionista* | *first world problem* |
| *full monty (as in to strip)* | *happy slapping* | *laddette* |
| *metrosexual* | *rave (first used late eighties, took off in the nineties)* | *soccer mom (US)* |
| *step aerobics* | *whatever (as in 'Whatever!')* | *wicked (as in 'Great!')* |
| *world wide web* | | |

## From the 2000s:

| | | |
|---|---|---|
| *alpha mom* (US) | *bailout* | *barista* |
| *car crash TV* | *cougar (as in an older woman who dates younger men)* | *credit crunch* |
| *crackBerry (someone who is addicted to their BlackBerry)* | *flashmob* | *frappucino* |
| *global warming* | *helicopter mum* | *hot-desking* |
| *peeps (as in 'people')* | *WAG* | *9/11* |

## From the 2010s:

| | | |
|---|---|---|
| *adultescent (a middle-aged person whose clothes, interests and activities are typically associated with youth culture)* | *clickbait (an internet link you are tempted to click on, designed to lure you to a website or blog)* | *fracking* |
| *frankenfood* | *guyliner (eye liner make-up worn by men)* | *hater (a person who can't be happy for others)* |
| *hipster (a follower of a certain fashion)* | *jeggings* | *mankini* |
| *muffin top* | *onesie* | *photo bomb* |
| *pop-up restaurants* | *twerking* | *upcycle (making new things from old)* |
| *vajazzle (a sparkly make-over for a female's private parts)* | *vape (to inhale from an e-cigarette)* | |

New words, like *vape*, are getting into the atmosphere all the time. Each year around two hundred make their way into *The Oxford English Dictionary*. Here are ten that got there in 2014:

| | | |
|---|---|---|
| *Blu-tack (n., v.)* | *chugger (n.)* | *demotivated (adj.)* |
| *exfoliator (n.)* | *hero-worshipping (adj., n.)* | *heroine-worship (v.)* |
| *Old Etonian (n., adj.)* | *scissor-kick (v.)* | *toilet-paper\* (v.)* |
| *wackadoodle (n., adj.) (Pertaining to an eccentric person)* | | |

*(NB This is a verb not a noun. Sometimes known as TPing, which also made its way into* The Oxford English Dictionary *this year, it is the act of covering someone's house or possessions with toilet paper.)*

Like me, you may be surprised to find that 'Blu-tack', 'hero-worshipping' and 'Old Etonian' weren't in the dictionary already, but you have to remember that *The Oxford English Dictionary* records the written use of language and cites sourced examples of each word and phrase it includes – and that takes time. Here are ten new words and phrases that have yet to make it to the printed dictionary. They are in the running, we know, because already they feature in *The OED* online version. Definitions courtesy of OxfordDictionaries.com:

> **adorbs** *arousing great delight, cute or adorable:* **all the pets are totally adorbs; check out the adorbs photos**
>
> **al desko** *a play on* **al fresco** *(for food eaten outside, literally 'in the fresh [air]' in Italian), it is an adjective and adverb denoting food eaten 'while working at one's desk in an office'*
>
> **amazeballs** *extremely good or impressive; amazing:* **the atmosphere was nothing special, but the food was amazeballs; she looks amazeballs.**
>
> **binge watching** *watch multiple episodes of (a television programme) in rapid succession, typically by means of DVDs or digital streaming*
>
> **catnip** *someone or something that is very attractive or appealing to a particular person or group:* **both men are aggressive self-promoters and catnip for the media; Biotech stocks have become catnip to investors this year**
>
> **cool beans** *used to express approval or delight:* **they went to Europe? Cool beans**
>
> **duck face** *an exaggerated pouting expression in which the lips are thrust outward, typically made by a person posing for a photograph*
>
> **humblebrag** *an ostensibly modest or self-deprecating statement whose actual purpose is to draw attention to a quality, achievement, or possession of which one is proud:* **I look dreadful today, so why have so many people bought me drinks?**
>
> **man crush** *a typically non-sexual liking or admiration felt by one man for another*

**spit take** *an act of suddenly spitting out liquid one is drinking in response to something funny or surprising*

The language is constantly evolving. As far as I'm concerned, that's cool beans. Who knows what words next year will bring?

# O

**is for**

## OLL KORRECT, OK?

Too much nonsense has been talked about the expression 'OK'. I'm here
to set the record straight, and I intend to be quick about it. OK?

'OK' does *not* come from the Native American Choctaw word *oke*
meaning 'it is' or from *hoke* meaning 'yes'.

'OK' does *not* come from the practice of grading woods for
furniture-making – the best oak, of course, being *Oak A.*

'OK' does *not* come from the O.K. Club named after Old Kinderhook,
Martin Van Buren's birthplace in New York. (Martin Van Buren was the
eighth president of the United States, 1837–41, but don't worry: I hadn't
heard of him either.)

OK, are you ready for the truth?

In New England, two hundred or so years ago, there was a craze for
abbreviations, and 'OK' and 'O.K.' first appeared in print then, in various
Boston newspapers, along with many other abbreviations. 'RTBS' was
'remains to be seen'; 'SP' was 'small potatoes'; 'OFM' was 'our first men'.

Inevitably, a number of the abbreviations had to be explained for the benefit of uninitiated readers – e.g. the *Boston Morning Post* of 12 June 1838 spoke of 'a duel W.O.O.O.F.C. (with one of our first citizens)'. Bizarrely, the craze went so far as to produce the abbreviations of international misspellings, so that 'NG' for 'no go' and 'AR' for 'all right' became 'KG' for 'know go', and 'OW' for 'oll right'. 'OK' comes from 'oll correct'. Of all the varied and colourful abbreviations and misspellings of the time, 'OK' alone spread and survived.

So now you know. OK?

# P

### is for

### PORTMANTEAUS & TELESCOPES

Portmanteaus and telescopes, as well as being suitcases and optical instruments, are useful ways of creating new words. (And, pedants, please note, 'portmanteau', while French in origin, is now used as an English word, so the plural is correctly portmanteaus rather than *portmanteaux*.)

. . . . . . . . . . . . . . . . . . . . . . . . . . . . . . . . . . . . . . . . . . . .

### PORTMANTEAUS DE LUXE

Lewis Carroll adopted and adapted the existing French word *portmanteau* to describe a new word created by packing two other words together. A portmanteau is a travelling case hinged in two; it is also a portmanteau itself: a combination of '*porter*' (to carry) and '*manteau*' (cloak/coat).

*Galumph* is one of Carroll's most famous portmanteaus: he created it by combining 'gallop' and 'triumph'. Of more modern, post-Carroll portmanteaus, here are some of my prizners:*

   *affluenza* affluence + influenza (first-world man-flu)
   *anecdotard* anecdote + dotard, a dotard given to telling anecdotes (the
      word dates from 1894, but my wife tells me the phenomenon is
      alive and well in 2015)

*biopic* biography + picture
*blog* web + log
*brunch* breakfast + lunch (1896)
*beautility* beauty + utility
*cheeseburger* cheese + hamburger (1938)
*citrange* citrus + orange, a hybrid fruit
*dat* dog + cat, a crossbreed hoax
*demopublican* democrat + republican, another crossbreed, though no
    hoax
*diplonomics* diplomacy + economics, use of economic power for
    diplomatic ends
*gawkward* gawky + awkward
*glommentary* glossary + commentary, such as you are presently reading
*guesstimate* guess + estimate, also to be found in our list of most
    loathed words (page 309)
*liger* lion + tiger, the offspring of a lion and tigress
*macon* not a wine, but mutton + bacon: mutton smoked and salted
    like bacon (a culinary creation dating from the Second World War)
*motel* motor + hotel (1925)
*promptual* prompt + punctual
*seascape* sea + landscape
*sexcapade* sex + escapade
*stagflation* stagnation + inflation
*swelegant* swell + elegant

*prize + *winners, a portmanteau designed to capture your attention.*

And it almost seems like dog-eat-dog when you get to the world of canine portmanteaus. Among the hybrids created by the crossing of purebred dogs in recent years we have had the beaglier (a cross of beagle and cavalier King Charles spaniel), the bichpoo (bichon frise and poodle), the borador (border collie and Labrador retriever), the cockapoo (poodle and cocker spaniel), the chorkie (Chihuahua and Yorkshire terrier), the labradoodle (poodle and Labrador retriever) and the pekeapoo (Pekinese and poodle).

. . . . . . . . . . . . . . . . . . . . . . . . . . . . . . . . . . . . . . . .

## TELESCOPES

Some people don't call portmanteaus 'portmanteaus': they call them 'telescopes' instead. To keep them happy, here are ten telescopes that have gained currency and at least one admirer (me):

*administrivia* administrative + trivia, what most administrators do
    most of the time
*bitini* itsy bitsy + bikini
*chillaxing* chilling + relaxing, my grandson Rory's favourite word
    (and occupation!) – but David Cameron favours it, too, so that's
    fine by me
*chugger* charity + mugger
*ecotecture* ecological + architecture
*flexitime* flexible + time, an arrangement that allows workers to set
    their own schedules
*glamping* glamorous + camping
*internet* international + network
*medevac* medical + evacuation, as from a battlefield or rock concert
*vodkatini* vodka + Martini

. . . . . . . . . . . . . . . . . . . . . . . . . . . . . . . . . . . . . . . .

## JUMBLES

Jumbles are the portmanteaus and telescopes devised by people who don't like calling them portmanteaus and telescopes. Here are fifteen of the best:

*Chunnel* Channel + tunnel
*croissandwich* croissant + sandwich
*fantabulous* fantastic + fabulous
*glitz* glamour + Ritz
*imagineer* imagine + engineer
*infomercial* information + commercial

*malware* malicious + software
*muppet* marionette + puppet
*outpatient* outside + patient
*plotboiler* literary work with a trite, improbable plot
*sextrovert* sexual + extrovert
*telethon* telephone + marathon
*televangelist* television + evangelist
*travelogue* travel + monologue
*tripewriter* typewriter used exclusively for political speeches

**is for**

# Q WITHOUT U AND I BEFORE E

. . . . . . . . . . . . . . . . . . . . . . . . . . . . . . . . . . . . . . . . . . . .

## ONLY Q

Just as we are brought up to believe that 'i before e except after c' is a rule that must always be obeyed (it isn't: see the end of this chapter), most of us go to our graves believing that a q is always followed by a u. Well, it ain't necessarily so.

English has absorbed quantities of words from other languages where the rule does not apply and all of the words listed below can now be found comfortably ensconced in the pages of quality English dictionaries.

*qabbala* a mystical interpretation of the Scriptures
*qadi* a Muslim judge interpreting and administering Islamic religious
    law
*qaf* the twenty-first letter of the Arabic alphabet
*qaid* a local Muslim administrator in Spain or North Africa
*qaimaqam* a minor official serving the Ottoman empire
*qanat* an underground tunnel used to convey water

*qaneh* a Hebrew measurement equalling 10.25 feet
*qantar* a unit weight used around the Mediterranean
*qasab* an ancient measure used in Arabia equalling 12.6 feet
*qasida* a laudatory or satiric poem in Arabic
*qat* an Arabian shrub used as a narcotic
*qhat* an obsolete spelling of what
*qhwom* an obsolete spelling of whom
*qibla* the point to which Muslims turn to pray
*qinah* a Hebrew dirge or lament
*qintar* An Albanian unit of money
*Qlana* the trade name of a fabric related to nylon
*qobar* a dry fog that forms in the area of the Upper Nile
*qvint* a Danish weight

You will have noticed those are all words that begin with the letter *q*.

Here's a selection which have u-less *q*s hiding among them. This list holds a particular gem: the only word I have yet found which contains both a *q* with a *u* and a *q* without one.

*bathqol* a divine revelation in Hebrew tradition
*burqa* a veiled garment worn by Muslim women
*cinq* the number five in dice or cards
*coq* a trimming of cock feathers on a woman's hat
*faqih* a Muslim theologian versed in Islamic religious law
*faqir* a Muslim ascetic
*fuqaha* a plural of '*faqih*'
*Iraqi* a resident of Iraq
*miqra* Hebrew text of the Bible
*muqaddam* a headman
*nastaliq* Arabic script used principally in Persian verse
*pontacq* a still wine from the South of France, red or white
*sambuq* a small Arab boat
*shoq* an East Indian tree
*shurqee* a south-easterly wind that blows in the Persian Gulf
*suq* a marketplace in the Muslim world

*taluq* an Indian estate including subtenants
*taluqdar* a collector of a taluq's taxes
*taqlid* the uncritical acceptance of Muslim orthodoxy
*tariqa* the Sufi path of spiritual development
*trinq* a toast, used in Rabelais's *Pantagruel*
*waqf* a charitable trust in Muslim law
*yaqona* an intoxicating beverage made from the crushed root of an
    Australasian shrubby pepper
*zaqqum* a tree with bitter fruit, mentioned in the Koran
*zindiq* a heretic showing extreme infidelity to Islam

. . . . . . . . . . . . . . . . . . . . . . . . . . . . . . . . . . . . . . . . . . . . . . .

## I BEFORE E?

When I taught English at the Park School in Baltimore, Maryland, I encouraged my students to learn what I had always regarded as one of the basic rules of spelling: 'It's *i* before *e* except after *c*.'

And so it is with *piece* and *ceiling* and *thief* and *deceive* and a multitude of other words. But unfortunately for me – and all the other English teachers who want a quiet life – it seems this time-honoured rule isn't as reliable as we thought. A fellow teacher introduced me to this new version of the rhyme:

*I before e except after c or when sounded like **a** as in neighbour and weigh*

I thought all my problems had been solved, until some smart alec at the front of the class piped up: '*Weird.* I'm *disagreeing* with you, sir, but from *herein* onwards *neither* my *leisure* time nor my *scientific* endeavours will be devoted to anything but *seeing* your theory proved *deficient.* I don't mean to be *feisty*, but one doesn't get a *surfeit* of chances to *seize wherein* to prove *their* professor wrong.'

The English language turns out to be riddled with words in which an *e* comes before an *i* and there's no *c* to be seen and in which an *i* comes before an *e* immediately after a *c*.

If you need proof that rules are made to be broken, here it is:

| | | |
|---|---|---|
| *ageism* | *heifer* | *reimburse* |
| *agencies* | *heinous* | *rein* |
| *ancient* | *heir* | *reindeer* |
| *beige* | *reitbok* | *being* |
| *inveigle* | *science* | *Beirut* |
| *Keith* | *seize* | *caffeine* |
| *Leicester* | *sheik* | *codeine* |
| *leishmaniasis* | *Sheila* | *conscience* |
| *leisure* | *skein* | *counterfeit* |
| *Marcie* | *sleigh* | *deficient* |
| *mercies* | *sovereign* | *deign* |
| *species* | *Deirdre* | *neigh* |
| *surfeit* | *eider* | *Neil* |
| *tenancies* | *eighth* | *neither* |
| *their* | *either* | *nonpareil* |
| *theism* | *Fahrenheit* | *nuclei* |
| *unpolicied* | *fancied* | *obeisance* |
| *veiled* | *feign* | *omniscient* |
| *vein* | *feint* | *onomatopoeic* |
| *weigh* | *financier* | *pharmacopoeia* |
| *weir* | *foreign* | *plebeian* |
| *weird* | *forfeit* | *freight* |
| *policies* | *zein* | *geisha* |
| *poltergeist* | *glacier* | *proficient* |

'Leishmaniasis', by the way, is an unpleasant disease spread by sandflies. It was identified by the British Army doctor Lieutenant General Sir William Boog Leishman around 1900. A 'reitbok' is a bushy-tailed South African reedbuck. And 'zein' is the principal protein of maize.

To make matters twice as bad, here are a dozen words where the golden rule is broken not once but twice:

| | |
|---|---|
| alliciences | efficiencies |
| anciencies | Einstein |
| cleidomancies | omnisciencies |
| deficiencies | oneiromancies |
| pleistoseist | sufficiencies |
| proficiencies | zeitgeist |

OK, so Einstein's a name and *zeitgeist* isn't English, and the rest won't mean much to you unless you have a dictionary to hand, but you get the point – or is that piont? (Spelling was never my strong suit.)

# R

## is for

## REJECTION

Famously, J. K. Rowling's *Harry Potter and the Philosopher's Stone* was rejected by twelve publishers before one took a chance on it. And then it was only because the publisher's nine-year-old daughter said she wanted to find out what happened at the end.

Margaret Mitchell's novel *Gone with the Wind* was rejected a staggering thirty-eight times before someone decided it might be worth taking a punt on it. More recently, Eimear McBride's debut, *A Girl Is a Half-formed Thing*, endured a decade of constant rejection before being published in 2014, winning acclaim and the Bailey's (previously the Orange) Prize for Fiction.

If you find yourself on the sharp end of a publisher's rejection letter, you can console yourself that you are in the company of the greats:

*75 Wiley Street*
*New York, N.Y.*
*U.S.A.*
*June 14th, 1925.*

*Dear Mr. Hemingway:*

*Thank you for sending us your manuscript, The Sun Also Rises. I regret to inform you that we will not be offering you publication at this time.*

*If I may be frank, Mr. Hemingway – you certainly are in your prose – I found your efforts to be both tedious and offensive. You really are a man's man, aren't you? I wouldn't be surprised to hear that you had penned this entire story locked up at the club, ink in one hand, brandy in the other. Your bombastic, dipsomaniac, where-to-now characters had me reaching for my own glass of brandy – something to liven up 250 pages of men who are constantly stopping to sleep off the drink. What Peacock & Peacock is looking for, in a manuscript, is innovation and heart. I'm afraid that what you have produced here does not fit that description.*

*A great story, Mr. Hemingway, is built on a foundation of great characters. I had trouble telling yours apart. Remind me, which is the broken-hearted bachelor who travels aimlessly across Europe? Ah, yes! They all do! As I understand it, Jake Barnes is intended to be your hero. A hero, Mr. Hemingway, is a person the reader can care about, root for. Jake Barnes is too detached, too ineffective; I doubt he'd have the energy to turn the page and find out what happened to himself. I take exception, also, to your portrayal of Mike. There is nothing less appealing than a character who sits blithely by while his wife sleeps with half of the continent. I have not yet said anything about Brett, your only prominent female character. As a woman, was I intended to identify with this flighty girl who takes in men the way the others take in after-supper coffees? Let me tell you, Mr. Hemingway, I did not. Your languid characters deserve each other, really each one is more hollow than the next.*

*Of course, I doubt it's possible to create a three-dimensional character with such two-dimensional language. Have you never heard of crafted prose? Style? Complexity of diction? It's hard to believe an entire novel's worth of pages could be filled up with the sort of short, stunted sentences you employ here. Let me be specific: at the start of the novel, you sum up a key character, Robert Cohn, with just five short words, "I was his tennis friend." This tells us nothing. Later, when Jake is looking out on the Seine – the beautiful, historic, poetic Seine – you write, "the river looked nice." Nice? The river looked nice? I dare say my young son could do better!*

*In short, your efforts have saddened me, Mr. Hemingway. I was hopeful that by 1925 the brutes would have stopped sending me their offerings. We at Peacock & Peacock are looking to publish novels that will inspire. God knows, it's what people need at this time. Certainly, what is not needed are treatises about bullfights and underemployed men who drink too much.*

*Sincerely,*

*Mrs Moberley Luger*

The following caustic letter sees London publisher Arthur Fifield not only rejecting Gertrude Stein but mocking her writing style as he does it.

*April 19, 1912.*

*Dear Madam,*

*I am only one, only one, only one. Only one being, one at the same time. Not two, not three, only one. Only one life to live, only sixty minutes in one hour. Only one pair of eyes. Only one brain. Only one being. Being only one, having only one pair of eyes, having only one time, having only one life, I cannot read your M.S. three or four times. Not even one time. Only one look, only one look is enough. Hardly one copy would sell here. Hardly one. Hardly one.*

*Many thanks. I am returning the M.S. by registered post. Only one M.S. by one post.*

*Sincerely yours,*

*A. C. Fifield*

The New York publishers Knopf managed some cracking rejections in the 1950s: Anne Frank and Vladimir Nabokov were just two of the writers they decided weren't right for them. Here editor 'jbj' rejects Sylvia Plath's *The Bell Jar*, not once but twice, first when it was submitted under a pseudonym and again once its true authorship had been revealed.

*REJECT RECOMMENDED*

*I'm not sure what Heinemann's sees in this first novel unless it is a kind of youthful American female brashness. But there certainly isn't enough genuine talent for us to take notice.*

*jbj*

*REJECT RECOMMENDED*

*I have now re-read – or rather read more thoroughly – "The Bell Jar" with the knowledge that it is by Sylva Plath which has added considerably to its interest for it is obviously flagrantly autobiographical. But it still is not much of a novel. The trouble is that she has not succeeded in using her material in a novelistic way; there is no viewpoint, no sifting out of the experiences of being a Mademoiselle contest winner with the month in New York, the subsequent mental breakdown and suicide attempts, the brash loss of virginity at the end. One feels simply that Miss Plath is writing of them because [these] things did happen to her and the incidents are in themselves good for a story, but throw them together and they don't necessarily add up to a novel. One never feels, for instance, the deep-rooted anguish that would drive this girl to suicide. It is too bad because Miss Plath has a way with words and a sharp eye for unusual and vivid detail. But maybe now that this book is out of her system she will use her talent more effectively next time. I doubt if anyone over here will pick this novel up, so we might well have a second chance.*

*jbj*

George Orwell's *Animal Farm* was famously rejected by T. S. Eliot, when he was a director at Faber and Faber in London. Eliot declared the novel 'unconvincing' and was not very happy with the characterisation of the pigs. The book was also rejected by our old friends at Knopf in New York, who described it as: '[a] stupid and pointless fable in which the animals take over a farm and run it . . . damn dull'.

*Animal Farm* went on to sell more than fifty million copies.

Here are a few further snippets from rejection letters – plus the sales totals the publishers have been kicking themselves about ever since.

THE DIARY OF ANNE FRANK
*'a dreary record of typical family bickering, petty annoyances and adolescent emotions'.*
Over 30,000,000

LOLITA BY VLADIMIR NABOKOV
*'It is overwhelmingly nauseating, even to an enlightened Freudian. To the public, it will be revolting, absurd and uninteresting. It will not sell, and will do immeasurable harm to a growing reputation...I recommend that it be buried under a stone for a thousand years.'*
Over 50,000,000

VALLEY OF THE DOLLS BY JACQUELINE SUSANN
*'a painfully dull, inept, clumsy, undisciplined, rambling and thoroughly amateurish writer whose every sentence, paragraph and scene cries for the hand of a pro'.*
Over 30,000,000

CATCHER IN THE RYE BY J. D. SALINGER
*'We feel we do not know the main character well enough.'*
65,000,000

CHICKEN SOUP FOR THE SOUL BY JACK CANFIELD AND MARK VICTOR HANSEN
*'Anthologies don't sell.'*
Over 125,000,000 (for the series)

THE DA VINCI CODE BY DAN BROWN
*'It is so badly written.'*
80,000,000

*JONATHAN LIVINGSTON SEAGULL* BY RICHARD BACH
*'Nobody will ever want to read a book about a seagull.'*
44,000,000

*THE WIND IN THE WILLOWS* BY KENNETH GRAHAME
*'An irresponsible holiday story that will never sell.'*
Over 25,000,000

*THE FOUNTAINHEAD* BY AYN RAND
*'Unsaleable and unpublishable.'*
Over 8,000,000

*CATCH-22* BY JOSEPH HELLER
*'I haven't the foggiest idea about what the man is trying to say. Apparently the author intends it to be funny.'*
10,000,000

And, finally, my favourite: one publisher's verdict on the man who created *The Jungle Book* and wrote 'If', the verse most often voted Britain's best-loved piece of poetry:

> *'I'm sorry, Mr Kipling, but you just don't know how to use the English language.'*

. . . . . . . . . . . . . . . . . . . . . . . . . . . . . . . . . . . . . . . . . . . . . . . . . . .

## VICIOUS CIRCLE

If, through persistence, you managed to get your poem published, your book in print or your play staged, congratulations. You have done well, but don't rest easy. There is no room for complacency in the world of words. The knocking never stops. A publisher may have accepted you, or a producer decided to put you on . . . Now it's time to face the critics.

Playwright Christopher Hampton once said: 'Asking a working actor what he thinks about critics is like asking a lamppost how it feels about dogs.' It does happen and some playwrights have a ready answer. This was Brendan Behan's:

> *Critics are like eunuchs in a harem. They're there every night, they see it done every night, they see how it should be done every night, but they can't do it themselves.*

The German playwright Bertolt Brecht had a similarly jaundiced view of critics: 'They tell you your play isn't yellow enough when it's blue.'

The heyday of coruscating criticism in America was also the heyday of the Algonquin Round Table – roughly the years from 1919 to 1929 when some of New York's leading writers and critics gathered at a rectangular table in the Pergola Room at the Algonquin Hotel for lunch. The Table's leading lady, Dorothy Parker, managed to sum up one play in five words: '*House Beautiful* is play lousy.' She was often as caustic, but not always so concise.

Here she is reviewing Margot Asquith's *Lay Sermons*:

> In this book of essays, which has all the depth and glitter of a worn dime, the Countess walks right up to subjects such as Health, Human Nature, Fame, Character, Marriage, Politics and Opportunities. A rather large order, you might say, but it leaves the lady with unturned hair. Successively, she knocks down and drags out each topic. And there is something vastly stirring in the way in which, no matter where she takes off from, she brings the discourse back to Margot Asquith. Such a singleness of purpose is met but infrequently.

> When she does get around to less personal matters, it turns out that her conclusions are soothingly far from startling. A compilation of her sentiments, suitably engraved upon a nice, big calendar, would make an ideal Christmas gift for your pastor, dentist or Junior's music teacher. Here, for instance, are a few ingots lifted from her golden treasury: 'The artistic temperament has been known to land people in every kind of dilemma...', 'Pleasure will always make a stronger appeal than Wisdom...', 'It is only the fine natures that profit by Experience...', 'It is better to be a pioneer than a passenger, and best of all to try and create...', 'It is not only what you See but what you feel that kindles appreciation and gives Life to beauty...', 'Quite apart from the question of sex, some of the greatest rascals have been loved...', 'I think it is a duty women owe not only to themselves, but to everyone else to dress well.'

The Thames I hear remains as damp as ever in the face of these observations.

Through the pages of *Lay Sermons* walk the great. I don't say that Margot Asquith actually permits us to rub elbows with them ourselves, but she willingly shows us her own elbow, which has been, so to say, honed on the mighty. 'I remember President Wilson saying to me'; 'John Addington Symonds once said to me'; 'The Master of Balliol told me' – thus does she introduce her anecdotes. And you know those anecdotes that begin that way; me, I find them more efficacious than sheep-counting, rain on a tin roof, or Alanol tablets. Just begin a story with such a phrase as 'I remember Disraeli – poor old Dizzy! – once saying to me, in answer to my poke in the eye', and you will find me and Morpheus off in a corner, necking.

For brevity it would be hard to beat Alexander Woollcott's review of a show called *Wham!* His entire notice read: 'Ouch!'

It was Woollcott who, after yet another disappointing evening at the theatre, reported: 'The audience strummed their catarrhs.' And taking a designer to task in another play, he singled out one piece of furniture and observed, 'The chair... was upholstered in one of those flagrant chintzes, designed apparently, by the art editor of a seed catalogue.'

Heywood Broun was one of the more down-to-earth of the Algonquin set. He greeted a new arrival on Broadway with the deathly sentence: 'It opened at 8:40 sharp and closed at 10:40 dull.' And when the English actor Montague Love appeared in New York, Broun summed up his performance with the observation: 'Mr Love's idea of playing a he-man was to extend his chest three inches and then follow it slowly across the stage.'

When Walter Kerr went to see *Hook and Ladder* he concluded, 'It is the sort of play that gives failures a bad name.' And on the opening night of a new comedy, George S. Kaufman reported: 'There was laughter at the back of the theatre, leading to the belief that someone was making jokes back there.'

Though known as the Vicious Circle, not everything the Algonquin set produced was knocking copy. Here is Franklin Pierce Adams enthusing over actress Minnie Maddern Fiske in verse:

*Somewords she runs runstogether*
*Some others are distinctly stated.*
*Somecometoofast and*
*s o m e t o o s l o w*
*and some are sy$^n$c$_o$p$^a$ted*
*And yet no voice – I am sincere –*
*Exists that I prefer to hear.*

Adams was less charitable when he saw Helen Hayes as Cleopatra in Bernard Shaw's *Caesar and Cleopatra* in 1925. In his review Adams remarked that it seemed as if the Egyptian queen was suffering from 'Fallen Archness'.

And in the Hall of Fame for acid criticism, there has to be a special place for James Agee's verdict on the movie *Random Harvest*: 'I would like to recommend this film to those who can stay interested in Ronald Colman's amnesia for two hours and who could with pleasure eat a bowl of Yardley's shaving soap before breakfast.'

# S

### is for

### SEVEN WORDS OF WISDOM

What is the most powerful word in the world? According to a recent public opinion poll survey, most people reckon it's 'love' – closely followed by 'freedom', 'money', 'hope', 'laughter', 'fame' and 'democracy'.

I am inclined to think the most powerful word in the world might simply be 'Yes!' I have thought that since I first heard the favourite prayer of Dag Hammarskjöld, the Swedish diplomat and secretary-general of the United Nations from 1953 until his death in a plane crash in September 1961. Hammarskjöld is the only person to have been awarded the Nobel Peace Prize posthumously. This was his prayer:

> *For all that has been,*
> *Thank you.*
>
> *For all that is to come,*
> *Yes!*

I once asked Margaret Thatcher, the former British prime minister, what she thought was the most powerful word in the language. 'Persistence,' she said at once, and pointed me in the direction of her favourite quotation from Calvin Coolidge:

> Nothing in this world can take the place of persistence. Talent will not: nothing is more common than unsuccessful men with talent. Genius will not; unrewarded genius is almost a proverb. Education will not: the world is full of educated derelicts. Persistence and determination alone are omnipotent.

For concise words of wisdom I think it's hard to beat these three. If you are looking for success in life, this should be your mantra:

*Don't dabble, focus.*

(Of course, if you are looking to lose weight, it's an equally simple four-word mantra that you need to know: 'Eat less, move more.' It really does do the trick.)

Albert Einstein had a three-word mantra that he very much believed in:

*Keep it simple.*

It came with a rider: 'Keep it simple: as simple as possible, but no simpler.'

Whenever I am fortunate enough to meet one of life's great achievers I ask them for advice. As a boy, I was lucky enough to encounter the poet T. S. Eliot. He said: 'Only those who will risk going too far can possibly find out how far one can go.' Thornton Wilder was even more on the money in my book: *'My advice to you is not to inquire why or whither, but just enjoy your ice cream while it's on your plate.'*

Wilder's wise words echo those of the great Robert Baden-Powell, founder of the Boy Scouts and Girl Guides movement. On 4 July 1911, in a letter to a friend, he wrote: 'I know my weak points and am only thankful that I have managed to get along in spite of them! I think that's the policy for this world: Be glad of what you have got, and not miserable about what you would like to have had, and not over-anxious about what the future will bring.'

If you approached Aristotle Onassis for advice, the shipping magnate who married Jackie Kennedy had a ready answer:

> No matter how good your business is, no matter how bad; no matter how good your sex life is, no matter how bad; no matter how good your health is, no matter how bad – always have a little bit of suntan.

A century ago, the British writer and soldier T. E. Lawrence went to the Middle East in search of the Seven Pillars of Wisdom. His account of his adventures in Arabia brought him fame and adulation – which he then tried to escape by joining the RAF under the assumed name of John Ross, Aircraftman 338171. Noël Coward wrote to him at the time: 'Dear 338171, or may I call you 338?'

More recently I, too, went to the Middle East in search of wisdom. And there I met one of the more remarkable men of our time, Sheikh Mohammed bin Raschid al Maktoum, ruler of Dubai and prime minister of the United Arab Emirates. I asked him for his secret.

Without hesitation he replied, 'God. Faith is everything. It gives you the strength, the energy, the power. I am a leader because it is a gift from God. I am a happy man because I never keep things in my heart. If something is wrong, I tell people. I take decisions. I don't feel burdened. I sleep well.'

'How much do you sleep?' I asked him.

'Four hours,' he replied. 'Two hours.'

'Truly? Look into my eyes and tell me the truth.'

He leant forward and pushed his face into mine. 'I tell you the truth. In the day it is all rush. At night it is quiet. I am alone. I write my notes with my green pen. I read. I read a lot of classical Arabic. It is a beautiful language. How many words did Shakespeare use? Forty thousand? In Arabic there are forty thousand words for different fish. At night, I write my poetry. And I think. I am never idle.'

I asked Sheikh Mohammed for any words of wisdom that he might have for me.

'For you?' he said. I nodded. He looked at me with a beady eye. 'Every morning in Africa a gazelle wakes up. It knows it must outrun the fastest lion or it will be killed. Every morning in Africa a lion wakes up. It knows it must run faster than the slowest gazelle or it will starve. It doesn't matter whether you're a gazelle or a lion, Mr Brandreth. When the sun comes up, you'd better be running.'

Sheikh Mohammed knew that the day of our meeting happened to be my birthday. 'I will give you a present,' he said, smiling. For a fleeting moment I pictured an Arab stallion or even a white Rolls-Royce (he has several of both that he could spare), but evidently the sheik could sense I wasn't one for mere material gewgaws. He gave me a collection of his love poetry and a calendar featuring photographs of his favourite horses and more intriguing words of wisdom:

> *Extraordinary determination. That's what makes ordinary people real leaders.*

> *At the root of all creation is imagination, because before you achieve you must first conceive.*

> *It is the leader who sets the pace of the pack.*

> *Begin when you are sure of yourself, and don't stop because someone else is unsure of you.*

> *Watch your thoughts, they become words.*
> *Watch your words, they become actions.*
> *Watch your actions, they become habits.*
> *Watch your habits, they become character.*
> *Watch your character, it becomes your destiny.*

# T

**is for**

## TEXTS & TELEGRAMS

The word 'text' has been with us for a thousand years. The 'text message' has not yet notched up a quarter of a century. The first mobile phone text was sent in December 1992 when Neil Papworth, then a twenty-two-year-old engineer at a US cell-phone company, sent the cheery words 'Merry Christmas' to a Vodafone employee in the United Kingdom.

Globally we are now sending trillions of text messages every year: the annual total was 8.6 trillion at the last count. In the UK alone we are responsible for more than 35 billion of those. Three-quarters of American teens send more than sixty texts a day – and a lot of those come with an emoticon attached.

An emoticon? That's the portmanteau for 'emotion icon', the pictorial representation of a facial expression designed to underscore the mood of the message.

In the west, according to ESA (the self-styled Emoticons Standards Agency): 'Emoticons are usually written from left to right as though the head is rotated counter-clockwise 90 degrees. One will most commonly see the eyes on the left, followed by the nose, if included, and then the mouth. Typically, a colon is used for the eyes of a face, unless winking, which uses a semicolon. However, an equals sign, a number 8, and a capital letter B are also used interchangeably to refer to normal eyes, widened eyes, or those with glasses. One can also add a "}" after the mouth symbol to indicate a beard.'

The point is: thanks to the emoticon, you can create a world of meaning with a few simple symbols – for example:

| ICON | MEANING |
| --- | --- |
| :-) | Happy – known as a 'smiley' |
| :-)) | Very happy (or 'You've got a double chin') |
| >:[ :-( :( | Sad |
| ;( | A 'winky' or a 'frowney' used to signify sadness, with a bit of sarcasm |
| :-\|\| :@ >:( | Angry |
| :'-( :'( | Crying |
| :'-) :') | Tears of happiness |
| D:< D: D8 D; D= DX v.v D-': | Dismay, disgust, distress |
| >:O :-O :O :-o :o 8-0 O_O o-o O_o o_O o_o O-O | Surprise, shock or boredom (the yawn) |
| :* :^* ( '}{' ) | Kissing |
| ;-) ;) *-) *) ;-] ;] ;D ;^) :-, | Winking |
| >:P :-P :P X-P | Tongue sticking out, blowing a raspberry |
| :\| :-\| | Straight face, neutral response |
| :$ | Embarrassed |
| :-X :X :-# :# | Sealed lips (or, in the USA wearing braces) |
| O:-) 0:-3 0:3 0:-) 0:) | Angelic, innocent |
| >:) >;) >:-) | Evil |

| }:-) }:) 3:-) 3:) | Devilish |
| #-) | Partied all night |
| %-) %) | Drunk, confused |
| :-###.. :###.. | Being sick |

The research suggests that women are twice as likely as men to use emoticons. I avoid them, though I am a keen general texter and I enjoy keeping up to date with my txt spk. Here are some of the abbreviations and acronyms you need to know if you want to feel fully on top of the sub-text as the messages roll in.

**ABT2**
About to

**AFAIC**
As far as I'm concerned

**AFAIK**
As far as I know

**ALOL**
Actually laughing out loud

**AML**
All my love

**ASAP**
As soon as possible

**ATST**
At the same time

**AWOL**
Absent without leave

**AYK**
As you know

**AYSOS**
Are you stupid or something

**AYTMTB**
And you're telling me this because?

**B4**
Before

**B4N**
Bye for now

**BBT**
Be back tomorrow

**BRB**
Be right back

**BTW**
By the way

**BW**
Best wishes

**BYKT**
But you knew that

**CID**
Consider it done

**CSL**
Can't stop laughing

**CU**
See you

**CYL**
See you later

**CYT**
See you tomorrow

**DGA**
Don't go anywhere

**DIKU**
Do I know you?

**DLTM**
Don't lie to me

**FF**
Friends forever

**FYM**
For your misinformation

**GBH**
Great big hug

**GG**
Good game

**GL**
Good luck

**GR8**
Great

**GTG**
Got to go

**HAK**
Hugs and kisses

**ILU**
I love you

**IMO**
In my opinion

**JK**
Just kidding

**LMAO**
Laughing my ass off

**M8**
Mate

**NE1**
Anyone?

**NP**
No problem

**ONNA**
Oh no, not again

**OTT**
Over the top

**PAW**
Parents are watching

**PM**
Personal message

**QL**
Quit laughing

**ROLF**
Rolling on the floor laughing

**SO**
Spouse/girlfriend/boyfriend

**SYS**
See you soon

**HAND**
Have a nice day

**IM**
Instant message

**IMS**
I am sorry

**KISS**
Keep it simple stupid

**LOL**
Laugh out loud

**MSG**
Message

**NMP**
Not my problem

**OMDB**
Over my dead body

**OOTO**
Out of the office

**P911**
Parent alert

**PIR**
Parents in room

**POOF**
Goodbye

**QT**
Cutie

**ROTFLMAO**
Rolling on the floor laughing my ass off

**SOHF**
Sense of humour failure

**TAH**
Take a hike

**IH8U**
I hate you

**IMHO**
In my humble opinion

**IOH**
I'm outta here

**L8R**
Later

**LTW**
Loving the weather

**N1**
Nice one

**NOYB**
None of your business

**OMG**
Oh my gosh

**OT**
Off topic

**PAL**
Parents are listening

**PLS**
Please

**POS**
Parents over shoulder

**RBTL**
Reading between the lines

**SMEM**
Send me an email

**SWALK**
Sealed with a loving kiss

**TBC**
To be continued

| | | |
|---|---|---|
| **TGIF** | **THX** | **TM** |
| Thank God it's Friday | Thanks | Trust me |
| **TOM** | **TTFN** | **TTG** |
| Tomorrow | Ta ta for now | Time to go |
| **TVM** | **VM** | **WC** |
| Thank you very much | Voice mail | Who cares? |
| **WDYMBT** | **WFM** | **WTG** |
| What do you mean by that? | Works for me | Way to go |
| **WYD** | **WYP** | **WYWH** |
| What are you doing? | What's your problem? | Wish you were here |
| **XOXO** | **YOLO** | **YOYO** |
| Hugs and kisses | You only live once | You're on your own |
| **ZZZ** | | |
| Sleeping, bored | | |

It is heartwarming to see some old acronyms finding new life with a new generation. AWOL has been around in America since the time of their Civil War. SWAK (and SWALK), sealed with a (loving) kiss, gained popularity during the Second World War when it was scribbled on the back of letters sent home from the front. Another popular acronym of yesteryear was NORWICH – kNickers Off Ready When I Come Home – but that probably takes us into the realm of 'sexting', which, happily, is beyond the scope of *Word Play*.

. . . . . . . . . . . . . . . . . . . . . . . . . . . . . . . . . . . . . . . . . . .

## PREDICTIVE TEXT FAILS

Predictive text, or 'autocorrect' as the Americans call it (see page 259 for the *Word Play* guide to Anglo-American speech), is a source of frustration to many and amusement to many more.

Here is an exchange of messages that shows you what risky territory we are now entering:

## *The first text message*

Hi Bob,

This is Alan next door. I'm sorry buddy, but I have a confession to make to you. I've been riddled with guilt these past few months and have been trying to pluck up the courage to tell you to your face, but I am at least now telling in text as I can't live with myself a moment longer without you knowing. The truth is, I have been sharing your wife, day and night when you're not around. In fact, probably more than you, particularly in the mornings after you've left for work. I haven't been getting it at home recently, but that's no excuse I know. The temptation was just too much . . . I can no longer live with the guilt and I hope you will accept my sincerest apologies and forgive me. I promise that it won't happen again. Regards, Alan

## *The response*

Bob, feeling anguished and betrayed, immediately went into his bedroom, grabbed his gun from the cabinet, and without a word, shot his wife twice, killing her instantly. He returned to the lounge where he poured himself a stiff drink and sat down on the sofa. He took out his phone to respond to the neighbour's text and saw he had another message:

## *The second text message*

Hi Bob, This is Alan next door again. Sorry about the slight typo on my last text, I expect you worked it out anyway, but as I'm sure you noticed, my predictive text changed 'WiFi' To 'Wife'. Technology hey?!? Hope you saw the funny side of that. Regards, Alan

Here are a dozen of my favourite predictive text mishaps: the initial message is on the left, the response on the right. They are all genuine and all SFW (that's Safe For Work :-) ) (And, yes, that's a smiley. And, yes, I also have a double chin.)

**1.**

Picking up meds anything else for the house?

Not that I can think of. Would you want a small salad and maybe a naked pastor for dinner.

OMG!!!! BAKED POTATO...
NOT NAKED PASTOR

**2.**

We're watching Harry Potato and the sorcerers' stove.

*potter *stone sweet jesus

harry potato and the sorcerer's stove sounds like the lamest movie ever.

**3.**

Are you doing the nutcracker this year?

Yep! I'm auctioning kids tomorrow.

Suctioning kids.

Ridiculous auto cat rectal.

Birdseed!

I AM AUDITIONING KIDS FOR PLAY.

Wow, I am sorry I asked. Hahahahahah

**4.**

Great news – Grandma is homosexual!

Okay?

Homo hot lips

Hot tulips

Grandma is home from hospital.

Hahaha homo hot lips!!

5.

I love thunder.

I know me too! Except when it makes my dog bark.

My dad barks too we have to comfort him.

I'm so sorry, I imagine his manly vocal cords cause much more commotion than a small dog.

OH DID YOU MEAN DOG??

Yeah!

6.

u home?

yea watching the game.

good i'm coming over and I'm bringing cold hermaphrodites with me.

Uh . . . No thanks bro

hermaphrodites!

Heineken! Jesus crust.

Christ!

LOL

**7.**

Do you still need help sewing?
I can come over Sunday.

No – I urinated my pants today.

I urinated my pants.

I heard you. Why?? Are you ok?

I am trying to say unhemmed!
I did not pee myself!

**8.**

Night wifey

Good night dead husband . . . Sweet dreams

LOL dear

OMG

Damn autocorrect lol

Haha! That was scary.

**9.**

Did you guys eat dinner yet?

Yep. Just had pasta.

Oh by the way, I laid the babysitter.

Uh, excuse me? You what????

Haha PAID. I paid her. Sorry to give you a heart attack babe.

I hate you! lol

**10.**

Hi Karen, I'd love to bring my ladybits in for grooming this week. Is Wednesday at 4 okay?

Hi Kay! Wed at 4 is fine but we don't do that kind of grooming here . . . lol.

Oh my gosh! Labrador. Not sure what my phone did there. I'm bright red!

No worries. See you then.

**11.**

How's the morning sickness?

Not too bad today. I can't believe we're having another baby :)

I'm leaving you.

WHAT???!!!!!!!!

now. I'm leaving NOW. I am not leaving you!

Now I'm really gonna throw up.

**12.**

I've got something to tell you.
Are you sitting down?

> I am actually. What's up?

> Your brother was adopted.

> What??? What are you talking about?

> Why are you telling me this over text? Call me.

> Oh this damn phone.
> Accepted, he got accepted to Yale!

. . . . . . . . . . . . . . . . . . . . . . . . . . . . . . . . . . . . . . . . . . . . . . . .

## TELEGRAMS

Before the text, we had the telegram.

I remember it well. But, then, I was around before 1981 when the last telegrams were sent in the United Kingdom. What was a telegram? A message sent by telegraph and delivered in handwritten or printed form – usually by a telegraph boy in a smart uniform on a bicycle.

The world's first telegram was sent by an American. Nearly 150 years before Neil Papworth dispatched his seasonal greetings across the Atlantic by text, Samuel Morse, on 24 May 1844, sent this message from Washington DC to Baltimore: 'What hath God wrought?'

The last telegram was sent and delivered in India (where its popularity as a method of communication outlasted the rest of the world) in July 2013. Now the telegram has gone the same way as the smoke signal and the carrier pigeon, and I reckon the world of wordplay is the poorer. For old times' sake, here are a few celebrated telegraphic exchanges from the golden age of the telegram.

The writer G. K. Chesterton wired his wife:

AM IN MARKET HARBOROUGH STOP WHERE OUGHT I TO BE?

She replied:

HOME

When the actress Gertrude Lawrence married Richard Aldrich, her wedding day messages included this:

DEAR MRS A, HOORAY HOORAY
AT LAST YOU ARE DEFLOWERED
ON THIS AS EVERY OTHER DAY
I LOVE YOU. NOEL COWARD.

Thomas Mann's daughter, Erika, labelled an enemy by Hitler's Third Reich, needed a British passport to escape Germany in a hurry. She wrote to W. H. Auden asking if he would marry her. The couple had never met, but Auden wired back:

DELIGHTED.

Famously, the editor of a magazine, keen to verify copy, sent a telegram to Cary Grant's agent:

HOW OLD CARY GRANT?

The star replied in person:

OLD CARY GRANT FINE. HOW YOU?

During a performance of *Of Thee I Sing*, Bill Gaxton, one of the cast, received this telegram from the playwright George S. Kaufman:

WATCHING YOUR PERFORMANCE FROM LAST ROW. WISH YOU WERE HERE.

Kaufman's friend and fellow writer Robert Benchley sent a telegram to the *New Yorker* from Venice:

STREETS FULL OF WATER. PLEASE ADVISE.

Noël Coward, taken ill in Italy on one occasion, telegraphed his friend Cole Lesley from Florence:

HAVE MOVED HOTEL EXCELSIOR COUGHING MYSELF INTO A FIRENZE.

When a group of Oxford undergraduates found out that Rudyard Kipling earned ten shillings for every word he wrote they posted him ten shillings asking for one of his very best words in reply. Back came a telegram from Kipling reading simply:

THANKS.

Sir Arthur Conan Doyle, the creator of Sherlock Holmes, used to claim that he had sent the same message by telegram to a dozen distinguished men. It read:

ALL IS DISCOVERED. FLY AT ONCE.

According to Conan Doyle all twelve had fled the country within twenty-four hours.

In 1897, when Mark Twain was in London, he heard that his obituary had been published in the United States. The story goes that he wired his publishers: 'The reports of my death are greatly exaggerated.' It seems he did no such thing. On 31 May 1897 he sent a note to a reporter saying this: 'James Ross Clemens, a cousin of mine, was seriously ill two or three weeks ago in London, but is well now. The report of my illness grew out of his illness; the report of my death was an exaggeration.' The misquotation as we know it, and the story of the telegram, were further exaggerations.

During his 1960 presidential campaign John F. Kennedy used to joke that he had just received a telegram from his father: 'DEAR JACK DON'T BUY ONE MORE VOTE THAN NECESSARY. I'LL BE DAMNED IF I PAY FOR A LANDSLIDE.'

Another story goes that the actor Peter Sellers was at home working in his study. The doorbell rang and Peter's then wife, Anne, answered it. It was a telegram, addressed to her. She opened it and read:

BRING ME A CUP OF COFFEE. PETER

I met Peter Sellers and I reckon the story could be true. I am not so sure about the next one, but I like it. In the United States in 1933 Western Union introduced 'the singing telegram'. The telegraph boy wouldn't just arrive on his bicycle, bringing you your message in a small buff-coloured envelope: he would sing the message to you. One morning that summer, in Dayton, Ohio, the doorbell rang at a small house in the suburbs and the lady of the house, whose birthday had just passed, opened her front door to see a young man in his Western Union uniform standing on the doorstep. 'Ooh, a singing telegram,' she exclaimed. No, she was told, this was just a regular telegram. The woman protested gaily, 'But I want a singing telegram!' The telegraph boy stood his ground. The lady pleaded some more. Eventually the young man relented and sang the message to her: 'Trala,lala,la,la, YOUR SISTER ROSE IS DEAD.'

# U

### is for

### UNMENTIONABLES

Can you guess the nature of the garment that once upon a time – say, a century and a half ago – could have been described as:

| | | |
|---|---|---|
| *irrepressibles* | *indispensables* | *indescribables* |
| *innominables* | *ineffables* | *inexplicables* |
| *inexpressibles* | *unwhisperables* | *unutterables* |
| *unmentionables* | | |

Well, you're wrong. They weren't euphemisms for underpants. They were euphemisms for ordinary trousers. What went under those 'unmentionables' (which were trousers to the early Victorians but, more daringly, underpants to the late Victorians) were **benders, understandings, underpinners, extremities** or even – wait for it – **crural appendages.** The Victorian piano didn't have legs: it was supported on **limbs.**

Euphemism – 'the substitution of a mild or vague expression for a harsh or blunt one, – is an instinct as old as language itself. The Greek historian Plutarch, writing in the first century AD about life in the sixth century BC, recorded that 'the ancient Athenians used to cover up the ugliness of things with auspicious and kindly terms, giving them polite and endearing names. Thus they called harlots *companions*, taxes *contributions*, and prison a *chamber*.'

To the genteel of only a generation or two ago a bitch was always a *lady dog* and a bull a *he-cow* or a *gentleman cow* or a *male beast* or a *critter* or a *sire* or a *brute* or *the big animal* or anything but a bull. And I admit until recently I often referred to going to the lavatory by means of euphemism. I was cured of the habit when an acquaintance came to dinner. On arrival I asked him if he'd like to go upstairs to 'wash his hands'. 'No, thanks,' he replied. 'I washed them in the bushes on the way here.'

A lavatory, after all, is a lavatory: it is not *the throne room*, *the holy of holies*, *the Chamber of Commerce*, *the little boys' room* or *the little girls' room*; and when you do want to go there, you do not want to *powder your nose* or *discover the geography of the house*, let alone *make a telephone call* or *spend a penny*. A lavatory may well be *the smallest room in the house* but it could never be described wholly accurately as a *toilet* (which is where one attends to one's toilet) or a *cloakroom* (which is where one leaves one's cloak) or a *restroom* (which is where, presumably, one rests) let alone a *comfort station* (which is where one – what *does* one do in a comfort station?). To call a lavatory *the john*, as some Americans still do, is sexist and unkind to people called John, and the same goes for *ruth*. *WC* at least stands for *water closet*, which is what it is, and *crapper* was at least the name of the Victorian plumber who pioneered the design of the modern lavatory – though, intriguingly, the vulgar word 'crap' predates Mr Thomas Crapper, sanitary engineer. I suppose *thunder box* and *biffy* have onomatopoeia on their side, but the English *loo* and the American *can* have little but their brevity to commend them.

Public lavatories are indeed *public conveniences* and when labelled frankly are simply marked *Men* and *Women*. At Disneyland they may be *Princes* and *Princesses*; at English holiday camps *Lads* and *Lasses*; at pony clubs *Colts* and *Fillies*; at the seaside honeymoon hotel *Buoys* and *Gulls*; at a pub in Stratford-upon-Avon *Romeos* and *Juliets*; at the Four Seasons in New York *Gentlemen* and *Ladies*; and at the House of Lords, in London, *Peers* and *Peeresses*. When the words fail the sign writers, they draw pictures instead – of a man and a woman, or a king and a queen, a cock and a hen, a bull and a cow or two dogs: a pointer for the men and a setter for the women.

When we use a euphemism it's usually because we feel it's more discreet. Sometimes, however, discretion is forced upon us. In 1973 in New York automobiles began to display their new golden licence plates with three numbers and three letters in blue. The Department of Motor Vehicles was proud that the new plates, designed to replace the old blue plates with yellow numbers, 'offer an infinite number of combinations', but was nervous about where some of those combinations might lead. The department was 'determined to avoid sequences of letters that are obscene, suggestive or insulting', and so put a ban on WET and DRY, on PIG and RAT, on ODD and POT, as well, of course, as the more obvious SEX and SIN.

The department's attitude, however laudable, is surprising in an age when, in linguistic terms, anything goes and the taboos themselves have become taboo. There was a time when you never saw obscenities in print. They may have been there implicitly, but all you got were euphemisms and well-placed asterisks:

*An author owned an asterisk*
*And kept it in his den*
*Where he wrote tales which had large sales*
*Of erring maids and men,*
*And always, when he reached the point*
*Where carping censors lurk,*
*He called upon the asterisk*
*To do his dirty work!*

It was about the time that D. H. Lawrence's notorious *Lady Chatterley's Lover* made its first unexpurgated appearance in the United States in 1959 (thirty-one years after Lawrence had intended it should be published) that attitudes began to change and the unmentionables became mentionable even in the politest society. *Lady Chatterley's Lover* tells the story of an English aristocrat, his wife and their gamekeeper, Mellors. It's a novel featuring plenty of uninhibited sex and no asterisks. Here is an extract from the celebrated review of the book by Ed Zern, originally published in *Field & Stream*, the magazine for the lovers of country pursuits:

> Although written many years ago, *Lady Chatterley's Lover* has just been reissued by Grove Press, and this fictional account of the day-by-day life of an English gamekeeper is still of considerable interest to outdoor-minded readers, as it contains many passages on pheasant raising, the apprehending of poachers, ways to control vermin, and other chores and duties of the professional gamekeeper. Unfortunately one is obliged to wade through many pages of extraneous material in order to discover and savor these sidelights on the management of a Midlands shooting estate, and in this reviewer's opinion this book cannot take the place of J. R. Miller's *Practical Gamekeeping*.

## TRIED AND TESTED

We are all familiar with the euphemisms of modern life. Once your boss starts talking about 'rightsizing' you know you're about to be fired – especially if, the last time you floated an idea past him, he said, 'Interesting... I must think about that.' In Britain, when someone greets your idea with the word 'interesting' you can be certain they are not interested and if they promise to think about it you can be certain you won't be hearing about it again.

Here are some more euphemistic phrases that we are using all the time. It's odd that we do because we all know *exactly* what they mean.

> You're looking well – *you've put on at least six pounds*
> She's tired and emotional – *she's hopelessly drunk*
> He's very good company – *he gets hopelessly drunk*
> courtesy call – *it's anything but*
> economical with the truth – *lies*
> lower ground floor – *basement*

cosy – *you can't swing a cat in it*
full-figured/curvy/big-boned/heavy-set/matronly/ample
    proportions – *fat*
vertically challenged and a little thin on top – *short and bald*
up the duff/bun in the oven/knocked up/in the club/in the family way
    – *unexpectedly pregnant*
wardrobe malfunction – *hideous* or *you've fallen out of it*
fell off the back of a lorry – *stolen*
going to see a man about a dog – *whatever you're about to do it's not that*
one step closer to the end of the buffet – *at death's door*

. . . . . . . . . . . . . . . . . . . . . . . . . . . . . . . . . . . . . . . . . . . . . . . .

## SEX AND DEATH

Shakespeare gave us 'the beast with two backs' and Wilfred Owen,
'pushing up the daisies'. Nothing inspires a euphemism like sex and death.
'A bit of rumpy-pumpy' is old hat, but while I don't approve of 'parking
your car in the wrong driveway' (a euphemism for cheating) I quite like
the sound of:

| | |
|---|---|
| making whoopee | hiding the sausage |
| baking the potato | extreme flirting |
| doing the four-legged foxtrot | jingling-jangling |
| having horizontal refreshments | playing pelvic pinoche |
| sharpening the pencil | taking Grandma to Applebee's |
| thumping thighs | tying the true lovers' knot |

As long as there's ink in the biro and snap in the celery, I'm still up for a
bit of paddling up Coochie Creek. Eventually, when my time comes to
meet my maker and I am immortally challenged, I will hand in my dinner
pail, put on the wooden overcoat and leave the building. That's the way it
goes for all of us.

# V

**is for**

**VERBARRHEA**

Compare this

> To everything there is a season and a time to every purpose under the heaven: a time to be born, and a time to die; a time to plant, and a time to pluck that which is planted.

with this:

> Over the past ten years the school has evolved a child-centred individual learning situation with a degree of integrated day organisation and close co-operation between each year's mixed ability classes. Basic-work morning programmes are carefully structured but allow for integration . . .

Both passages are exemplars of their times. The first comes from the King James version of the Bible (1611). The second is from an advertisement for a junior secondary-school teacher (2014).

What happened to the language between 1611 and now? The answer, in a word, is verbarrhea. It's a contagion, it's spreading, and I believe something needs to be done about it.

Over the years, my love of language has led me to some interesting places, not least Dictionary Corner on the Channel 4 word game, *Countdown*. In the 1980s, in the early days of *Countdown*, I always appeared on the programme wearing colourful knitwear. In the 1990s, when I gave up my place in Dictionary Corner for a seat in the House of Commons, I was surprised to find that my reputation had preceded me. Speaking in a committee one day I was interrupted from the opposition front bench by John Prescott MP. Looking at me scornfully, Mr Prescott called out, 'Woolly jumper! Woolly jumper!' I struggled on with my speech and Mr Prescott continued with his barracking – until I paused to observe that the joy of a woolly jumper is that you can take it off at will, whereas the blight of a woolly mind is that you are lumbered with it for life.

Of course, John Prescott got the last laugh because he became deputy prime minister and is now, wrapped in ermine, seated in the House of Lords, whereas I . . . Well, I am here . . . And, frankly, I am happy to be where I am and proud of the fact that when I was an MP I did what I could on behalf of the English language.

Yes, as a back-bench Member of Parliament I took up arms against the sea of verbarrhea. People seem unable to resist the temptation to use two or three or, better still, four words where one will do. The simple is eschewed in favour of the complex, the monosyllabic in favour of the polysyllabic, the easily comprehensible in favour of the almost incomprehensible. That's why, in Parliament in 1992, I introduced a Private Member's Bill designed to encourage the use of plain language in commercial contracts. I hope, after hearing my argument, you would have voted in its favour. You can decide now, because here is the essence of what I had to say:

> Language is what distinguishes the human race: it is the characteristic that sets us apart and makes us unique. And we in this country are born with the privilege of having a unique language as our parent tongue – English, the richest language in the history of humanity.
>
> It is the language of Chaucer, and the King James Bible; of Keats, Joyce, Anthony Trollope and Anthony Burgess. It has taken two

thousand years to reach this far – and where is it now, in 1992? Let me show you, Madam Speaker, by quoting from the terms of sale offered by a certain excellent builders' merchant:

> 'If and to the extent that any person by whom the Seller has been supplied with the goods supplied hereunder (hereinafter referred to as "the Supplier") validity excludes, restricts or limits his liability to the Seller in respect of the said goods or of any loss or damage arising in connection therewith, the liability of the Seller to the Buyer in respect of the said goods or of any loss or damage arising in connection therewith shall be correspondingly excluded restricted or limited.'

There you have it, Madam Speaker: the English language today – and those were just five or more than a hundred such lines that feature on the back of the delivery note. When the driver drops off the breeze block and says, 'Sign 'ere, guv', what I have just read out constitutes five per cent of what the recipient is agreeing to – whether he likes it or not.

Does it matter? Yes, I believe that it does. It cannot be good that people regularly sign contracts that they do not understand, and, indeed, are not meant to understand . . .

Costly mistakes can be made. A constituent of mine discovered that when he signed an incomprehensible contract to lease a photocopier. When he wanted to change the photocopier, he was faced with the option of a so-called settlement charge of about ten thousand pounds, which was three times the value of the original equipment, or the prospect of leasing the equipment, whose lifetime, according to the manufacturer, was three years, for a total of seven years. None of that was clear from the contract, whose wording was deliberately obfuscatory and arcane.

The Bill is designed to encourage the use of clear, plain language in commercial contracts and to prevent the unscrupulous, arrogant or incompetent from hiding behind legalese, jargon, gobbledygook, or small print. It would apply to consumer contracts, consumer credit contracts – think of all the confusion that we would all be spared if we understood the small print that comes with our credit card – and housing contracts.

A plain language law might appear to be a contradiction in terms, because is it not the law and lawyers which are responsible for much of the gobbledygook found in contracts? I believe I am right in saying that in 1595 an English chancellor chose to make an example of a particularly wordy document filed in his court. He ordered a hole to be cut in the centre of the document – all 120 pages of it – and had the author's head stuffed through it. The offender was then led around Westminster Hall, a hundred yards from where we are now – even a hundred metres – as an example to all and sundry. Alas, that Elizabethan lesson did not stick; and that is where I come in, four centuries later but not a moment too soon.

I propose that the contracts covered by the Bill should be written in clear and readily understandable language using words with common and everyday meanings, to be arranged in logical order, be suitably divided into paragraphs and headings, be clearly laid out and easily legible.

The experience in the United States is that plain language law such as this would immediately improve practice and standards but, if a contract did not comply with the Act, the party which made the contract in the course of business would be liable to an action for damages brought by the other party – so there is also something in this for the lawyers.

I trust that the advantages of the Bill will be obvious to the House. Inevitably, some people will not see its virtues, but then, as the saying has it, a slight inclination of the cranium is as adequate as a spasmodic movement of one optic to an equine quadruped utterly devoid of visionary capacity.

My proposed legislation never reached the statute book, alas. Verbarrhea is still with us. And to prove that it is as virulent as ever, and very much part of the current political discourse, step forward, actor/performer/activist Russell Brand. Here he is in 2014 – in full flow:

> The internal mayhem I'm feeling is spilling out everywhere. I loved it, and felt very connected to activism – particularly activism that feels loaded with potential. Not the oppositional activism that seems like there's a stasis around it – earnestly sincere, but a monolith equal to the establishment.

I met Russell not long ago on the sofa in *The One Show* studio and warmed to him. I felt his passion, even if I could not quite follow his argument:

> I find it [capitalism] hard to understand. It obfuscates truth and I think an economic ideology is oppositional to the spiritual ideologies that are what we need to adopt if we're to save our planet and humankind. Capitalism, the economic arm of the individualism and materialism ideologies that keep us framed in a narrow bandwidth of consciousness, prevents us from seeing that we're all connected.

The Plain English Campaign, which has been going strong since 1979, and supported my Plain Language Bill in 1992, honoured Russell with their special Foot in Mouth Award in 2014, giving pride of place to 'a representative bit of codswallop' from Russell's book, *Revolution*, in their citation:

> This attitude of churlish indifference seems like nerdish deference contrasted with the belligerent antipathy of the indigenous farm folk, who regard the hippie-dippie interlopers, the denizens of the shimmering tit temples, as one fey step away from transvestites.

According to the Plain English Campaign: 'There could be only one winner this year: bravo, Russell. Your message is entertainingly garbled and may well be meaningful – we just have no idea what you're talking about and we're not sure you do.'

**is for**

**WHAT'S IN A NAME?**

. . . . . . . . . . . . . . . . . . . . . . . . . . . . . . . . . . . . . . . .

## WHAT AM I?

If you don't know who you are, I can't help you. But if you don't know *what* you are, perhaps I can. I know what I am.

'Gyles' is quite simply the plural form of *gyle* and, depending on the dictionary you care to consult, *gyle* is defined as:

- *wort in the process of fermentation added to a stout or ale*
- *the beer produced at one brewing*
- *a quantity of beer brewed at one time*
- *a brewing*
- *the vat in which the wort is left to ferment*
- *an obsolete spelling of guile*
- *a channel on a beach that the high tide fills, leaving a small island within*
- *an island of sand*
- *a quicksand*
- *a ravine, a narrow valley or glen, with precipitous or rocky banks,*

*generally wooded and with a stream running at the bottom*
*– a dingle*
*– a rivulet or mountain stream*
*– the bed of a stream*
*– a waterfall*
*– a ditch*

And, as I mentioned earlier, 'brandreth' is variously defined as a gridiron, a tripod or trivet, and a substructure of piles to support a house. Of course, I'm not alone. Numerous surnames have meanings as ordinary words – I know a Butcher and a Baker, and I believe there's a man in Florida called Hans Candlestickmaker – and there are plenty of forenames that are also words in their own right. For example, Jenny is a female bird or animal, especially a female donkey; Jemima is an elastic-sided boot; Mike is short for microphone; and Will is a document bequeathing one's possessions at death.

Here, with definitions, are more than a hundred of them. I hope you find your name in the list.

| | | | |
|---|---|---|---|
| *Abigail* | a lady's maid | *Albert* | a short kind of watch chain |
| *Alma* | an Egyptian dancing girl | *Ann* | from 1672 to 1925, a half-year's stipend payable to the wife of a parish minister after his death |
| *Anna* | an obsolete coin from India and Pakistan | *Basil* | an aromatic plant |
| *Ben* | a mountain peak | *Beryl* | a precious stone |
| *Bertha* | a woman's collar | *Beth* | the second letter of the Hebrew alphabet |
| *Betty* | a burglar's jemmy (a short metal bar used as a lever: also known as a jimmy) | *Bill* | a bird's beak |
| *Billy* | an Australian teapot | *Bob* | to move up and down |
| *Bobby* | a policeman | *Carol* | a Christmas song |
| *Cicely* | the name of several plants | *Clement* | mild |

| | | | |
|---|---|---|---|
| Colin | the Virginian quail | Craig | a crag, a rough steep rock or point |
| Dan | a box for carrying coal | Dicky | a false shirtfront |
| Dolly | a trolley | Don | to put on |
| Emma | a signaller's name for the letter M | Eric | a fine for committing murder in old Irish law |
| Faith | confidence | Fay | a fairy |
| Flora | the vegetation of a region | Frank | open |
| Grace | favour | Guy | a fellow |
| Hank | a loop | Harry | to harass |
| Hazel | light brown | Heather | a common shrub |
| Henry | in physics, the unit of inductance | Iris | part of the eye |
| Ivy | an evergreen climbing plant | Jack | a device for raising heavy weights |
| Jake | a country lout | Jane | a woman |
| Jean | a twilled cotton cloth | Jeff | in circus slang, a rope |
| Jerry | a chamber pot | Jess | a short strap around the legs of a hawk |
| Jill | a female ferret | Jimmy | see Betty above |
| Jo | a beloved one | Joey | a young kangaroo |
| Josh | to ridicule | Ken | to know |
| Kirk | a church | Laura | a group of recluses' cells |
| Louis | an old French gold coin | Luke | tepid |
| Madge | a magpie | Maria | dark areas on the moon and Mars |
| Martin | a bird | Matt | dull |
| Molly | a milksop | Mona | a West African monkey |
| Mungo | waste cloth | Nelly | a large petrel, a type of bird |
| Nelson | a wrestling hold | Nick | to steal |
| Norma | a rule or a standard | Norman | a bar inserted in a windlass |
| Olive | a tree with oily fruit | Oliver | a forge hammer worked by hand |
| Otto | a fragrant oil | Pansy | the name of various plants |

| | | | |
|---|---|---|---|
| *Patrick* | a seventeenth-century Irish halfpenny | *Patty* | a little pie |
| *Paul* | an obsolete papal silver coin | *Peggy* | a small warbler, a type of bird |
| *Peter* | to dwindle away | *Polly* | a tube of mineral water |
| *Rex* | pranks | *Rob* | to plunder |
| *Robin* | a bird with a red-orange breast | *Rose* | got up |
| *Rosemary* | a fragrant shrub | *Ruby* | a highly prized stone |
| *Ruth* | pity | *Sally* | to rush out suddenly |
| *Sam* | together | *Saul* | a Scots form of 'soul' |
| *Taffy* | flattery | *Ted* | to spread new-mown grass for drying |
| *Terry* | a Scottish sweetheart | *Timothy* | a grass for feeding cattle |
| *Toby* | robbery on the road | *Tommy* | a private in the British Army |
| *Tony* | fashionable | *Victor* | a winner |
| *Wally* | excellent | | |

. . . . . . . . . . . . . . . . . . . . . . . . . . . . . . . . . . . . . .

## THE ORDINARY AND EXTRAORDINARY

Ursula Woop is alive and well and living in Germany where she was once the National Typewriting Champion.

Adolph Blaine Charles David Earl Frederick Gerald Hubert Irvin John Kenneth Lloyd Martin Nero Oliver Paul Quincy Randolph Sherman Thomas Uncas Victor William Xerxes Yancy Zeus Wolfchlegsteinhausenbergerdorffvoralternwarengewissenhalftschafter-swessenschafewarenwohlgepfflegeundsorgfaltigkeitbeschutzenvonangre-ifendurcheinenvanderersteerdemenschderraumschiffgebrauchlichtalssein-ursprungvonkraftgestartseinlangefahrthinzwischensternartigraumaufder-suchenachdiesternwelchegehabtbewohnbarplanetenkreisedrehensichun-dwohinderneurassevonverstandigmenschlichkeitkonntefortpflanzenund-sicherfreuenanlebenslanglichfreudeundruhemitnichteinfurchtvorangreifen-vonandererintelligenentgeschopfsvonhinzwischensternartigraum Senior is alive, well and living in Philadelphia, where he has taken to calling himself Mr Wolfe + 585, Sr, for short.

When I was last there, the last name in the telephone directory in Madison, Wisconsin, was Hero Zzyzzx, son of Xerxes Zzyzzx.

The world is full of ordinary people with quite extraordinary names.

If you want to be one of the crowd be a Chang. Estimates vary, but there are considerably in excess of 100 million Changs on earth.

If you want to stand out in the crowd, you'll need to have a name as unusual as these, all of which have been borne at some time by otherwise ordinary people:

A. Moron, who occupied the position of Commissioner of Education for the Virgin Islands
Mr Groaner Digger, a Texas undertaker
Dr Zoltan Ovary, a New York gynaecologist
Safety First, lives in Leisure World, Sea Beach, California. 'Every time I get a traffic ticket, I get a column in the newspaper... I've been in Ripley's "Believe It or Not" three times. My sister June has been in only once'
Jean Sippy, recently divorced but still calls herself Mrs Sippy
Sam Sparks, fire chief
Mark Clark Van Ark, a resident of Toledo, Texas
B. Brooklyn Bridge, who had a policy with the John Hancock Life Insurance Company
Reverend Christian Church, who was active in the Italian city of Florence
DeFred Go Folts, a university administrator at Harvard University
Lettice Goedebed, of Johannesburg, South Africa
T. Hee, who worked in a restaurant in New York City
Rapid Integration, who featured in *Newsweek* magazine
Buncha Love, who also came to the attention of *Newsweek*
Judge Judge, who administered justice in Pasadena, California, and Lord Chief Justice Judge, who was head of the judiciary in England

and Wales
Moon Bong Kang, a Korean diplomat
Santiago Nudelman, who worked as a publisher in Brazil
Violet Organ, an art historian in New York City
Luscious Pea, a citizen of New Orleans, Louisiana
Rosebud Rosenbloom, who was enrolled at the Ethical Culture School
    in New York City
Cardinal Sin, sometime Archbishop of Manila
Justin Tune, chorister from the class of 1947, Westminster Choir,
    Princeton, New Jersey
Peninnah Swingle Hogencamp Umbach, a spiritualist minister from
    Charleston, South Carolina
Mr Vroom, a motorcycle dealer from Port Elizabeth, South Africa
Ms Filet Minon, a real estate agent from Atlanta
Ms Tahra Dactyl, American activist
Sue H. Yoo, a New York lawyer
Marijuana Pepsi Sawyer, a college counsellor from Wisconsin.
    (Disappointingly, her sisters are simply called Kimberly and Robin.)

Sadly, I don't believe the British politician Ed Balls has a sister called
Ophelia, but Ophelia Egypt is a real person. These people are real, too,
and all living somewhere in the United States, Canada or Britain.

| | | |
|---|---|---|
| Eve Adam | Bent Korner | Etta Apple |
| Joseph Wood Krutch | Philip Brilliant | Hunt A. Lusk |
| Betty Burp | Spanish McGee | Upson Downs |
| Asa Miner | Luscious Easter | Savage Nettles |
| Belle Nuddle | Alice Everyday | Elly Oops |
| Wanda Farr | Victor Overcash | Lo Fat |
| Ure A. Pigg | Thaddeus Figlock | Freeze Quick |
| Yetta Gang | Wanton Rideout | Solomon Gemorah |
| Pious Riffle | Bess Goodykoontz | Viola Rubber |
| Fair Hooker | Bea Sharpe | Melvin Intrilligator |
| Bess Sinks | Hannah Isabell Jelly | Adelina Sloog |
| Amazing Grace Jones | Love Joy | Daily Swindle |
| Verbal Snook | | |

| Evan Keel | Pleasant Kidd | Brutus Twitty |
| Royal Knights | Superman Wheaton | Fuller Zest |

. . . . . . . . . . . . . . . . . . . . . . . . . . . . . . . . . . . . . . . . . . . . . . . . . . .

## CELEBRITY ENDORSEMENT

The first names we give our children often reflect our aspirations, our interests or our experiences.

Jay Z and Beyoncé named their daughter Blue Ivy. Michael Jackson called his children Prince, Paris and Blanket. Jermaine Jackson's son glories in the name Jermajesty. Sylvester Stallone's son also has a name with a ring to it: Sage Moonblood. If there is a reason for that, I don't know it. However, I can tell you that the name of Gwyneth Paltrow and Coldplay frontman Chris Martin's daughter, Apple, was inspired by the Bible. As Gwyneth explained, before she 'consciously uncoupled' from Chris, 'Apples are so sweet, and they're wholesome, and it's biblical – and I just thought it sounded so lovely and . . . clean!'

Singer/activist Bono called his daughter Memphis. Nurse/heroine Florence Nightingale was born in Florence, Italy. Actress/singer Ashlee Simpson and her ex-husband, musician Pete Wentz, named their son Bronx Mowgli after the New York City borough. He's in good company, of course, because he's joined by Brooklyn, the son of David and Victoria Beckham. The Beckhams' youngest, however, is named after a position rather than a place. Harper Seven Beckham is named in honour of her dad's shirt number when he played for Manchester United and the English national team.

By some standards, Paris Hilton's name seems quite tame. Actor Nicolas Cage went for something a bit out of this world: he called his son Kal-El, which is Superman's birth name. Another actor, Jason Lee, named his son Pilot Inspektor, after a song by the band Grandaddy called 'He's Simple, He's Dumb, He's The Pilot'. Kim Kardashian and Kanye West named their daughter North, making her North West.

If you have a new offspring in the offing and you are looking for
inspiration, look no further. Here's a selection of memorable first names
registered in either the United Kingdom or the United States since the
start of the twenty-first century.

| GIRLS | BOYS |
|---|---|
| Disney | Kartier |
| Ikea | Princeton |
| Money | ESPN (after the |
| Vegas | American sports channel) |
| Pancake | Del Monte |
| Armani | Canon |
| L'oreal | Courvoisier |
| Chardonnay | Google |
| Fanta | Guinness |
| Nivea | |
| Champagne | |

· · · · · · · · · · · · · · · · · · · · · · · · · · · · · · · · · · · · · · · · · · · · ·

## IDENTITY CRISIS

Edward Banks, Leonard Douglas, William Elliott, Don Reynolds and
Leonard Spalding are one and the same man: novelist Ray Bradbury. J. K.
Rowling is also Robert Galbraith.

It is not unusual for authors to adopt different pen names for books
written in differing styles, but few (if any) eminent writers can have
assumed as many *noms de plume* as this distinguished gentleman. He was
born in 1811 and died in 1863. Who was he?

| | |
|---|---|
| Mr Brown | Groley Byles |
| Folkestone Canterbury | John Corks |
| Fitzroy Clarence | Jeames de la Puche |
| Frederick Haltamont de Montmorency | Henry Esmond, Esq. |
| Boldomero Espertero | Fat Contributor, the |

| | |
|---|---|
| George Savage Fitz Boodle, Esq. | Major Goliam Gahagan |
| A Gentleman in Search of a Manservant | M. Gobemouche |
| Leontius Androcles Hugglestone | Jeames of Buckley Square |
| Theresa MacWhorter | Master Molloy Molony |
| Mulligan of Kulballymulligan | One of Themselves |
| Arthur Pendennis | Peter Perseus |
| Harry Rollicker | The Honourable Wilhelmina Amelia Skeggs |
| Ikey Soloms, Esq., Junior | Miss Tickleboty |
| Michael Angelo Titmarsh | Lancelot Wagstaff |
| Theophile Wagstaff | Charles James Yellowplush |

These were all aliases used by one man: the author of *Vanity Fair* and *Barry Lyndon*, William Makepeace Thackeray.

. . . . . . . . . . . . . . . . . . . . . . . . . . . . . . . . . . . . . . . . . . .

## NAME GAMES

Name games are games you play with names. Could Alistair Cooke? Did Ezra Pound? Does Saul Bellow? Was Clare Boothe Luce?

*John*
*Was Gay*
*But Gerard Hopkins*
*Was Manley*

*Dame May*
*Was Whitty*
*But John Greenleaf*
*Was Whittier*

*Oscar*
*Was Wilde*
*But Thornton*
*Was Wilder*

*Immanuel Kant*
*But Kubla Khan*

. . . . . . . . . . . . . . . . . . . . . . . . . . . . . . . . . . . . . . . . . . .

## WEDDING BELLS

In the Wedding Name Game you make up marriages. If dancer Ginger Rogers had married novelist Thomas Mann she'd have been Ginger Mann. If Mitzi Green had married Orson Bean she'd have been Mitzi Green Bean. If lawyer and political activist Bella Abzug had married comedian and actor Red Buttons she'd have been Bella Buttons. If Tuesday Weld had married Frederic March II, she'd have been Tuesday March 2nd.

. . . . . . . . . . . . . . . . . . . . . . . . . . . . . . . . . . . . . . . . . . .

## CALL ME ADAM

You will need to be of a certain vintage to know that Red Buttons's real name was Aaron Chwatt. Ditto knowing that Judy Garland, Douglas Fairbanks, Jack Benny, Cary Grant, Peter Lorre, Mike Nichols, Marlene Dietrich, El Greco, and King Edward VII started life as plain Frances Gumm, Nicholas Bronstein, Benjamin Kubelski, Archie Leach, László Löwenstein, Michael Igor Peschkowsky, Maria Magdalena von Losch, Domenico Teotocopulo and Albert of Saxe-Coburg and Gotha.

Coming more up to date, here are the real names of a few more famous folk:

*Eric Bishop* – Jamie Foxx
*Farrokh Bulsara* – Freddie Mercury
*Margaret Hyra* – Meg Ryan
*Demetria Guyunes* – Demi Moore
*Allen Konigsberg* – Woody Allen
*Cornelius Chase* – Chevy Chase
*Krishna Pandit Bhanji* – Ben Kingsley
*Alphonso D'Abruzzo* – Alan Alda

*Georgios Panayiotou* – George Michael
*Terry Bollette* – Hulk Hogan
*Love Harrison* – Courtney Love
*Peter Hernandez* – Bruno Mars
*Ilyena Mironov* – Helen Mirren
*Eileen Edwards* – Shania Twain
*Clare Woodgate* – Kim Cattrall

**is for**

**XEME**

A 'xeme' is a bird or bucket or a bison or a butterfly.

Which is it?

You're quite right: it's a bird, a fork-tailed gull. Your vocabulary is obviously impressive – but is it good enough? How many words do you know? How many words would you expect to know?

You are nearly half-way through the book now, properly soaked in the world of *Word Play*, and consequently ready, I reckon, to rise to the challenge and take the tests.

The tests that follow – scientifically devised by experienced and demanding educationalists and philologists, then developed and refined over a period of years – will tell you accurately the size of your vocabulary. There are six tests. Try one, try all. And take your time. This is not an exam. You are not up against the clock. You are just looking down each list and counting the number of words that you recognise and understand. In each test, every single word you find you know stands for 600 words in your overall general vocabulary. If you get 30 words right out of 60, your vocabulary is about 30 x 600 words = 18,000 words.

Average your results for as many of the six tests as you care to take. The more tests you complete, the more accurate the average will be. Bear in mind that the vocabulary featured in the tests is Anglo-American and conventional. This is testing traditional English. Will.i.am has a glorious vocabulary, but not a lot of it features here.

What do your score and size of vocabulary signify?

LEVEL 1: 0–6,000 WORDS
Most of those who score from 0 to 10 out of 60 are children aged six to nine. Don't worry: you are going to do better than that.

LEVEL 2: 6,600–12,000 WORDS
A score of 11 to 20 out of 60 is usually attained at age 10 or soon after. Those who reach it at age 10 are likely to score 40 or more out of 60 as adults. About 25 per cent of adults have vocabularies no larger than 12,000 words.

LEVEL 3: 12,600–18,000 WORDS
Among adults this score of 21 to 30 out of 60 is the most common range. If this is where you find yourself, don't be surprised: most other people are here, too. In the range 12,000–15,000 are most of the adults who left school as soon as the law would let them; and they haven't done much reading since. In the range 15,000–18,000 are adults who may have left school early, but continued with some reading or are in jobs that involve language skills. An 18-year-old who intends to pursue further education should have reached the top of this range.

LEVEL 4: 18,600–24,000 WORDS
Adults with little or no higher education may get 31 to 40 out of 60 if they have maintained a keen interest in what is going on in the world, plus a wide range of reading. Most graduates are in this range, and so are the members of most professions. This is where you will find me, so you are in good company.

LEVEL 5: 24,600–30,000 WORDS

Those in this range (41 to 50 out of 60) are well educated and do a lot of reading. They are in the top echelons of their professions or heading in that direction. In some of the tests, I managed to hit 47, and I am someone who has spent a lot of time leafing through dictionaries, so if you got here effortlessly, I am impressed. And envious.

LEVEL 6: 30,600–36,000 WORDS

The few who fall into this category (51 to 60 out of 60) do not necessarily achieve more in their professions than those at Level 5. At this level, the tests become more an intellectual game than a significant scientific measurement.

On the whole the words that feature in the tests are well established, traditional, non-technical, and feature in Anglo-American dictionaries. If you are in doubt as to whether one of your answers is correct, consult a dictionary. If you are at Level 6, it will need to be a big dictionary.

And if there are words in the test that you did not know before, you do now. Most people's vocabularies grow through adulthood at the rate of about a word a day until they hit their forties. Using the tests to build your vocabulary as well as to measure it means you can go on increasing your word power for as long as you like. That's the joy of wordplay: you can know more and more even as bits of you start drooping and dropping off.

. . . . . . . . . . . . . . . . . . . . . . . . . . . . . . . . . . . . . . . . . . . . .

## TEST 1

| LEVEL 1 | LEVEL 2 | LEVEL 3 |
|---|---|---|
| 1. abroad | 11. abandon | 21. abridge |
| 2. binoculars | 12. ballot | 22. aggregate |
| 3. daily | 13. chaos | 23. bivouac |
| 4. expedition | 14. contraband | 24. chronology |
| 5. horizon | 15. excavate | 25. credulous |
| 6. jangle | 16. fatigue | 26. hireling |

7. limit
8. pattern
9. rate
10. stroke

17. laboratory
18. manual
19. purchase
20. shuttle

27. indolent
28. meagre
29. nomadic
30. occidental

LEVEL 4
31. abhorrent
32. amorphous
33. crustacean
34. declivity
35. emaciated
36. fabrication
37. galaxy
38. heretical
39. igneous
40. nomenclature

LEVEL 5
41. abscissa
42. badinage
43. cartel
44. daemon
45. dendrite
46. exordium
47. inchoate
48. moraine
49. rubric
50. soutane

LEVEL 6
51. abulia
52. bicuspid
53. caracole
54. chalybeate
55. croton
56. dysphoria
57. gazebo
58. kymograph
59. ortolan
60. quadrat

. . . . . . . . . . . . . . . . . . . . . . . . . . . . . . . . . . . . . . . . . . . . . . .

# TEST 2

LEVEL 1
1. alter
2. barometer
3. distinct
4. festival
5. hardship
6. harpoon
7. matinée
8. reign
9. report
10. waste

LEVEL 2
11. beverage
12. cardinal
13. demolish
14. graph
15. humdrum
16. impulsive
17. memorial
18. parallel
19. terminate
20. vivacious

LEVEL 3
21. biography
22. decarbonize
23. domicile
24. facet
25. impunity
26. lore
27. mercenary
28. phantasm
29. restive
30. taboo

LEVEL 4
31. actuate
32. bravura

LEVEL 5
41. antinomy
42. carronade

LEVEL 6
51. antonomasia
52. cartouche

33. comber
34. gouache
35. hieroglyphic
36. hybrid
37. iconoclast
38. maelstrom
39. muezzin
40. resurgent

43. dithyrambic
44. hebdomadal
45. infusoria
46. linage
47. medusa
48. myrmidon
49. paradigm
50. topology

53. dorter
54. elvan
55. filemot
56. isomer
57. lasher
58. noumenon
59. pulvinate
60. velleity

. . . . . . . . . . . . . . . . . . . . . . . . . . . . . . . . . . . . . . . . . . .

# TEST 3

LEVEL 1
1. explosion
2. impatient
3. kangaroo
4. pirate
5. prowl
6. referee
7. slant
8. solo
9. unique
10. waste

LEVEL 2
11. fledgling
12. hatchet
13. impact
14. javelin
15. landlubber
16. novelist
17. primitive
18. renown
19. tradition
20. urban

LEVEL 3
21. cosmopolitan
22. diverge
23. interpose
24. lateral
25. niche
26. porous
27. rampant
28. territory
29. voodoo
30. yeoman

LEVEL 4
31. ecology
32. laconic
33. linden
34. maxilla
35. paragon
36. prolixity
37. redolent
38. stertorous
39. timbre
40. vellum

LEVEL 5
41. asymptotic
42. burlap
43. echidna
44. henry
45. interfacial
46. jeton
47. paregoric
48. rachitic
49. tanager
50. syncretism

LEVEL 6
51. bisque
52. colporteur
53. decuman
54. grallatorial
55. isomorphous
56. orc
57. parataxis
58. rivière
59. tanagra
60. Urticant

## TEST 4

LEVEL 1
1. ballad
2. canoe
3. external
4. icicle
5. lame
6. magazine
7. martyr
8. mass
9. patriot
10. patrol

LEVEL 2
11. abyss
12. bale
13. canyon
14. exterminate
15. instrument
16. lizard
17. obvious
18. password
19. rhythm
20. stoppage

LEVEL 3
21. adaptable
22. capsule
23. daub
24. embargo
25. gargoyle
26. justify
27. liberate
28. memento
29. naturalise
30. oblivion

LEVEL 4
31. calculus
32. debouch
33. gargantuan
34. ibid.
35. lassez-faire
36. literati
37. neurology
38. obloquy
39. patois
40. rabid

LEVEL 5
41. aclinic
42. banshee
43. illation
44. keelson
45. lachrymal
46. martingale
47. newton
48. occipital
49. petrology
50. ratline

LEVEL 6
51. babbittry
52. calumet
53. dehiscent
54. gault
55. hypocaust
56. kenosis
57. knap
58. limnology
59. mithridatism
60. unau

## TEST 5

LEVEL 1
1. belfry
2. bulge
3. outlaw

LEVEL 2
11. besiege
12. bronze
13. gorge

LEVEL 3
21. aquiline
22. botanist
23. captious

4. package
5. pillar
6. rental
7. riddle
8. shellfish
9. vanish
10. varnish

14. import
15. judo
16. ledger
17. limpet
18. penetrate
19. resort
20. warbler

24. furtive
25. initiate
26. jaded
27. kaleidoscopic
28. limerick
29. mutual
30. stratagem

LEVEL 4
31. aurochs
32. beriberi
33. cornice
34. denary
35. gratuitous
36. hertz
37. hiatus
38. medial
39. teredo
40. valetudinarian

LEVEL 5
41. bergamot
42. brevier
43. deemster
44. homologous
45. lamina
46. largo
47. pantheon
48. refulgence
49. savoury
50. triolet

LEVEL 6
51. ablegate
52. algorism
53. baltimore
54. bezel
55. leat
56. mittimus
57. myosotis
58. peneplain
59. prunella
60. windlestraw

• • • • • • • • • • • • • • • • • • • • • • • • • • • • • • • • • • • • • • • • • • • • • •

# TEST 6

LEVEL 1
1. anthill
2. climate
3. container
4. endeavour
5. immediately
6. jingle
7. outcast
8. rhyme
9. signal
10. tank

LEVEL 2
11. absurd
12. collapse
13. entire
14. generation
15. immigrate
16. jealous
17. mature
18. raid
19. satellite
20. slipshod

LEVEL 3
21. acoustics
22. bicker
23. bison
24. centripetal
25. emancipation
26. garbled
27. lichen
28. mattock
29. outshine
30. perimeter

| LEVEL 4 | LEVEL 5 | LEVEL 6 |
|---|---|---|
| 31. botulism | 41. chamfer | 51. champlevé |
| 32. cutaneous | 42. eschatology | 52. demersal |
| 33. datum | 43. giaour | 53. enchiridion |
| 34. distrait | 44. imprest | 54. geodic |
| 35. encyclical | 45. lapidate | 55. jokul |
| 36. gamma | 46. nadir | 56. laches |
| 37. lacerate | 47. oblate | 57. maud |
| 38. mandate | 48. samphire | 58. pedicular |
| 39. martinet | 49. satrap | 59. spandrel |
| 40. nacelle | 50. ukase | 60. vavasor |

# Y

**is for**

## YOUR VERY GOOD HEALTH

If you need an excuse for a drink, you are going to like this chapter. It's the only one in the book I won't allow you to read until you have a drink in your hand – even if it's only an innocent glass of elderflower cordial. Not only do I want you to enjoy yourself with some liquid refreshment before reading any further, I also want you to read the chapter standing up.*
Why? Because, ladies and gentlemen, I am about to propose a toast – or, to be more accurate, I'm about to propose seventeen, so I hope you've got strong legs and you're feeling thirsty.

Once upon a time, when a toast was proposed it was done with wit and charm and style. While you do occasionally come across an amusing modern toast ('Here's to staying positive and testing negative'), on the whole most people when raising a glass, these days, fail to rise to the occasion. That's why I want to revive the best of the good old days with the best of traditional toasts. Whatever the occasion – a civic banquet, a family wedding, a modest meal with two or three friends – you should be able to find something here to fit the bill. So, without more ado, would you kindly raise your glasses and be upstanding, for the Toasts.

*To your good health, old friend,*
*may you live for a thousand years,*
*and I be there to count them.*

*May the road rise to meet you.*
*May the wind be always at your back.*
*May the sun shine warm upon your face.*
*And rains fall soft upon your fields.*

*And until we meet again,*
*May God hold you in the hollow of His hand*

*May your joys be as deep as the ocean*
*and your sorrows as light as its foam.*

*Drink not to my past, which is weak and indefensible,*
*nor to my present, which is not above reproach;*
*but let us drink to our futures, which, thank God, are*
*immaculate.*

*Here's wishing you the kind of troubles that will last as long as*
*your New Year resolutions!*

*Here's to the lasses we've loved, my lad,*
*here's to the lips we've pressed;*
*for of kisses and lasses,*
*like liquor in glasses,*
*the last is always the best.*

*Here's to the bride that is to be,*
*happy and smiling and fair.*
*Here's to those who would like to be*
*and wondering when and where.*

*Here's champagne to our real friends,*
*and real pain to our sham friends.*

*Drink! for you know not whence you come, nor why.*
*Drink! for you know not why you go, nor where.*

*Drink to me only with thine eyes,*
*and I will pledge with mine;*
*or leave a kiss but in the cup*
*and I'll not look for wine.*

*Here's to matrimony, the high sea for which no compass has yet*
*been invented.*

*Here's to my bride: she knows everything about me, yet loves me*
*just the same.*

*Here's to the red of the holly berry,*
*and to its leaf so green;*
*and here's to the lips that are just as red,*
*and the fellow who's not so green.*

*The Ladies – we admire them for their beauty, respect them for*
*their intelligence, adore them for their virtue, and love them*
*because we can't help it.*

*May friendship, like wine, improve as time advances, and may*
*we always have old wine, old friends, and young cares.*

*Here's to lying, cheating, stealing, and drinking...*
*If you're going to lie, lie for a friend.*
*If you're going to cheat, cheat death.*
*If you're going to steal, steal a heart.*
*If you're going to drink, drink with me.*

My penultimate toast is one I was introduced to by the actor Derek Nimmo:

*Let us raise our glasses to the beautiful people*
*and a night like tonight – spent eating with the beautiful people,*

*drinking with the beautiful people,
and sleeping... with a clear conscience*

I have left my favourite toast till last. It was first proposed by Mark Twain:

*Let us toast the fools; but for them the rest of us could not succeed.*

\* Correct. If you are reading this book at sea, you do not need to stand for
the toasts. By tradition long established, sailors may drink toasts sitting
down because on board their ships there may not be room enough to stand.
And, by tradition, too, in the Royal Navy, the loyal toast to the sovereign is
always followed by a second toast depending on the day of the week:

Monday: our ships at sea
Tuesday: our sailors (this used to be 'our men', but there are women at
  sea, too, nowadays)
Wednesday: ourselves ('As no one else gives a fig for us' is the retort –
  more or less)
Thursday: a bloody war or a sickly season (meaning the prospect of
  promotion because of colleagues dying due to war or sickness)
Friday: a willing foe and sea room (because of the traditional payment
  of prize money after a successful engagement)
Saturday: our families (formerly 'our wives and sweethearts' with the
  retort of 'May they never meet')
Sunday: absent friends

# Z

**is for**

**ZAP!**

Professor Abel T. Jackson, head of the English department at Western Community College in Indiana, has concluded an unusual piece of research, on the use of onomatopoeic exclamations in twentieth-century comic books. He and his students have carefully examined several hundred thousand strips – from *Crazy Kat*, *Batman* and *Popeye* right the way through to *The Incredible Hulk*, *Star Wars* and *Shriek!* – and have listed each and every exclamation. Says the professor: 'We deliberately excluded from the scope of the survey everyday exclamations like "Oh!" and "Ah!" and "Hi!" and "Hey!" What interested us were the exclamations used as stage directions within the strips – the dramatic sounds that gave life and meaning to the action.'

Here are the top fifty of the twentieth century's most popular onomatopoeic exclamations:

| | | |
|---|---|---|
| Zap! | Wow! | Aw! |
| Pow! | Ooo! | Yuk! |
| Bang! | Gulp! | Splosh! |
| Ugh! | Smash! | Boof! |
| Bonk! | Thwack! | Slurp! |

| | | |
|---|---|---|
| Splat! | Woweee! | Oik! |
| Fut! | Zing! | Clang! |
| Eee! | Oi! | Splot! |
| Whizz! | Scrunch! | Clatter! |
| Jeepers! | Koing! | Ulp! |
| Cripes! | Ping! | Kersplat! |
| Klunk! | Kerr-unch! | Yikes! |
| Aaagh! | Weee! | Vroomvroom! |
| Crack! | Jipes! | Kerplop! |
| Klonk! | Crumbs! | Klink! |
| Crash! | Krunk! | Yarooo! |
| Bong! | Och! | |

Compiling the list – which includes at least a thousand words – has taken Professor Jackson and his team three years. Was it all worthwhile? 'Definitely,' says the professor. 'This has been no dry semantic exercise. Comic strips and comic books are an integral part of American culture. These extraordinary exclamations have given a new richness to our language. They add a vital dimension to the twentieth-century experience.'

Ouch.

# Y

**is for**

## YOU GO URUGUAY AND I'LL GO MINE

Since I first heard that line – at the Classic Cinema in Baker Street, London, in about 1960 – I have been a confirmed Marxist.

The great Groucho Marx spoke the line in the 1930 movie *Animal Crackers*. His co-stars were his brothers, Harpo, Chico, Zeppo, and the magnificent Margaret Dumont. The script was by Bert Kalmar, Harry Ruby and George S. Kaufman and, boy, those guys sure loved a pun.

Groucho encounters a Welsh woman. 'Did you ever meet a fellow named Jonah? He lived in Wales for a while.' In *The Cocoanuts*, Groucho says, 'What's a thousand dollars? Mere chicken feed. A poultry matter.' And in the same movie (with Kaufman again taking the writing credit), Groucho shares a truly awful pun with Chico:

GROUCHO: We're going to have an auction.

CHICO: I came over here on the Atlantic auction.

Whoever wrote them, these are my favourite Groucho Marx lines:

'Outside of a dog, a book is man's best friend. Inside of a dog it's too dark to read.'

'Anyone who says he can see through women is missing a lot.'

'A child of five could understand this. Send someone to fetch a child of five.'

'When you're in jail, a good friend will be trying to bail you out. A best friend will be in the cell next to you, saying, "Damn, that was fun."'

'From the moment I picked up your book until I put it down, I was convulsed with laughter. Some day I intend reading it.'

'Learn from the mistakes of others. You can never live long enough to make them all yourself.'

'I never forget a face, but in your case I'll be glad to make an exception.'

'I sent the club a wire stating, PLEASE ACCEPT MY RESIGNATION. I DON'T WANT TO BELONG TO ANY CLUB THAT WILL ACCEPT ME AS A MEMBER.'

'Politics is the art of looking for trouble, finding it everywhere, diagnosing it incorrectly and applying the wrong remedies.'

'I've had a perfectly wonderful evening, but this wasn't it.'

'Those are my principles, and if you don't like them . . . well, I have others.'

'One morning I shot an elephant in my pajamas. How he got in my pajamas I'll never know.'

'I'm not crazy about reality, but it's still the only place to get a decent meal.'

'He may look like an idiot and talk like an idiot but don't let that fool you. He really is an idiot.'

'If a black cat crosses your path, it signifies that the animal is going somewhere.'

'I have nothing but respect for you – and not much of that.'

'Well, art is art, isn't it? Still, on the other hand, water is water! And east is east and west is west, and if you take cranberries and stew them like applesauce they taste much more like prunes than rhubarb does. Now, uh . . . now you tell me what you know.'

'I intend to live for ever, or die trying.'

'Just give me a comfortable couch, a dog, a good book and a
        woman. Then if you can get the dog to go somewhere and
        read the book, I might have a little fun.'
'Whatever it is, I'm against it.'

. . . . . . . . . . . . . . . . . . . . . . . . . . . . . . . . . . . . . . . . . . . . .

## TOM SWIFTIES

Groucho Marx first came to fame in the 1920s, the era that introduced the
world to another pun-loving phenomenon: Tom Swifties.

Tom Swifties are a type of pun based on adverbs or adverbial phrases. They
take their name from one Tom Swift, a character in a series of books by
Edward Statemeyer. They work like this:

'Turn on the radio,' said Tom, with a short wave.
'How about a game of draughts?' asked Tom, airily.
'I'll try to dig up a couple of friends,' said Tom, gravely.
'I got the first three wrong,' said Tom, forthrightly.
'*Drei . . . fünf,*' said Tom, fearlessly.
'Let's trap that sick bird,' said Tom, illegally.
'That's a very large herring,' said Tom, superficially.
'Pass the cards,' said Tom, ideally.
'Drop that gun,' said Tom, disarmingly.
'I bequeath,' said Tom, willingly.
'Brothers,' said Tom, grimly.
'I can't find the apples,' said Tom, fruitlessly.
'I've just had a serious operation,' said Tom, half-heartedly.
'Walk this way,' said Tom, stridently.
'Where did all the carpet on the steps go?' asked Tom, with a
        blank stare.
'I have no flowers,' said Tom, lackadaisically.
'I know not which groceries to purchase,' said Tom, listlessly.
'Did you say to zip up my sleeping bag or the door?' Tom asked,
        inattentively.

'Careful with that chainsaw,' Tom said, offhandedly.
'I'm here,' said Tom, presently.
'Zero,' said Tom, naughtily.
'Coda,' said Tom, finally.

. . . . . . . . . . . . . . . . . . . . . . . . . . . . . . . . . . . . . . . .

## CROAKERS

Tom had a cousin called Croaker. With him the pun is purely verbal:

'I'm dying,' he croaked.
'I decided to come back to the group,' he rejoined.

Roy Bongartz was the man responsible for the Croaker craze. Here are half a dozen of his gems:

'You can't really train a beagle,' he dogmatised.
'That's no beagle, it's a mongrel,' she muttered.
'The fire is going out,' he bellowed.
'Bad marksmanship,' the hunter groused.
'You ought to see a psychiatrist,' he reminded me.
'My experiment was a success,' the chemist retorted.

James I. Rambo and Mary J. Youngquist have novel names and an equally novel collection of Croakers. Here are the best, in ascending order of complexity:

'You snake,' she rattled.
'Someone's at the door,' she chimed.
'Company's coming,' she guessed.
'Dawn came too soon,' she mourned.
'I think I'll end it all,' Sue sighed.
'I ordered chocolate, not vanilla,' I screamed.
'Your embroidery is sloppy,' she needled cruelly.
'Where did you get this meat?' he bridled hoarsely.

Alun F. G. Lewis is the fellow who observed that 'A true adman writes the prose and cons.' He is also the chap who asked this question: 'Is a group of trainee secret service agents aspiring?' Here is Lewis the punster at his best – or worst:

*I'll be with you –*
*in two sex, said the hermaphrodite*
*in half a tick, said the vivisectionist*
*in two shakes, said the freemason*
*in half a mho, said the electrician*
*in a trice, said the Third Man*
*in necks to no time, said the executioner*
*in a flash, said the magician*
*in an instant, said the marketing man*
*in a twinkling, eye said*

## OCCUPATIONAL HAZARDS

Violinists are unstrung.
Bankers are disinterested.
Butchers are delivered.
Models are denuded.
Songwriters are decomposed.
Castle owners are demoted.
Surveyors are dislocated.
Accountants are disfigured.
Witch doctors are dispelled.
Train drivers are derailed.
Symphony conductors are disconcerted.
Orchestra leaders are disbanded.
Diplomats are disconsolate.
Cannibal victims are disheartened.
Winemakers are deported.
Mathematicians are discounted.

Advertisers are declassified.
Admirals are abridged.
Tailors are unsuited.
Neurologists are unnerved.
Brides are dismissed.
Committee members are disappointed.
Electricians get discharged.
Authors are described.
Choristers are unsung.
Mathematicians are nonplussed.
Politicians are devoted.
Hairdressers are distressed.
Tree surgeons are uprooted.
Prisoners are excelled.
Bridge players are discarded.
Teachers are outclassed.
Eulogists are distributed.
Puzzlers are dissolved.
Clubs are dismembered.
Private eyes are undetected.
Botanists are deflowered.
Tennis players are unloved and defaulted.
Arsonists are unmatched and fired.
Gunsmiths, they're just plain fired.

. . . . . . . . . . . . . . . . . . . . . . . . . . . . . . . . . . . . . . . . . . . . .

## JESTER STORY

A pun my soul, it can be a dangerous business this punning. Witness the story of the medieval court jester who was an inveterate punster from a family of inveterate punsters and punned knight and day until his master, the monarch – an ace of a king and quite a card by all accounts – was driven beyond reason and ordered the fool to be carried away to the gallows, there to be strung up and executed. No sooner had the jester been dragged from the royal presence than the king began to reflect on the problems of acquiring a replacement, and it didn't take him long to have a pardon speeding towards the condemned jester.

The messenger carrying the pardon reached the gallows just in time to save the hapless fool, who was already standing with the rope around his neck. The pardon proclaimed the jester's freedom on condition that he and every member of his pun-loving family never uttered another pun in their lives. But old habits die hard, and without thinking the jester grinned at the messenger and remarked: 'No noose is good news.'

So they hanged him.

But that isn't the end of the story. The jester's brother was the undertaker, charged with carting the jester's coffin to the burial ground. Unfortunately, on the way, the road was rough and the coffin slipped its moorings and fell to the ground. 'We'll have to rehearse that,' said the undertaker, gravely. They hanged him, too.

# X

### is for

### X MARKS THE SPOT

. . . . . . . . . . . . . . . . . . . . . . . . . . . . . . . . . . . . . . . . . .

## THE JOY OF X

I like some letters of the alphabet much more than others. My analyst – if I had one – could probably tell me why, but I can't. All I know is that I don't care much for *j* and *r*, but *x* I just adore. It's the look of the letter, I suppose. And the sound. And the suggestion of something forbidden. When I was a boy, X-rated movies were the ones I couldn't go to.

Xan is my son's second name and *x* is the first letter I turn to when I open a new dictionary. Everyone is familiar with 'xylophone' and 'X-ray' and 'xenophobia', but many more intriguing words begin with *x*.

Here are thirty of my favourites:

| | |
|---|---|
| *xanorphica* | a stringed musical instrument |
| *Xanthippe* | an ill-tempered woman |
| *xanthocyanopsy* | colour blindness in which the ability to distinguish only yellow and blue is present |

| | |
|---|---|
| *xanthoderm* | a person with yellow skin |
| *xarque* | jerked meat |
| *xat* | a carved pole erected as a memorial to the dead by some of the Native American tribes |
| *xebec* | a Mediterranean sailing ship |
| *xenagogue* | a guide |
| *xenelasia* | the banishment of aliens from ancient Sparta by official action |
| *xenia* | gifts sometimes given compulsorily to medieval rulers and churches |
| *xenodocheionology* | the lore of hotels and inns |
| *xeriff* | a gold coin, at one time currency in Turkey and Egypt |
| *xerophagy* | the eating of dry food |
| *xerosis* | abnormal dryness of the skin |
| *Xibalba* | in Maya religion, the abode of the dead |
| *Xicaque* | a native people of northern Honduras |
| *xilinous* | of cotton |
| *xiphoid* | sword-shaped |
| *xoanon* | a primitive image of carved wood |
| *xu* | a monetary unit of Vietnam |
| *xurel* | a fish |
| *xya* | a genus of mole-crickets, mainly tropical |
| *xylanthrax* | charcoal |
| *xylography* | artistic wood carving |
| *xylomancy* | divination by means of pieces of wood |
| *xylopolist* | a timber merchant |
| *xylosistron* | a musical instrument |
| *xysma* | membraneous shreds in the stools of patients with diarrhoea or dysentery |
| *xyster* | an instrument for scraping bones |
| *xystus* | a walk lined with trees |

. . . . . . . . . . . . . . . . . . . . . . . . . . . . . . . . . . . . . . . . . . . . . . .

# THE JOY OF LEX

If *x* is my favourite letter, next to 'yes' and 'yex', 'lex' is my favourite three-letter word. I reckon there are about fifty words in the English language that begin with the letters *l, e, x*. Here are my top thirty – and, as you will see, many of them have something to do with language:

| | |
|---|---|
| *Lexa* | a town in Arkansas |
| *Lexden* | a town in Essex |
| *lexeme* | a meaningful speech form that is an item of the vocabulary of a language |
| *lexemic* | relating to a lexeme |
| *lexer* | a student of law |
| *lexia* | a soft raisin produced chiefly in Spain and Australia |
| *lexica* | a plural of lexicon |
| *lexical* | relating to words of the vocabulary of a language |
| *lexicalise* | to accept into the vocabulary of a language |
| *lexicographer* | a dictionary compiler |
| *lexicographian* | relating to lexicography |
| *lexicographical* | relating to lexicography |
| *lexicography* | the principles and practices of dictionary-making |
| *lexicological* | relating to lexicology |
| *lexicologist* | one versed in lexicology |
| *lexicology* | the science of the derivation and significance of words |
| *lexicon* | a dictionary of word stock |
| *lexiconist* | a compiler of a lexicon |
| *lexiconize* | to make a lexicon |
| *lexicostatistic* | pertaining to the statistics of vocabulary |
| *lexigram* | any figure or symbol used to represent a word |
| *lexigraphic* | pertaining to lexigraphy |
| *lexigraphy* | the art of defining words |
| *Lexington* | A town in Massachusetts, the site of the first engagement of the American Revolution |
| *lexiphane* | a phrasemonger |
| *lexiphanic* | pretentious |
| *lexiphanicism* | pretentious phraseology |
| *lexipharmic* | an antidote |
| *lexis* | the wording of a piece of writing |

And here are thirty words that end with *-lex*:

| | |
|---|---|
| *apoplex* | to strike with a sudden loss of consciousness |
| *circumflex* | an accent mark |
| *complex* | complicated |
| *Culex* | a genus of mosquitoes |
| *decemplex* | having ten parts |
| *duplex* | twofold |
| *exlex* | without legal authority |
| *flex* | to bend |
| *googolplex* | ten raised to the power of a googol |
| *ilex* | an evergreen oak of southern Europe |
| *implex* | intricate |
| *multiplex* | having numerous parts |
| *octuplex* | relating to a system of telegraphy in which eight messages can be sent simultaneously |
| *perplex* | to bewilder |
| *plex* | to make like a network |
| *pollex* | thumb |
| *proplex* | a complicated network of nerves |
| *Pulex* | a genus of fleas |
| *quadruplex* | relating to a specific system of telegraphy |
| *reflex* | an act performed automatically |
| *retroflex* | bend abruptly backwards |
| *scolex* | the head of a tapeworm |
| *silex* | a pure form of silica |
| *simplex* | single |
| *supellex* | furniture |
| *telex* | a communication service |
| *triplex* | threefold |
| *Ulex* | a genus of spiny shrubs |
| *uncomplex* | simple |

. . . . . . . . . . . . . . . . . . . . . . . . . . . . . . . . . . . . . . . . . . . . . . .

## TWO OUT OF THREE

Running through the alphabet looking for three-letter words ending in *-ex* isn't so easy.

| | |
|---|---|
| *Aex* | a genus of short-legged perching duck |
| *bex* | an obsolete plural of beak |
| *cex* | an obsolete spelling of six |
| *Dex* | a diminutive form of the masculine forename Dexter |
| *eex* | ??? |
| *fex* | a variant spelling of 'fax'; the hair on the head |
| *gex* | an English dialect word meaning 'to guess' |
| *hex* | a spell or jinx |
| *iex* | ??? |
| *Jex* | A surname, related to Geake and Jacks |
| *kex* | the dry stalk of various plants |
| *lex* | law |
| *Mex* | a Mexican |
| *nex* | an obsolete spelling of next |
| *OEX* | an abbreviation for the Office of Educational Exchange |
| *pex* | an obsolete spelling of pax, peace |
| *qex* | ??? |
| *rex* | king |
| *sex* | gender |
| *Tex* | a nickname for Texas or someone from Texas |
| *uex* | an obsolete spelling of vex |
| *vex* | to worry or annoy |
| *wex* | a dialectical spelling of wax |
| *xex* | ??? |
| *yex* | to belch or hiccup |
| *zex* | a variant spelling of 'sax'; a chopping tool for trimming slates |

It seems we don't yet have meanings for *eex, iex, qex* and *xex*. We ought to have. Perhaps *eex* should be the first spouse of a twice-divorced person, *iex* an English form of 'Eureka!', *qex* someone who gets kicks out of spelling badly and *xex* a point on the map – as in 'Xex marks the spot.' If you have any deft definitions of your own, send me a tweet and tell your friends. I think we should do all we can to spread the words.

## is for

## THE WORLD WIDE WEB

The internet has given us email, Facebook and funny-cat videos. It has changed the way we communicate and brought closer to reality Andy Warhol's prophecy that one day we will all be famous for fifteen minutes.

When Tim Berners-Lee created the first website in 1989, who could have predicted that the internet would have so much influence? And mostly for the good. I was encouraged to discover that the most searched female on the internet at the last count was not Kim Kardashian, as I supposed, but Malala Yousafzai, the Pakistani schoolgirl and now Nobel Peace Prize-winner who became a symbol of the struggle for women's rights when she was shot for pursuing an education.

As well as adding something extraordinary to our lives, the internet and the world wide web have brought new words to our language. I will leave you with some of them. (I'll only be next door. I just want to catch this video of a bulldog skateboarding.)

. . . . . . . . . . . . . . . . . . . . . . . . . . . . . . . . . . . . . . . . .

# NETLINGO – WORDS WE GET FROM THE INTERNET

We all know our email from our snail mail, our Twitter from our Facebook, and our downloading from our uploading, don't we? Here's a selection of other words and phrases that the internet has either given us or changed for ever.

*App.* App is short for 'application': it's a program you download to your mobile device or tablet. From games to cinema listings, dating, mating, shopping and socialising, there is an app out there for everything. The top ten most downloaded apps of 2014 were: 10. Apple music, 9. Instagram, 8. Google+, 7. Facebook Messenger, 6. gmail, 5. Google Maps, 4. Google Play, 3. YouTube, 2. Google Search, 1. Facebook.

*Avatar.* In times gone by, 'avatar' was a Hindu term meaning the bodily incarnation of a deity on earth. These days, it has the rather more prosaic meaning of a graphic or character that represents a player or program-user within a computer game.

*Bitcoin.* Bitcoins are a digital currency. They are virtual. They have no physical form, you can't put them in a bank and it is almost impossible to use them in the real world. They came into existence in 2009. There are 21 million bitcoins and their value has fluctuated from $5 to $1000 per coin. (Don't worry: I don't really understand it, either.)

*Cookie.* I love a cookie. I'm particularly fond of white chocolate chip. I'm not so fond of the ones that seem to ask my permission to do something every time I visit a website. It turns out they are files that the site downloads to store information about me and what I've been up to on their website.

*Grindr.* This is not for the pepper: it's the gay man's Tinder (see below) – or, rather, Tinder is the straight Grindr. (Oh, yes, dear reader, it's all happening out there. We're missing quite a bit curled up in our armchairs leafing through the pages of *Word Play*.)

*Hashtag.* This is one of the best-known words to have leapt from our computer screen and started a new life in the language. The ubiquitous hashtag # is put before a #word or #phrase on a social media site, most famously Twitter, to tag it so that what precedes it comes up when that word is searched for. It is now used by people as a conversational quirk, though hopefully not for much longer. #pastitssellbydate

*Meme.* A meme can be anything from a hashtag, or vine (see below), or a viral video (see below below), that gets passed from user to user on the internet. In the words of Paul Gill from *abouttech.com*: 'A meme is a virally-transmitted cultural symbol or social idea. A meme (rhymes with "team") behaves like a flu or a cold virus, travelling from person to person quickly, but transmitting an idea instead of a life form.' The word was coined in 1976 by Richard Dawkins, who, doubtless, was not anticipating it would one day be used to describe such assorted viral sensations as Nuts the Squirrel, LOLcats, RickRolling, Gangnam Style or the Pope's Easter Message.

*Noob.* Noob comes from 'newbie' and is used to describe those new to the internet or any kind of programming or site. It is often written n00b. According to the Texas-based and self-styled Global Language Monitor, in 2009 'noob' almost became the one-millionth word in the English language. Instead, at the last minute, that honour went to another geeks' favourite: 'Web 2.0'.

*Phablet.* A large smart phone. Somewhere between the size of a phone and a tablet.

*Phishing* is when you get an email that seems to come from your bank, energy provider or any other quasi-reputable institution asking you to reveal personal details to them. Don't take the bait. This is phishing, a fraudulent way of getting hold of your passwords, bank details or identification so that they can be used to rob you blind or steal your identity.

*Selfie.* This is the word of the age and some think it sums up the age, too. A selfie is a photo you take of yourself, normally on your phone and normally to post on social media. And normally making the obligatory duck face (see page 123).

*Sexting* is sending someone sexually explicit photos or messages via mobile phone. Often over Snapchat (see above). But don't do it. Really don't do it. Especially if you are a prospective parliamentary candidate.

*Silver surfer.* Yup, that's me: someone over sixty who regularly uses the internet.

*Snapchat* is a photo-messaging app with a difference. You send your photo or video: the recipient can only view it for ten seconds before it disappears.

*Social media.* This isn't an easy phrase to define precisely, but essentially it's a concept that has altered the way we communicate with our friends and with our culture. The most famous social media sites are Facebook and Twitter. Facebook was created in 2004 and claims around 1.39 billion active users around the world. Twitter was created in 2006 and now has around 300 million users worldwide. Here are our friends at *abouttech.com* again with a silver-surfer-friendly description of 'social media':

> a website that doesn't just give you information, but interacts with you while giving you that information. This interaction can be as simple as asking for your comments or letting you vote on an article, or it can be as complex as Flixster recommending movies to you based on the ratings of other people with similar interests. Think of regular media as a one-way street where you can read a newspaper or listen to a report on television, but you have very limited ability to give your thoughts on the matter. Social media, on the other hand, is a two-way street that gives you the ability to communicate too.

The nation that spends the most time engaging with social media is Malaysia, with Russia coming second.

*Spam.* The tinned meat of my childhood is now electronic junk mail. It made this leap via a Monty Python sketch, which featured singing Vikings and a restaurant where all they served was Spam.

*Tinder.* Light my fire! This is not what you need to start a conventional blaze, but a dating app that allows you to see all the single people within a certain radius of you. The potential date's picture comes up: if you like the look of them you swipe right; if they are not your cup of tea you swipe left. The app lets you know if you have any matches – when both of you have swiped right.

*Troll.* A traditional troll is an ugly cave-dwelling creature favoured by Norse mythology. Some would argue that the internet troll is even more pernicious. Hiding behind their computers, trolls post deliberately offensive and nasty messages.

*Tweet.* A tweet is a message of 140 characters or fewer that people post on Twitter to be read by their followers, also known as their tweeps.

*Unfriend.* When you remove someone from your friends list, primarily on Facebook. The gesture has come to be one of symbolic significance.

*Vine.* Vines are six- or seven-second-long video clips. They get their name from the video-sharing service onto which people upload their clips.

*Viral.* In the same vein as a meme (see above), a viral is something, usually a photograph or video, that has spread across the net.

· · · · · · · · · · · · · · · · · · · · · · · · · · · · · · · · · · · · · · · · · ·

## INTERNEAUS: INTERNET + PORTMANTEAUS

The internet is brimming with new words that have come to us courtesy of our old friend, the portmanteau. Here are just a few.

*blog*: web + log
*blogebrity*: blog + celebrity
*cybrarian*: cyber + librarian
*email*: electronic + mail
*freeware*: free + software
*internet*: international + network
*malware*: malicious + software
*netiquette*: internet + etiquette
*netizen*: internet + citizen
*wi-fi*: wireless + fidelity

By the way, you will know that you are spending too much time in the world of the world wide web when . . .

   . . . you refer to going to the lavatory as downloading.
   . . . you go to the bathroom in the middle of the night and check your emails on the way back. It says 'no new messages'. So you check again.
   . . . you turn off your modem and get this awful empty feeling, as though you have just pulled the plug on a loved one.
   . . . you eventually get to sleep and find your nightmares are in HTML.
   . . . all of your friends have an @ in their names.

# V

**is for**

## VICTORIAN AMUSEMENTS

The heyday of wordplay was the Victorian era, when education was starting to spread, and before the advent of radio, television, cinema, the home computer and the Xbox. In the nineteenth century more people than ever were learning to read and write – and discovering how to amuse themselves by playing with words and language.

• • • • • • • • • • • • • • • • • • • • • • • • • • • • • • • • • • • • • • • • • • • •

### ACROSTICS

An acrostic is a verse in which the initial letters of the lines form words. Lewis Carroll loved creating acrostics and here is his most famous example, dedicated to Alice Pleasance Liddell, the little girl who inspired *Alice's Adventures in Wonderland*:

> *A boat, beneath a sunny sky*
> *Lingering onward dreamily*
> *In an evening of July –*
>
> *Children three that nestle near,*
> *Eager eye and willing ear,*

*Pleased a simple tale to hear –*
*Long has paled that sunny sky:*
*Echoes fade and memories die:*
*Autumn frosts have slain July.*

*Still she haunts me, phantomwise,*
*Alice moving under skies*
*Never seen by waking eyes.*

*Children yet the tale to hear,*
*Eager eye and willing ear,*
*Lovingly shall nestle near.*

*In Wonderland they lie,*
*Dreaming as the days go by,*
*Dreaming as the summers die:*

*Ever drifting down the stream –*
*Lingering in the golden gleam –*
*Life, what is it but a dream?*

A double acrostic is one in which the initial and the final letters of the lines make up words and a triple acrostic is one in which the initial letters, the final letters and a middle letter of each line make up words. If you have trouble getting to sleep (as Lewis Carroll did), you can try composing an acrostic beneath the duvet.

If you are a proper insomniac, you can try composing a telestich. A telestich is a more complex cousin of the acrostic, in which the initial letters of the lines spell one word, while the final letters of the lines spell another word with a meaning contrary to the first. Here is a neat Victorian example, using the words 'unite' and 'untie' and so adding a pleasing anagrammatical dimension to the whole:

*Unite and untie are the same – so say yoU*
*Not in wedlock, I ween has this unity beeN*

*In the drama of marriage each wandering gouT*
*To a new face would fly – all except you and I –*
*Each seeking to alter the spell in their scenE*

Acrostics were popular with Victorians as puzzles as well as verses. Queen Victoria herself was very taken with double acrostics and she is credited with the authorship of this geographic puzzle 'for the royal children'. It amused her. I hope it amuses you. (It isn't easy, but bear in mind that Queen Victoria lived 150 years ago and so was closer in time to the Battle of Lepanto of 1571 and more familiar with old Bothnia than we are.)

The initial letters spell out the name of a town in Great Britain and the last letters spell, in reverse order, something for which it is famous. Can you work it out?

A city in Italy
A river in Germany
A town in the United States
A town in North America
A town in Holland
The Turkish name of Constantinople
A town in Bothnia
A city in Greece
A circle on the globe

Answer:
Naple**S**
Elb**E**
**W**ashingto**N**
**C**incinnat**I**
**A**msterda**M**
**S**tambou**L**
**T**orne**A**
**L**epant**O**
**E**clipti**C**
(Newcastle: coalmines)

. . . . . . . . . . . . . . . . . . . . . . . . . . . . . . . . . . . . . . . . . . . . .

## ALPHABETICS

In 1842, in the fifth year of Queen Victoria's reign, *The Times* carried this unusual advertisement:

> To widowers and single gentlemen – wanted by a lady, a Situation to superintend the household and preside at table. She is Agreeable, Becoming, Careful, Desirable, English, Facetious, Generous, Honest, Industrious, Keen, Lively, Merry, Natty, Obedient, Philosophic, Quiet, Regular, Sociable, Tasteful, Useful, Vivacious, Womanish, Xantippish, Youthful, Zealous, etc.

The lady in question was obviously a prize worth winning, for as well as all her stated virtues she was also a mistress in the art of alphabetics. To master the art yourself all you need to do is devise an essay or poem or a story or an advertisement in which each word begins with a successive letter of the alphabet. It can even be done with a toast, as the Jacobite Lord Duff showed in 1745 when he called on those around him to raise their glasses to this alphabet. Students of the current political scene in Scotland will probably be familiar with the names of the Earl of Mar and the Duke of Ormond and will be gripped by the poem's political thrust. The rest of us can just enjoy the alphabetical ingenuity of it.

| | |
|---|---|
| ABC | A Blessed Change |
| DEF | Down Every Foreigner |
| GHJ | God Help James |
| KLM | Keep Lord Mar |
| NOP | Noble Ormond Preserve |
| QRS | Quickly Resolve Stewart |
| TUVW | Truss Up Vile Whigs |
| XYZ | 'Xert Your Zeal! |

The toast, of course, contains no 'I'. To merge 'I' and 'J' was once an allowable practice among puzzlers.

Here is another historical gem, probably the most famous alphabetic verse of all, an alliterative epic called 'The Siege of Belgrade'. It doesn't feature any *j*s this time, but it brings the dramatic events of 1789 thrillingly to life. The 'Suwarrow', who features in the poem, is the Russian general you would recognise as Suvorov. Enjoy.

*An Austrian army, awfully arrayed,*
*Boldly, by battery, besieged Belgrade;*
*Cossack commanders cannonading come,*
*Dealing destruction's devastating doom;*
*Every endeavour, engineers essay,*
*For fame, for fortune, fighting furious fray:*
*Generals 'gainst generals grapple – gracious God!*
*How honours Heaven, heroic hardihood!*
*Infuriate, indiscriminate in ill,*
*Kindred kill kinsmen, kinsmen kindred kill!*
*Labour low levels loftiest longest lines,*
*Men march 'mid mounds, 'mid moles, 'mid murderous mines:*
*Now noisy, noxious, noticed nought*
*Of outward obstacles opposing ought:*
*Poor patriots, partly purchased, partly pressed:*
*Quite quaking, quickly quarter, quarter quest,*
*Reason returns, religious right redounds.*
*Suwarrow stops such sanguinary sounds,*
*Truce to thee, Turkey – triumph to thy train!*
*Unjust, unwise, unmerciful Ukraine!*
*Vanish vain victory, vanish victory vain!*
*Why wish we warfare? Wherefore welcome were*
*Xerxes, Ximenes, Xanthus, Xaviere?*
*Yield! ye youths! ye yeomen, yield your yell!*
*Zeno's, Zapater's, Zoroaster's zeal,*
*And all attracting – arms against acts appeal.*

Alaric Alexander Watts is the Victorian journalist credited with creating the poem. Apparently, he was a forebear of Adolph Blaine Charles David Earl Frederick Gerald Hubert Irvin John Kenneth Lloyd Martin Nero

Oliver Paul Quincy Randolph Sherman Thomas Uncas Victor William Xerxes Yancy Zeus Wolfeschlegelsteinhausenbergerdorrf Senior whom we met back on page 176.

There is no better way to ease yourself to sleep than by composing an alphabetical verse in your head. It can help you in even the most trying circumstances. Here is the start of one that dates from the grim nights of the London Blitz at the beginning of the Second World War:

> *Air raid shelters, damp and black*
> *Bombs exploding, back to back*
> *Children crying, adults too*
> *'Down the cellar – after you.'*
> *Evacuees on the train*
> *Farewells said in pouring rain*
> *Gone to live in some strange place*
> *Hoping for a friendly face . . .*

. . . . . . . . . . . . . . . . . . . . . . . . . . . . . . . . . . . . . . . . . . . . . . . . .

## LOGOGRAMS

The dictionary definition of a logogram is 'a sign representing a word in shorthand'. In the world of Victorian wordplay, however, logograms are word puzzles in which a word changes its meaning as it loses certain of its letters. Here is an example:

> *Beginning with a fruit*
> *you move to the part of a kitchen where you cook*
> *and go on to do what the telephone did*
> *and then what the four-minute miler did*
> *before becoming a sun god*
> *and an indefinite article.*

The word you are looking to start with is ORANGE, which becomes other words as you drop one letter in turn:

ORANGE
RANGE
RANG
RAN
RA
A

My Twitter friend Phil Taylor (@pstni) tells me that the best-known logogram is this one:

STARLING
STARING
STRING
STING
SING
SIN
IN
I

Another of my Twitter followers, Whale Gangsta (@handgunwales), offered me these two:

PALPATES
PALATES
PLATES
PATES
PATS
PAS
AS
A

WRAPPING
RAPPING
RAPING
APING
PING

PIN
IN
I

Whale Gangsta has actually created a computer program that will generate logograms for you. I think it's more fun to self-generate them. Here is my all-time favourite, a versified logogram from the pen of Lord Macaulay (1800–59). The great historian wants you to uncover a common three-letter word. Can you?

*Cut off me head, how singular I act!*
*Cut off my tail, and plural I appear,*
*Cut off my head and tail – most curious fact –*
*Although my middle's left, there's nothing there!*
*What is my tail cut off? A flowing river!*
*Amid their mingling depths I fearless play,*
*Parent of softest sounds, though mute forever!*

The starting word in Macaulay's logogram is COD – of course.

. . . . . . . . . . . . . . . . . . . . . . . . . . . . . . . . . . . . . . . . . . . . . . . . . .

## METAGRAMS

A metagram is a word that can be turned into a number of other words by the simple process of changing its initial letter.

KINK is a perfect metagram:

KINK
LINK
MINK
PINK
RINK
SINK
WINK

Metagrams can take the form of riddles and the Victorians were great ones for constructing them in verse:

> A vessel, when empty I make a great sound . . . . . CAN
> For frying I'm used, in shape I am round . . . . . PAN
> My lady she carries me off in her hand . . . . . FAN
> All the boys did it when they heard the band . . . . . RAN
> The King of creation, and proud of his race . . . . . MAN
> A pretty girl's name if it's short's no disgrace . . . . . NAN
> The law on the rebel laid me, alack . . . . . BAN
> I'm an old Jewish tribe that existed long back . . . . . DAN
> The sun takes your faces and paints them with me . . . . . TAN
> Where the brave soldier stands, who never would fall . . . . . VAN

Here's another fairly simple metagram based on three-letter words. Can you solve the riddle?

> Well known to all as a covering for the head;
> Change my initial, a doze I mean instead.
> Once more, and an opening you will see;
> Exchange again, I'm found inside a tree.
> Once more, I mean then to befall.
> Again, I'm used by travellers, one and all.
> Again, in this my mother often nursed me.
> Exchange again, and this my food would be.
> Again, and a sharp blow you've spelled.
> Once more, and a blow that's hardly seen or felt.

The answers? Cap, nap, gap, sap, hap, map, lap, pap, rap, tap

And with this one you are looking for five four-letter words:

> Of letters four, I do denote
> A man of wisdom great,
> But cooks do often me devote
> To share – alas! – a goose's fate;

*But change my head and then, instead,*
*Part of a book you'll find;*
*And if again I'm carefully read,*
*A youth who walks behind;*
*Change once again, and then you will*
*A furious passion see,*
*Which reason vainly tries to still,*
*Keep far removed from me;*
*Another change, and you will then*
*See I'm remuneration*
*Earned by all grades of working men*
*Throughout the British nation;*
*But change my head once more, and then*
*A prison I appear.*
*From which sweet sounds oft issue forth*
*That pleasant are to hear.*

The words you were after: sage, page, rage, wage and cage.

. . . . . . . . . . . . . . . . . . . . . . . . . . . . . . . . . . . . . . . . . .

## PANGRAMS

In 1818, the year before Victoria was born, Thomas Hartwell Horne published his justly noted *Introduction to the Critical Study and Knowledge of the Holy Scriptures.* For Horne, this was the culmination of a letter-by-letter analysis of the whole of the King James version of the Bible.

Dr Horne found that the Bible contains 774,476 words (593,493 in the Old Testament and 181,253 in the New Testament), with a total letter count of 3,566,480 letters (2,728,100 in the Old Testament and 838,380 in the New Testament). He highlighted the shortest verse in the good book, John 11:35, which runs to just two words: 'Jesus wept.' By contrast verse nine of the eighth chapter of the Book of Esther ranks as the longest verse with its ninety-word description of the Persian empire. (The Book of Esther is also the only book in the Bible in which God's name is not mentioned.)

Horne's real revelation, however, was his discovery that the twenty-first verse of the seventh chapter of the Book of Ezra contains every letter of the English alphabet, except one:

> And I, even I, Artaxerxes the king, do make a decree to all the treasurers, which are beyond the river, that whatsoever Ezra the priest, the scribe of the laws of the God of heaven, shall require of you, it be done speedily.

That sentence is a pangram – almost. Had it included the letter *j* it would have been one, because a pangram is a sentence that includes every letter of the alphabet.

Pangrams have long been testing the ingenuity of writers. We will never know whether Shakespeare deliberately set out to produce a pangram in these lines spoken by Coriolanus but, apart from *z*, he managed to include all twenty-six letters of the alphabet:

> *O, a kiss*
> *Long as my exile, sweet as my revenge!*
> *Now, by the jealous queen of heaven, that kiss*
> *I carried from thee, dear, and my true lip*
> *Hath virgin'd it e'er since.*

Here is a less poetic, albeit complete, pangram, consisting of just forty-eight letters:

> John P. Brady gave me a black walnut box of quite a small size.

Here is a even shorter one. It consists of only thirty-three letters and is often used by trainee typists who are trying to get to know all the letters on the keyboard:

> A quick brown fox jumps over the lazy dog.

This pangram is even more concise, consisting of thirty-two letters:

Pack my box with five dozen liquor jugs.

This one has thirty-one:

The five boxing wizards jump quickly.

And here is one with thirty:

How quickly daft jumping zebras vex.

Once you get down to twenty-nine and twenty-eight letters, you have to bring in names to help you out:

Quick, wafting zephyrs vex bold Jim.
Waltz, nymph, for quick jigs vex Bud.

The only way to create a twenty-six-letter pangram is to include names and initials:

J.Q. Schwartz flung D.V. Pike my box.

Or take the word 'vext' (an alternative spelling of vexed), bring in a 'quiz' (an archaic word for an eccentric), and some 'glyphs' (inscriptions) on the side of a 'cwm' (a Welsh valley) on the bank or side of a 'fjord' (Scandanavian or New Zealand estuary) and end up with this:

CWM FJORD-BANK GLYPHS VEXT QUIZ

. . . . . . . . . . . . . . . . . . . . . . . . . . . . . . . . . . . . . . . . . . . . . . . . .

## RIDDLES

Victorians liked riddles and the riddles they liked most are riddles like these:

Q. What grammatical term is unpopular with young lovers?
A. The third person.

Q. In what sort of syllables ought a parrot to speak?
A. In polly-syllables.

Q. When can you recognise the naked truth?
A. When you are given the bare facts.

Q. In what colour should a secret be kept?
A. Inviolate.

Q. When is longhand quicker than shorthand?
A. When it is on a clock.

Q. Why is a joke like a coconut?
A. Because it's of no use until it has been cracked.

Q. Why does a dishonest man stay indoors?
A. So that no one will find him out.

Q. When is a farmer best able to look at his pigs?
A. When he has a sty in his eye.

Q. Why are playing cards like wolves?
A. Because they come in packs.

We began this visit to the world of Victorian wordplay with Lewis Carroll. Let's end with him, too. Here is a multi-layered riddle he composed in 1866. He called it 'Enigma' and in the puzzle he invites you to find one three-letter word that contains all the other words that you will discover along the way. Do your best to unravel the enigma before you look at Carroll's 'explication'.

I have a large box, two lids, two caps, three established measures, and a great number of articles a carpenter cannot do without.

Then I have always by me a couple of good fish, and a number of a smaller tribe, besides two lofty trees, fine flowers, and the fruit of an indigenous plant; a handsome stag; two playful animals, and a number of a smaller and less tame herd.

Also two halls, or places of worship; some weapons of warfare; and many weathercocks; the steps of an hotel: the House of Commons on the eve of dissolution; two students or scholars, and some Spanish grandees, to wait upon me.

All pronounce me a wonderful piece of mechanism, but a few have numbered up the strange medley of things which compose my whole.

Did you solve the enigma?

Here is Carroll's 'explication'. Perhaps only an unmarried, insomniac clergyman and academic could find time for this.

The whole is: MAN.

The parts are as follows:

A large box – the chest
Two lids – the eyelids
Two caps – the kneecaps
Three established measures – the nails, hands and feet
A great number of articles a carpenter cannot do without – nails
A couple of good fish – the soles of the feet
A number of a smaller tribe – muscles (mussels)
Two lofty trees – the palms (of the hands)
Fine flowers – two lips (tulips), and irises
The fruit of an indigenous plant – hips
A handsome stag – the heart (hart)
Two playful animals – the calves
A number of a smaller and less tame herd – hairs (hares)
Two halls, or places of worship – the temples
Some weapons of warfare – the arms, and shoulder blades
Many weathercocks – the veins (vanes)

The steps of an hotel – the insteps (inn-steps)
The House of Commons on the eve of a Dissolution – the eyes and the
    nose (ayes and noes)
Two students or scholars – the pupils of the eye
Some Spanish grandees – the tendons (ten dons)

# U

### is for

## UPPERS AND DOWNERS AND U AND NON-U

. . . . . . . . . . . . . . . . . . . . . . . . . . . . . . . . . . . . . . . . . . . . . . . .

## THE LOOK OF THE THING

Can you judge a word by its appearance?

Apparently so. And among the people who do, this is the word that has the most to offer in the English language:

#### *overnumerousnesses*

Why? Because it is pleasing to the eye in a special way.

*Overnumerousnesses*, with eighteen letters, is the longest English word that consists only of letters that lack ascenders (or 'uppers' – parts of the letters that go upward when written, as in *b, d, f, h, k, l, t*), descenders (or 'downers' – parts of the letters that go down, as in *g, j, p, q, y*), and dots in the lower case (as in *i* and *j*). It is a word without excrescences – which 'excrescences' is, too.

*Overnervousnesses*, at seventeen letters, is similarly blessed.

Sixteen-letter words with this property include *curvaceousnesses* and *overnumerousness*, while fifteen-letter words include *erroneousnesses*, *nonconcurrences* and *overnervousness*.

Of course, some people don't mind the odd excrescence. In fact, what they really hanker after in a word are the uppers and the downers. These are the folk who get a positive kick out of *lighttight* (a kind of oil) and *lillypilly* (a type of tree), words with ten letters apiece, and the longest English words consisting *only* of letters with ascenders, descenders, or dots in lower case.

The only English words that consist entirely of letters with descenders in lower case are *gyp* and *gyppy*. These are old words, but best avoided because they originate in racial slurs. To gyp is to cheat and comes from the word 'gypsy'. A gyppy tummy is something our forebears feared they might contract when visiting Egypt.

CHECKBOOK, spelt the American way, is nine letters long, is the longest word in the English language composed entirely of letters with horizontal symmetry in upper case. Eight-letter words with this rather marvellous property include BEDECKED, BOOHOOED, CODEBOOK, COOKBOOK and EXCEEDED.

HOMOTAXIA, with nine letters, is the longest word in the English language composed entirely of letters with vertical symmetry in upper case. (No, homotaxis are not cabs for gay people. Homotaxis is a term from the world of geology.) Eight-letter words with this property include AUTOMATA, MAHIMAHI and THATAWAY – as in 'He went thataway!' You can increase the letter count if you include hyphenated terms such as HOITY-TOITY and MOUTH-TO-MOUTH.

I, OHO and IHI'IHI (a four-leaf clover lookalike from Hawaii) are the only words in the English language that, when written in upper-case letters, have horizontal and vertical symmetry and consist entirely of letters that have both horizontal and vertical symmetry.

*Zoonosis* is a disease that can be transmitted to humans from animals. ZOONOSIS, with eight letters, is also the longest word in the English language composed of letters with 180-degree rotational symmetry. (Oh, yes, I know my ONIONS.) MOW, SIS, and SWIMS, when written in upper-case letters, are complete words that have 180-degree rotational symmetry.

COUSCOUS, eight letters long, is the longest word in the English language where you cannot tell simply by looking at the letters whether it has been written in all upper-case or all lower-case letters. Four-letter words with this peculiar property include COCO, COOS, COWS, CUSS, SCOW (a type of boat), VOWS, WOOS, WUSS (a weak or ineffectual person) and ZOOS.

Some people are snobs about language. Some people are just snobs.

I was brought up in London in the 1950s, which was when I learnt about words that were considered either U or non-U. It was quite confusing for a child. It was explained to me that if you were unwell and in bed you should say you were 'ill' and not 'sick', but if you were unwell on a boat you should say you were 'sick' and not 'ill'.

The terms – 'U' for upper class and 'non-U' for non-upper class – were coined by a British professor of linguistics in a Finnish journal of linguistics. They were taken up by the English author Nancy Mitford, who produced a list of words and phrases that revealed to people where they belonged in the English social structure depending on their vocabulary:

| U | NON-U |
| --- | --- |
| *lavatory/loo* | *toilet* |
| *drawing/living room* | *lounge/front room* |
| *graveyard* | *cemetery* |
| *sofa* | *settee* |
| *spectacles* | *glasses* |
| *vegetables* | *greens* |
| *scent* | *perfume* |

| | |
|---|---|
| *die* | *pass on* |
| *ice* | *ice cream* |
| *jam* | *preserve* |
| *pudding* | *sweet, dessert* |
| *How d'you do* | *Pleased to meet you* |
| *napkin* | *serviette* |
| *lunch then dinner* | *dinner then supper* |
| *What?* | *Pardon?* |
| *a nice house* | *a lovely home* |
| *mad* | *mental* |
| *writing paper* | *notepaper* |
| *looking glass* | *mirror* |
| *riding* | *horse-riding* |
| *Your good health* | *Cheers* |

Sixty years after the arrival of U and non-U, most of the words that were then non-U still are. There are exceptions. These days, for example, Prince Harry calls the lavatory 'the toilet' and, as a consequence, his grandmother, the Queen, occasionally does, too. Of course, Harry still refers to the Queen as his granny or grandmother or grandmamma or even Her Majesty, but never as his nan. As Jilly Cooper noted in her book, *Class*: 'Nana is a big dog in *Peter Pan*, not your granny.'

# T

## is for

## TYPOS AND HOWLERS

In the world of words anyone can make a mistake, and plenty of us do. Over the years – as a child, then, briefly, as a teacher, and since then as a parent and grandparent – I have been collecting what were traditionally known as 'schoolboy howlers'. We can assume that schoolgirls never made them.

Here is the cream of my crop:

Drake circumcised the world in a small ship.
Oedipus Complex was a famous queen of Egypt.
'Marseillaise' is a French salad dressing.
A fjord is a Swedish automobile.
Robinson Crusoe was a great operatic singer.
Henry VIII found walking difficult because he had an abbess on his knee.
Telepathy is a code invented by Morse.
Livid was a famous Latin poet.
People living on the equator are called equestrians.
In the spring the lambs can be seen gambling in the fields.
Samuel Pepys worked in the Admiralty and was always going to bed.
Abstinence is a good thing if practised in moderation.

In France even the pheasants drink wine.

The inhabitants of Paris are called Parasites.

Siena is a place in Italy famous for being burnt.

The pope lives in a vacuum.

Jacob had a brother called Seesaw.

Abraham is in the Bible and is noted for his bosom.

A hostage is a nice lady on an aeroplane.

Barristers are pieces of wood, generally at the side of the stairs.

An optimist is a person who looks after your eyes and a pessimist looks after your feet.

Fidel Castro invented oil.

Waltz time is sometimes called cripple time.

Blood consists of red corkscrews and white corkscrews.

Psychology is a fairly modern disease invented by a man call Floyd.

An oxygen had eight sides.

The Gorgons had long snakes in their hair. They look like women only more horrible.

*-ster* is a female suffix. Example, *spinster, monster* and *sterile.*

There are eligible fish in the sea.

A blizzard is the inside of a chicken.

Herrings go about the sea in shawls.

The future of 'I give' is 'you take'.

The bowels are *a, e, i, o, u* and sometimes *w* and *y.*

Poetry is when every line starts with a capital letter.

Water is composed of oxygin and hydrogin. Oxygin is pure but hydrogin is gin and water.

There are four elements, mustard, salt, pepper and vinegar, although I think vinegar is really an acid.

A good cosmetic is salt and water. Cosmetics make you sick.

Homer wrote *The Oddity.*

Polonius was a sort of sausage.

The appendix is the part of the book for which nobody has found much use.

Washington was a great general who always began a battle with the fixed determination to win or lose.

Socrates died from an overdose of wedlock.

Reefs are what you put on coffins.
Austerity is an old religion but even today politicians preach it.
Income is a yearly tax.
Faith is believing what you know is untrue.
Ambiguity is telling the truth when you don't mean to.
An epitaph is a short sarcastic poem.
Pasteur found a cure for rabbits.
Pâté de foie gras is an outdoor circus held in New Orleans every year.
The crusaders were little children sent on a cruise to Jerusalem in
    Shakespeare's time.
When a man has more than one wife he is a pigamist.
Daniel Boone was born in a log cabin he built himself.
The eastern part of Asia is called Euthanasia.
Electric volts are named after Voltaire who discovered electricity.
A stowaway is the man with the biggest appetite on the ship.

Dr Alan Adell, professor of semantics at the University of Michigan
in Ann Arbor, recently completed a study of high-school vocabularies
and came to the conclusion that children are much more likely to
misunderstand a word if they hear it spoken than if they see it written.
The students were each asked to define one hundred words given to them
orally/aurally. These are some of the ones they got wrong.

| | |
|---|---|
| *agnostics* | behaviour of sound |
| *allegro* | chorus line |
| *amidst* | thick fog |
| *anthem* | quite good-looking |
| *antimony* | money inherited from an aunt |
| *asperity* | drug from which aspirins are made |
| *bibliography* | geography of the Holy Land |
| *chinchilla* | ice pack for the lower part of the face |
| *concubine* | merger of several businesses |
| *deciduous* | able to make up one's mind |
| *diatribe* | food for the whole clan |
| *effusive* | able to be merged |
| *executive* | man who puts others to death |

| | |
|---|---|
| *genealogy* | allergic to denim |
| *gullible* | to do with sea birds |
| *hackneyed* | opposite of knock-kneed |
| *hysterics* | letters in sloping type |
| *ingenious* | not very smart |
| *longevity* | being very tall |
| *nitrate* | off-peak charges |
| *semiquaver* | half afraid |
| *vicar* | masculine form of 'vixen' |

Of course, it's not only the young who get it wrong. As a writer prone to making mistakes, I am in excellent company. In Daniel Defoe's novel *Robinson Crusoe*, the shipwrecked hero decides to salvage some goods from his ship before it sinks completely. Defoe describes how Crusoe removes all of his clothes before swimming to the ship but, forgetting this fact, then has him fill his pockets with biscuits once he is on board. And, famously, Sir Arthur Conan Doyle gave Sherlock Holmes's loyal companion, Dr Watson, one war wound – but in two places. In *A Study in Scarlet* the wound is in the shoulder; in *The Sign of Four* it is in Watson's leg.

. . . . . . . . . . . . . . . . . . . . . . . . . . . . . . . . . . . . . . . . . . . . . .

## MEET THE PRESS

The world's press is rightly noted for its ability to misquote, misprint and misunderstand absolutely everything. If you've ever had anything to do with an event that's been written up in a newspaper, I guarantee there was at least one error in the report. There's no point sulking about it. After all, misprints and mistakes like these – taken from newspaper reports and magazine articles – add a certain something to any story.

The bride wore a long white lace dress which fell to the floor.
The landlord insisted that no female should be allowed in the bra
without a man.
Miss Patricia Muddleton, qualified vice instructor, sang *Christian, Dost*

*thou See Them?* on Sunday night.

In Germany a person cannot slaughter any animal unless rendered unconscious first.

The summary of information contains totals of the number of students broken down by sex, marital status and age.

Even more astonishing was our saving the lives of little babies who formerly died from sheer ignorance.

I never went through that ghastly adolescent phrase most girls experience. I went from child to woman in one go. One day I was a child. The next day, a man.

For those of you who have small children and don't know it we have a nursery downstairs.

Mrs Freda Wallace Brown of Baltimore, Md., dined this week at her home. Service and cremation will be held next Thursday at 2:00 p.m.

Never throw away old chicken bones, or those left from a roast. Put them in water and boil them for several hours with a few diced vegetables. It will make a very delicious soap.

The bride was gowned in white silk and lace. The colour scheme of the bridesmaids' gown and flowers was punk.

He spent his early life on the back of a horse with a pipe in his mouth.

A Boy Scout can cook himself.

Mr Bromsgrove suffered a stroke on 24 November, but with the loving care of his family and his kind and efficient nurse, he never fully recovered.

The ladies from the Helping Hands Society enjoyed a swap social on Friday evening. Everybody brought along something they no longer needed. Many of the ladies brought their husbands.

Over fifty children took advantage of the mobile clinic and were examined for tuberculosis and other diseases which the clinic offered free of charge.

The new bride is approximately eighteen feet wide from buttress to buttress.

We note with regret that Mr Willis Overing is recovering after a serious car crash.

Sex and violence came into Jane Morgan's life gradually, then she became a Christian and matters escalated.

Ms Turner has set up a campaign against incestuous relationships at the house where she loves with her parents.

The city which claims to have the largest outdoor mule market in the world recently held a parade of asses led by the governor.

Blend sugar, flour, and salt. Add egg and milk, cook until creamy in double boiler. Stir frequently. Add rest of ingredients. Mix well and serve chilled. Funeral service will be held Thursday afternoon at two o'clock.

Wash your face in the morning and neck at night.

A gentleman never crumbles his bread or rolls in his soup.

We apologise for the error in last week's paper in which we stated that Mr Arnold Smith was a defective in the police force. This was a typographical error. We meant of course that Mr Smith is a detective in the police farce, and are very sorry for any embarrassment caused.

. . . . . . . . . . . . . . . . . . . . . . . . . . . . . . . . . . . . . . . . . . . . . .

## HITTING THE HEADLINES

And where would we be without classic headlines like these?

MAN FOUND DEAD IN GRAVEYARD
PASSENGERS HIT BY CANCELLED TRAINS
BUFFALO SWEPT OFF FEET BY MENDELSSOHN CHOIR
MASSIVE ORGAN DRAWS THE CROWD
POLICE MOVE IN BOOK CASE
20-YEAR FRIENDSHIP ENDS AT THE ALTAR
NEWLY WEDS AGED 82 HAVE PROBLEM
LUCKY MAN SEES FRIENDS DIE
PRISONERS ESCAPE AFTER EXECUTIONS
FATHER OF TEN SHOT DEAD (MISTAKEN FOR A RABBIT)
'LENORE' ONLY OPERA BEETHOVEN WROTE ON MONDAY EVENING
PROTESTER TRIED TO SPOIL PLAY BUT THE ACTORS SUCCEEDED

. . . . . . . . . . . . . . . . . . . . . . . . . . . . . . . . . . . . . . . . . . . . . . . .

## JUST MY TYPO

And here, collected by Drummond Moir, are six gems where just one letter going awry creates a mountain of mischief:

Later that same evening after a vain search all around the village, Mary found the dog dead in the garden. She curried the body indoors.
*Life in Barnsthorpe*, Patricia Cox

From his left ear to the corner of his mouth ran a long scar, the result of a duet many years before.
*Flight from Germany*, William le Quex

He and his wife Gillian, who is a teacher, have three children, Gaven aged 13 and 11 year old twins ugh and Helen.
*Orpington New Shopper*

The speaking cock turns 75 years old on Sunday.
*The BBC news announcement of the speaking clock's birthday*, July 2011

Police yesterday called off a search for a 20 year old man who is believed to have frowned.
*Scotsman*

The bridal couple stood, facing the floral setting, and exchanged cows.
*Modesto News-Herald*, California

. . . . . . . . . . . . . . . . . . . . . . . . . . . . . . . . . . . . . . . . . . . . . . . .

## AUTOMATIC PILOT

If you are hooked on typos and howlers you are living in the right age. Thanks to the advent of automatic subtitling on television, you can turn on your TV at almost any time of day or night and catch every kind of linguistic horror. A computer 'listens' to the words being spoken, then prints them up on the screen for you. That is how...

... *Celebrity Mastermind* became *Celibacy Mastermind.*

... 'Welcome to the year of the whores' appeared on screen at the start of the Chinese year of the horse

... the news was broken that 'Andy Murray had become Midge Ure' when he was being saluted for becoming 'mature'

... 'The Arch Bitch of Canterbury' was the caption offered for the Archbishop and the nation was told 'We will now have a moment's violence at the Queen Mother's funeral'. It was silence we were after.

# S

### is for

## SAIPPUAKAUPPIAS

*Saippuakauppias* is the longest-known palindromic word. It is a fifteen-letter Finnish word meaning 'soap seller'.

A palindrome is a word like *deed* or *level* or *repaper* or *noon* or *redder* or *civic* or *tenet* or *kayak* or *nun* that reads the same backwards as forwards.

The longest palindromic word in everyday English is *redivider* with nine letters. *Rotavator* is a nine-letter registered trademark that has found its way into the dictionary, and *detartrated*, with eleven letters, is a contrived chemical term still hoping to find its way there. Dictionaries of Native American already feature the twelve-letter *kinnikkinnik*, a dried leaf and bark mixture sometimes smoked by Cree people.

*Tut-tut* is one of the oldest and most international palindromes. If they spoke English in the Garden of Eden, then 'Madam, I'm Adam,' was the first palindrome. If not, then it was probably one John Taylor who came up with the first palindromic sentence on record. At the beginning of the seventeenth century he wrote:

Lewd did I live & evil I did dwel

Spelling habits have changed; today a more acceptable version would read:

Evil I did dwell: lewd did I live

More recent palindromes involve people's names, some of them quite famous:

Was it Eliot's toilet I saw?

No mists reign at Tangier, St Simon!

Sums are not set as a test on Erasmus

Some palindromes are supposed to have been spoken by the famous. The composer Henry Purcell is said to have remarked:

Egad, a base tone denotes a bad age!

And it is well known that the Emperor Napoleon was wont to complain during his exile:

Able was I ere I saw Elba

For a modern palindrome that succinctly tells a story, it would be hard to beat this one by Leigh Mercer:

A man, a plan, a canal – Panama

And here are the runners-up on my scoresheet of top palindromic sentences. Each one makes sense – sort of.

Was it a car or a cat I saw?
Pull up if I pull up
Ten animals I slam in a net
In a regal age ran I
Yawn a more Roman way
Some men interpret nine memos

. . . . . . . . . . . . . . . . . . . . . . . . . . . . . . . . . . . . . . . . . . . . .

## TELL ME A STORY

The American humorist James Thurber enjoyed palindromes – 'He goddam mad dog, eh?' was one of his best efforts – but few other writers of note have attempted them. The problem is that once they stretch beyond a couple of dozen letters or so, they cease to make sense. This fifty-one-letter palindrome by Penelope Gilliatt is an exception:

Doc, note I dissent. A fast never prevents fatness. I diet on cod.

The poet and committed wordplayer J. A. Lindon is the author of the only known palindrome to include an eighteen-letter word. To understand it (and excuse it) you need to know that Beryl has a hippie husband who is both free-thinking and something of a sun-worshipper. Yes, he runs around the garden in the nude. His friend, Ned, asks him if he does this to annoy poor Beryl and this is his palindromic reply:

Named undenominationally rebel, I rile Beryl?
La, no! I tan. I'm, O Ned, nude man!

Apparently, two palindromic novels have been published: *Satire: Veritas* by David Stephens (1980, running to 58,795 letters), and *Dr Awkward & Olson in Oslo* by Lawrence Levine (1986, 31,954 words), but I have not read them. The longest palindromic composition I have struggled through ran to 2,769 letters, but it was mostly gobbledygook – to me, at least. The story began: 'Spot stops to hoot at a mad sung ari . . .' You can guess how it ended: 'Agnu's damn, at a too hot spot, stops.'

However, there is hope for palindromic fiction – if it is approached in the right way. The American wit and versifier Willard Espy reported an entertaining interview in the *Harvard Bulletin* between 'Professor R. Osseforp, holder of the Emor D. Nilap Chair in Palindromology at

Harvard, and Solomon W. Golomb (PhD '57)' in which the reply to every question was a neat palindrome:

'And what about your new novel, could you tell me the title?'
'*Dennis Sinned.*'
'Intriguing. What is the plot?'
'Dennis and Edna sinned.'
'I see. Is there more to it than that?'
'Dennis Krats and Edna Stark sinned.'
'Now it all becomes clear,' I agreed. 'Tell me, with all this concern about the ecology, what kind of car are you driving nowadays?'
'A Toyota.'
'Naturally, and how about your colleague, Professor Nustad?'
'Nustad? A Datsun.'

. . . . . . . . . . . . . . . . . . . . . . . . . . . . . . . . . . . . . . . . . . .

## PSEUDODROMES

As their name suggests, pseudodromes aren't the real thing, but they are linguistic curiosities all the same. And creating them is quite challenging. Pseudodromes are sentences where words, rather than individual letters, read the same backwards as forwards:

So patient a doctor to doctor a patient so!
You can cage a swallow, can't you, but you can't swallow a cage, can you?
Women understand men; few men understand women.
God knows man. What is doubtful is what man knows God.
Does milk machinery milk does?
Bores are people that say that people are bores.
Girl, bathing on Bikini, eyeing boy, finds boy eyeing bikini on bathing girl.

J. A. Lindon rose to the challenge of writing a poem where each line is a unit, so the poem can be read line by line from the top down or the bottom up:

*As I was passing near the jail*
*I met a man, but hurried by.*
*His face was ghastly, grimly pale.*
*He had a gun. I wondered why*

*He had a gun. I wondered: why?*
*His face was ghastly! Grimly pale.*
*I met a man, but hurried by,*
*As I was passing near the jail.*

## SEMORDNILAPS

Most people wouldn't know a semordnilap if they fell over one. Here are fifteen for you to fall over:

bard
deliver
desserts
devil
dog
golf
maps
mood
mail
redrawer
reknits
repaid
stop
strap
straw

If you don't yet see what these words have in common, take a closer look at *semordnilap*. Exactly. It's **palindromes** spelt backwards, and a semordnilap is a word that makes a different word when it's spelt backwards. Spell *bard* backwards and you get *drab*.

Semordnilapic sentences, making any sort of sense, composed of true semordnilapic words, are not easy to come by.

Here's one from England:

Dog a devil!

Here's one from America:

Was no diaper on Dennis?

As a cure for insomnia (or a distraction from toothache) you might try to devise a third. It could drive you mad – or knock you out. 'Kook. KO. OK?'

# R

**is for**

**RULES OF THE GAME**

A great American once observed:

> The Lord's Prayer has 56 words; at Gettysburg, Lincoln spoke only
> 268 long remembered words; and we got a whole country going on
> the 1,322 words in the Declaration of Independence. So how come it
> took the government 26,911 words to reissue a regulation on the sale
> of cabbages?

I don't know the answer to that one, but I do know we would all write
and speak better, clearer and more understandable English if only we had
learnt the rules of the game.

Which rules? you ask. These ten for a start:

> *Don't use no double negatives.*
> *Make each pronoun agree with their antecedent.*
> *Join clauses good, like a conjunction should.*
> *Verbs has to agree with their subjects.*
> *Just between you and I, case is important too.*
> *Don't use commas, which aren't necessary.*

*Try not to oversplit infinitives.*
*It is important to use your apostrophe's correctly.*
*Proofread your writing to if any words out.*
*Correct spelling is esential.*

And here are two extra rules that over the years, as a writer, I have found invaluable:

**The Oxford rule.** It's is not, it isn't ain't, and it's it's, not its, if you mean it is. If you don't, it's its. Then too it's hers. It isn't her's. It isn't our's either. It's ours, and likewise yours and theirs.

**Smith's writing rule.** In composing, as a general rule, run your pen through every word you have written; you have no idea what vigour it will give your style.

. . . . . . . . . . . . . . . . . . . . . . . . . . . . . . . . . . . . . . . . . .

## SIX BIG RULES

On more serious note, it would be hard to come across a better set of rules for writing than the six offered by George Orwell in 1946:

1. Never use a metaphor, simile, or other figure of speech which you are used to seeing in print.

2. Never use a long word where a short one will do.

3. If it is possible to cut a word out, always cut it out.

4. Never use the passive where you can use the active.

5. Never use a foreign phrase, a scientific word, or a jargon word if you can think of an everyday English equivalent.

6. Break any of these rules sooner than say anything outright barbarous.

Follow the rules and your writing may not be as good as Orwell's, but it will be clear and to the point. What's more, as Orwell noted, 'When you make a stupid remark, its stupidity will be obvious, even to yourself.'

. . . . . . . . . . . . . . . . . . . . . . . . . . . . . . . . . . . . . . . . . . . . . . . .

## SIX SMALL TIPS

*Who vs Whom.* Use 'who' when you are referring to the subject of a clause and 'whom' when you are referring to the object. A tip from *Grammar Girl's Quick and Dirty Tips for Better Writing* is to use the 'him' test. If you could answer the question with 'him', it needs to be 'whom'!

*Nor vs Or.* It's 'nor' when it's a negative and it goes with 'neither'. 'Or' with a positive and it goes with 'either'.

*Its vs It's.* The simplest way to remember this (as opposed to the *Oxford Rule* above!) is to take out the apostrophe and see if it still works. If 'it is' makes sense in the context of the sentence then it's 'it's'!

*Fewer vs Less.* 'Fewer' refers to things that can be counted, 'less' to things that cannot.

*Lie vs Lay.* 'Lie' means to recline. It does not take a direct object. 'Lay' means to place or set down. It always takes a direct object. 'I lay a plate on the table'; 'I lie down on the floor.'

*Me, myself and I.* 'I' when it's the subject of the sentence, 'me' when it's the object and 'myself' when you have used 'I' earlier in the sentence.

. . . . . . . . . . . . . . . . . . . . . . . . . . . . . . . . . . . . . . . . . . . . . . . .

## LETTER RULES

In these days of modern communication, old-fashioned letter-writing is fast becoming a lost art. However, there are still some general rules of thumb:

The sign-off depends on the salutation. If your letter begins 'Dear Mr Brandreth', it should conclude with 'Yours sincerely'. If it is 'Dear Sir/Madam', the correct sign-off is 'Yours faithfully'. For more personal correspondence, for example 'Dear Gyles', you can choose from a less formal selection such as 'Best wishes', 'With love', etc.

If you are writing a personal letter the date should be written out in full, not abbreviated, e.g. 15 August 2015, not 15/8/15.

If you aren't using letter-headed paper, you should write your own address in the top right-hand corner. The address of the person to whom you are writing should be on the left, starting below your address.

When it comes to matters of etiquette I always turn to *Debrett's* for guidance. They first published their guide to the peerage in 1769 and, in terms of social savvy, what they say goes. Here's what they have to tell us about whether a written thank-you is expected in today's world:

> *When thanking someone after an event, the form of the invitation signals the appropriate format of a thank you. Engraved invitation cards require a formal thank you letter.*

> *A verbal, telephone or email invitation needs only a telephone call of thanks after the event; telephone and email are interchangeable if all parties use both frequently.*

So now you know. But, that said, my personal rule on this is: *a handwritten note is worth a hundred texts.*

. . . . . . . . . . . . . . . . . . . . . . . . . . . . . . . . . . . . . . . . . . . . . . .

## LIFE RULES

From Staten Island, New York, a reader recently wrote to me:

*Dear Gyles, You seem to think you know a lot. Tell me, what is the meaning of life?*

Well, dear reader, I don't like admitting this – and you may find it hard to believe – but I don't know nothing about the Meaning of Life. At the same time, I hate disappointing anyone so, just for the fun of it, I have gathered together my favourite Life Lessons: the rules, observations, and maxims that may not explain all the mysteries of life, but at least make it more manageable. Here they are:

*Blick's Rule of Life.* You have two chances, slim and non-existent.

*Brenne's Laws of Life.* (1) You never get it where you want it. (2) If you think it's tough now, just wait.

*Freud's Observation.* Shunning women, drink, gambling, smoking and eating will not make one live longer; it will only seem like it.

*Gandhi's Observation.* There is more to life than increasing its speed.

*Hovanick's Wait-till-tomorrow Principle.* Today is the last day of the first part of your life.

*Howe's Verities.* (1) When you're in trouble, people who call to sympathise are really looking for the particulars. (2) When in doubt in society, shake hands. (3) Everyone hates a martyr; it's no wonder martyrs are burnt at the stake. (4) A good many of your tragedies probably look like comedies to others. (5) Put cream and sugar on a fly and it tastes very much like a black raspberry. (6) Families with babies and families without babies are sorry for each other. (7) Where the guests at a gathering are acquainted, they eat 20 per cent more than they otherwise would.

*Lee's Law.* Mother said there would be days like this, but she never said there would be so many.

*Lichtenberg's Insights.* (1) If life were 'just a bowl of cherries' . . . we would soon die of deficiency disease. (2) We can never get to the Promised Land, for if we did, it would no longer be the Promised Land. (3) We say that the plough made civilisation, but for that matter, so did manure. (4) The planning laws in most American neighbourhoods would not permit the construction of the Parthenon.

*Lucy's Law.* The alternative to getting old is depressing.

*Paige's Six Rules of Life* (guaranteed to bring anyone to a happy old age). (1) Avoid fried foods that angry up the blood. (2) If your stomach antagonises you, pacify it with cool thoughts. (3) Keep the juices flowing by jangling around gently as you move. (4) Go very lightly on the vices, such as carrying on in society, as the social ramble ain't restful. (5) Avoid running at all times. (6) Don't look back, something might be gaining on you.

*Quality of Life Constant.* Every time in your life when you think you are about to be able to make both ends meet, somebody moves the ends.

*Schwartz's Maxim.* Live every day as if it were your last . . . and some day you'll be right.

. . . . . . . . . . . . . . . . . . . . . . . . . . . . . . . . . . . . . . . . . . . . . . . . . .

## RULES OF MATURITY

Or How To Know You're Growing Older:

*Everything hurts, and what doesn't hurt doesn't work.*
*The gleam in your eye is from the sun hitting your bifocals.*
*You feel like the morning after the night before, and you haven't been anywhere.*
*Your children begin to look middle-aged. And when you look in the mirror, you see one of your own parents looking back at you.*
*A dripping tap causes an uncontrollable bladder urge.*

*You join a health club and don't go.*
*You look forward to a dull evening.*
*You turn out the lights for economic rather than romantic reasons.*
*You sit in a rocking chair and can't get it going.*
*Your knees buckle but your belt won't.*
*Your back goes out more than you do.*
*The little grey-haired lady you help across the street is your wife.*
*You have too much room in the house and not enough in the medicine cabinet.*
*You know all the answers, but nobody asks you the questions.*

# Q

**is for**

## QUEUE IN LINE

'The English have really everything in common with Americans, except of course, the language,' said Oscar Wilde, when he heard that audiences in New York weren't *queuing* to see his plays: they were *standing in line* at the box office.

There are scores of English words about which the British and Americans don't seem to agree. Here are twenty-five that cause confusion:

| | | | |
|---|---|---|---|
| *apartment* | flat | *back-up lights* | reversing lights |
| *Band-Aid* | plaster | *bathrobe* | dressing-gown |
| *bill* | banknote | *checkers* | draughts |
| *closet* | cupboard | *cream of wheat* | semolina |
| *elevator* | lift | *faucet* | tap |
| *flashlight* | torch | *hamburger meat* | mince |
| *lima bean* | broad bean | *molasses* | black treacle |
| *nightstick* | truncheon | *odometer* | mileometer |
| *pantyhose* | tights | *private school* | public school |

| | | | |
|---|---|---|---|
| *raisin* | sultana | *sidewalk* | pavement |
| *spool* | cotton reel | *thumbtack* | drawing pin |
| *tic-tac-toe* | noughts and crosses | *vest* | waistcoat |
| *zucchini* | courgette | | |

Is your English British or American?

Do you think a trainer is a running shoe, or the man who helps you work out at the gym?

If something was described as *à la mode*, would you think it was fashionable or about to be served with ice cream?

Confused? Don't worry. I'm here to help. Here is my concise Anglo-American dictionary. With the twenty-five pairs above, it includes all the everyday British words an American might misunderstand.

| BRITISH ENGLISH | AMERICAN ENGLISH | BRITISH ENGLISH | AMERICAN ENGLISH |
|---|---|---|---|
| *articulated lorry* | trailer truck | *bank holiday* | legal holiday |
| *bap* | hamburger bun | *bat (ping-pong)* | paddle |
| *bespoke (made to measure)* | custom-made | *big dipper* | roller-coaster |
| *bill (restaurant)* | check | *billion = million million* | billion = thousand million |
| *biscuit (sweet)* | cookie | *biscuit (unsweetened)* | cracker |
| *black or white? (milk/cream in coffee)* | with or without? | *block of flats* | apartment building |
| *bomb (success)* | bomb (disaster) | *bonnet (car)* | hood |
| *boot (car)* | trunk | *bowler hat* | derby |
| *box room* | lumber room | *braces* | suspenders |
| *candy floss* | cotton candy | *caravan* | trailer |
| *caretaker/porter* | janitor | *catapult* | slingshot |
| *chemist's* | drugstore | *chicory* | endive |

| BRITISH ENGLISH | AMERICAN ENGLISH | BRITISH ENGLISH | AMERICAN ENGLISH |
|---|---|---|---|
| *chips* | french fries | *cinema* | movie house/ theater |
| *cloakroom* | checkroom | *clothes peg* | clothespin |
| *conscription* | draft | *convoy* | caravan |
| *cooker* | stove | *cot* | crib |
| *cotton* | thread | *cotton wool* | absorbent cotton |
| *crisps* | potato chips | *cul-de-sac* | dead end |
| *diamanté* | rhinestone | *diversion* | detour |
| *dual carriageway* | divided highway | *dummy* | pacifier |
| *dungarees* | overalls | *dynamo* | generator |
| *eiderdown* | comforter | *estate car* | station wagon |
| *flannel* | washcloth | *funfair* | carnival |
| *first floor* | second floor | *fish slice* | spatula |
| *fitted carpet* | wall-to-wall | *flex* | electric cord |
| *flyover* | overpass | *football* | soccer |
| *fortnight* | two weeks | *foyer* | lobby |
| *full stop* | period | *gangway* | aisle |
| *gaol* | jail | *garden* | yard |
| *gear lever* | gearshift | *green fingers* | green thumb |
| *haberdashery* | notions | *hair grip* | bobby pin |
| *hair slide* | barrette | *hardware* | housewares |
| *hire purchase* | instalment plan | *holiday* | vacation |
| *homely = pleasant* | homely = ugly | *ice lolly* | popsicle |
| *icing sugar* | confectioner's sugar | *identification parade* | line-up |
| *immersion heater* | water heater | *interval* | intermission |
| *ironmonger* | hardware store | *jab (injection)* | shot |
| *joint (meat)* | roast | *jug* | pitcher |
| *jumper* | sweater | *label* | tag |
| *larder* | pantry | *lay-by* | pull-off |
| *leader (in a newspaper)* | editorial | *leader (first violin in orchestra)* | concertmaster |

| BRITISH ENGLISH | AMERICAN ENGLISH | BRITISH ENGLISH | AMERICAN ENGLISH |
|---|---|---|---|
| left luggage office | baggage room | level crossing (railway) | grade crossing |
| lorry | truck | lounge suit | business suit |
| mackintosh | raincoat | marrow | squash |
| methylated spirits | denatured alcohol | mincer | meat grinder |
| motorway | freeway | nappy | diaper |
| neat (drink) | straight | net curtains | sheers/ underdrapes |
| newsagent | news dealer | nought | zero |
| number-plate | license plate | off-licence | liquor store |
| oven gloves | pot holder | overtake (vehicle) | pass |
| packed lunch | sack lunch | paraffin | kerosene |
| pelmet | valance | petrol | gas |
| pillarbox | mailbox | predictive text | autocorrect |
| power point | outlet/socket | post | mail |
| postal code | zip code | postponement | rain check |
| public convenience | restroom | pudding | dessert |
| pushchair | stroller | put through (telephone) | connect |
| quay | wharf | rasher (bacon) | slice |
| reception (hotel) | front desk | receptionist | desk clerk |
| return ticket | round-trip ticket | robin (small red-breasted bird, symbol of Christmas) | robin (large red-breasted bird, first sign of spring) |
| roundabout | traffic circle | saloon (car) | sedan |
| scribbling pad | scratch pad | shop assistant | salesclerk |
| skipping rope | jump rope | sofa | love seat |
| skirting board | baseboard | solicitor | lawyer/attorney |
| sorbet | sherbet | spanner | monkey wrench |
| spirits | liquor | staff (academic) | faculty |
| stalls (theatre) | orchestra seat | state school | public school |
| stone (fruit) | pit | surgical spirit | rubbing alcohol |
| suspender belt | garter belt | suspenders | garters |

| BRITISH ENGLISH | AMERICAN ENGLISH | BRITISH ENGLISH | AMERICAN ENGLISH |
|---|---|---|---|
| *swede* | turnip/rutabaga | *sweets* | candy |
| *swiss roll* | jelly roll | *teat (baby's bottle)* | nipple |
| *tin* | can | *trousers* | pants |
| *turn-ups (trousers)* | cuffs | *undergraduate* | first year freshman |
| *undergraduate* | second year sophomore | *undergraduate* | third year junior |
| *undergraduate* | fourth year senior | *wardrobe* | closet |
| *wash up* | do the dishes | *wash your hands* | wash up |
| *Welsh dresser* | hutch | *windcheater* | windbreaker |
| *wing/mudguard* | fender | *zed (Z)* | zee |

They say that 'To understand America, you must first understand baseball.'

Except for the horse (*you can lead a horse to water...*, *horse of a different colour, cart before the horse*, etc.), no other subject has contributed as many terms to the English language in America as baseball: the 'horsehide' sport.

And in the United Kingdom, even those of us who have no idea about the rules of baseball, find that our language is infected with baseballese:

*He was born with two strikes against him.*
*He couldn't get to first base with that girl.*
*He threw me a curve that time.*
*I'll take a rain check on it.*
*He went to bat for me.*
*I liked him right off the bat.*
*He was way out in left field on that one.*
*I think you're way off base on that.*
*It was a smash hit.*
*I hope to touch all the bases on this report.*
*Major league all the way.*
*He was safe by a mile.*
*He really dropped the ball that time.*

# P

## is for

## POTTED POETRY

. . . . . . . . . . . . . . . . . . . . . . . . . . . . . . . . . . . . . . . . . . .

### RUTHLESS RHYMES

I like my verse terse. And to the point:

> *I had written to Aunt Maud*
> *Who was on a trip abroad*
> *When I heard she'd died of cramp –*
> *Just too late to save the stamp.*

Actually, I like my verse terse. And ruthless:

> *O'er the rugged mountain's brow*
> *Clara threw the twins she nursed*
> *And remarked, 'I wonder now*
> *Which will reach the bottom first?'*

What I love about these terse verses is the way they manage to be both
heartless and heart-warming at the same time:

> *Making toast at the fireside*
> *Nurse fell in the fire and died*
> *And, what makes it ten times worse,*
> *All the toast was burned with Nurse.*

It's the casual cruelty that appeals to me:

> *During dinner at the Ritz*
> *Father kept on having fits*
> *And, which made my sorrow greater,*
> *I was left to tip the waiter.*

And the sense of understanding exactly where the poet is coming from:

> *Late last night I slew my wife,*
> *Stretched her on the parquet flooring;*
> *I was loath to take her life,*
> *But I had to stop her snoring.*

Four lines, two rhymes and so much drama:

> *'There's been an accident!' they said,*
> *'Your husband's cut in half: he's dead!'*
> *'Indeed,' said Mrs Brown. 'Well, if you please*
> *Send me the half that's got my keys.'*

For challenging wordplay, in bed, in your head, compose your own ruthless rhyme – and be as ruthless as you dare:

> *Llewellyn Peter James Maguire*
> *Touched a live electric wire;*
> *Back on his heels it sent him rocking:*
> *His language (like the wire) was shocking.*

. . . . . . . . . . . . . . . . . . . . . . . . . . . . . . . . . . . . .

## POETIC INJUSTICE

*'Oh, Daddy dear, what is a basket?'*
*Asked a youthful, mischievous elf;*
*'All baskets, my boy, are children of joy,*
*In fact you're a basket yourself.'*

I enjoy short poems that not only pack a punch, but also involve linguistic ingenuity. Famously, some words are 'impossible' to rhyme. 'Month' is supposed to be one of them.

*'You can't,' said Jack to lisping Jill,*
*'Find any rhyme for month.'*
*'That'th what you think,' was Jill's reply,*
*'I'll find a rhyme at onth.'*

The lyricist and composer Stephen Sondheim rose to the challenge of finding a rhyme to go with another apparently unrhymable word: silver.

*To find a rhyme for silver*
*Or any rhymeless rhyme*
*Requires only will, ver-*
*Bosity and time.*

Tonight, as you make your way to the Land of Nod, have a go at finding rhymes for one of these three places:

Niagara
Massachusetts
Timbuktu

. . . . . . . . . . . . . . . . . . . . . . . . . . . . . . . . . . . . . . . . . . . .

## THE LIMERICK

*The limerick is furtive and mean*
*You must keep her in close quarantine*
*Or she sneaks to the slums*
*And promptly becomes*
*Disorderly, drunk and obscene.*

That's the trouble with the limerick. I'm not sure I know any that I can publish in a politically correct family-minded volume like this.

*There was a young farmer named Gorse*
*Who fell madly in love with his horse.*
*Said his wife, 'You rapscallion,*
*That horse is a stallion:*
*This constitutes grounds for divorce.'*

I like this one because it is both respectable and thought-provoking:

*There was a faith healer of Deal*
*Who said, 'Although pain isn't real,*
*If I sit on a pin,*
*And it punctures my skin,*
*I dislike what I fancy I feel.'*

And I love this one because it's so clever. It is the work of Monsignor Ronald Knox, who is supposed to have inserted it as an advertisement in the *Church Times*:

*Evangelical vicar in want*
*Of a portable second-hand font*
*Would dispose of the same*
*For a portrait (in frame)*
*Of the bishop-elect of Vermont.*

This limerick is the work of Clifford Witting. We know that **Slough** rhymes with **cow**, but **Slough** is spelt like **dough**, which rhymes with **know**. The poetic life is not a doddle:

> *A certified poet from Slough*
> *Whose methods of rhyming were rough*
> *Retorted, 'I see*
> *That the letters agree*
> *And if that's not sufficient I'm through.'*

. . . . . . . . . . . . . . . . . . . . . . . . . . . . . . . . . . . . . . . . . . . . . . . . . .

## WHAT'S IN A NAME?

My favourite poem about a person is this one by Joe Ecclesine, entitled 'Van Gogh, Van Gogh, Van Gogh':

> *It seems rather rough*
> *On Vincent Van Guff*
> *When those in the know*
> *Call him Vincent Van Go*
> *For unless I'm way off*
> *He was Vincent Van Gogh.*

I do like a potted poem that's a potted biography, too:

> *The Art of Biography*
> *Is different from Geography.*
> *Geography is about Maps,*
> *But Biography is about Chaps.*

The master of the genre was Edmund Clerihew Bentley (1875–1956) who gave his middle name to the form. Of his gems my favourite is this tribute to one of England's greatest architects:

> *Sir Christopher Wren*
> *Said, 'I am going to dine with some men.*
> *If anyone calls*
> *Say I am designing St Paul's.'*

What's brilliant about Bentley is that he gets beneath the skin of the folk he writes about:

> *'I quite realised,' said Columbus,*
> *'That the earth was not a rhombus,*
> *But I am a little annoyed*
> *To find it an oblated spheroid.'*

Here he is on another of England's greatest poets, John Milton. In four short lines, Bentley gets to the heart of the matter:

> *The digestion of Milton*
> *Was unequal to Stilton.*
> *He was only feeling so-so*
> *When he wrote* Il Pensoroso.

This clerihew is by Robert Longden:

> *The Emperor Caligula's*
> *habits were some irrigula.*
> *When he sat down to lunch*
> *He got drunk at onch.*

And this is the work of Louis Phillips:

> *Robert De Niro*
> *Is a screen hero*
> *Only a slob*
> *Would call him Bob.*

. . . . . . . . . . . . . . . . . . . . . . . . . . . . . . . . . . . . . . . . . . . . . . . . . . . .

## THE POETRY OF SCIENCE

Albert Einstein was born on 14 March 1879 in Ulm, Germany. In his honour, Tom Stoppard wrote one of my favourite poems. It is simply called '14 March':

> *Einstein born*
> *Quite unprepared*
> *For E to equal MC squared.*

Albert Einstein died on 18 April 1955 at Princeton, New Jersey:

> *Here Einstein lies.*
> *At least, they laid his bier*
> *Just hereabouts –*
> *Or relatively near.*

For a perfect poetic formula Einstein himself would be hard put to beat this:

$$\frac{12 + 144 + 20 + 3\sqrt{4}}{7} + (5 \times 11) = 9^2 + 0$$

Or:

> *A dozen, a gross and a score*
> *+ 3 times the square root of 4*
> *Divided by 7*
> *+ 5 times 11*
> *Is 9 squared*
> *And not a bit more.*

## HAIKUS

If you want to raise your game in the terse verse stakes, hitch your
intellectual wagon to a haiku. As Willard Espy put it in a perfect haiku:

> *Haikus show IQs.*
> *High IQs like haikus. Low*
> *IQs – no haikus.*

The haiku is a form of Japanese poetry, expressing a single feeling or
impression, and comprising just three lines and seventeen syllables, with
five syllables in the first and third lines and seven in the second. Here is
one translated from the Japanese:

> *Utter stillness! Through*
> *The rainy dark of midnight*
> *The sound of a bell.*

Nature is often at the heart of a haiku. Love often gets a look-in, too:

> *Refreshing and cool*
> *Love is a sweet summer rain*
> *That washes the world.*

I confess that there is no wordplay I enjoy more than the haiku. I am
addicted to their deceptive simplicity.

> *Haikus are easy,*
> *But sometimes they don't make sense.*
> *Refrigerator.*

. . . . . . . . . . . . . . . . . . . . . . . . . . . . . . . . . . . . . . . . . . .

## CAUSTIC COUPLETS

*Hatred is by far the longest pleasure:*
*Men love in haste – but they repent at leisure.*

That's the great Lord Byron (1788–1824). And here he is again:

*Society is now one polished horde,*
*Formed by two mighty tribes: the bores and the bored.*

Here is another proper poet, Matthew Prior (1664–1721):

*It is remarkable that they*
*Talk most who have the least to say.*

You will be familiar with this couplet from the mighty pen of Sir Walter
Scott (1771–1832):

*O what a tangled web we weave*
*When first we practise to deceive!*

To which Phyllis McGinley replied:

*Which leads me to suppose the fact is*
*We really ought to get more practice.*

J. R. Pope then added:

*But when we've practised for a while*
*How vastly we improve our style!*

Willard Espy rightly brought it all to a wise conclusion:

*Forget, dear friends, that practice angle!*

*You'll only tangle up the tangle.*

Through the Queen's English Society, I have come across the work of Roy Dean, a literary enthusiast with a fondness for the telling couplet. His problem is that he can usually·remember the first line, but sometimes the second escapes him and he has to improvise ... Here he is with Shakespeare:

*'Fear no more the heat o' the sun'*
*The English summer has begun.*
*'There is a bank whereon the wild thyme grows'*
*You can't get money there, it's had to close.*

And here he's adding a certain something to John Donne:

*'Go and catch a falling star'*
*Who's had too many at the bar?*

Here he is helping out Robert Herrick:

*'A sweet disorder in the dress'*
*Can soon become an awful mess.*

Lord Byron's next:

*'She walks in beauty, like the night'*
*But in the daylight, what a fright!*

And gives the last word to John Keats:

*'When I have fears that I may cease to be'*
*There's nothing nicer than a cup of tea.*

. . . . . . . . . . . . . . . . . . . . . . . . . . . . . . . . . . . . . . . . . . . .

## A RHYME IN TIME

And how did you get on finding a rhyme for Niagara? Did it drive you to suicide – almost?

> *Take instead of rope, pistol or dagger, a*
> *Desperate dash down the falls of Niagara.*

With Massachusetts you get a sporting chance:

> *Of tennis I played one or two sets*
> *On a court at Richmond, Massachusetts.*

And finally, a little rhyming masterpiece: the poem that manages to find a rhyme for the unrhymable:

> *If I were a cassowary*
> *On the plains of Timbuktu*
> *I would eat a missionary,*
> *Cassocks, bands and hymnbook too*

# O

**is for**

## OSCAR HOCKS AND PORRIDGE

. . . . . . . . . . . . . . . . . . . . . . . . . . . . . . . . . . . . . . . . . . . . . .

### HIP TALK

Man, it's cool –

| | |
|---|---|
| *electric* | *outasight* |
| *far out* | *together* |
| *freaky* | *too much* |
| *groovy* | *totally* |
| *heavy* | *way out* |

In my day, this was known as hip talk. We dug it.

Most of those expressions sound dated now, but a surprising number of phrases from the American urban slang of fifty years ago has managed to stand the test of time. Here are some of them – with translations that, almost certainly, you won't need:

| | |
|---|---|
| *blow your cool* | lose control |
| *bread* | money |
| *bum, v.* | cadge |
| *burn, v.* | swindle or cheat |
| *buzz, n.* | mild intoxicating effect from doing something ordinary |
| *cage, n.* | school |
| *crash, v.* | obtain a bed/floor in someone else's home |
| *dig* | understand |
| *flip* | lose control, break down |
| *freak out* | lose control, lose inhibitions |
| *hacked off* | angry, very annoyed |
| *laid back* | apathetic, uninvolved, relaxed |
| *out front* | honest, candid |
| *psyched out* | incapable of rational thought |
| *rap* | talk |
| *scene* | place of action, where it all happens |
| *score* | buy (anything) |
| *slide* | leave for a specific place |
| *split* | leave |
| *suss out* | find out about |
| *turn off* | lose interest in |
| *turn on* | sexual or pharmaceutical arousal |
| *walking soft* | humble, full of humility |
| *wheels* | transportation, usually a car |
| *where is it with you?* | how are you? |
| *wired* | nervous, tense |

If you are looking to add edge to your urban vernacular small-talk, here are some marginally more current words and phrases with which to pepper your conversation:

| | |
|---|---|
| *krunk* | to have a good time, typically on a night out – e.g. 'Let's get krunk' |
| *down low/DL* | to keep something quiet, to protect a secret – e.g. 'If I tell you something can you keep it on the DL?' |
| *crib* | a person's home |
| *stacked* | lots of muscles – e.g. 'Gyles is well stacked' |

| | |
|---|---|
| *bail* | to cancel a plan or arrangement |
| *cray* | crazy, also 'cray, cray' |
| *throw shade* | to criticise or express contempt for someone – e.g. 'I'm going to throw her some shade' |
| *diss* | to speak disrespectfully, to insult someone |
| *hood* | neighbourhood – e.g. 'He's not from my hood' |
| *grill* | face or personal space – e.g. 'He got all up in my grill' |

. . . . . . . . . . . . . . . . . . . . . . . . . . . . . . . . . . . . . . . . . . . . . . . . . .

## JAIL TALK

When I was a boy, I read stories about two American brothers called the Hardy Boys. They were amateur sleuths, hugely popular, hugely successful. In the early 1960s, as a young word enthusiast, I was particularly excited when I reached volume forty-five in the series, *The Mystery of the Spiral Bridge*. In the book, the Hardy Boys learnt some jailhouse language from the convicts they encountered. I can remember it still:

| | |
|---|---|
| *pair of bins* | binoculars |
| *clobby joint* | gambling house |
| *long nit* | look out |
| *bathe in the canal* | drown |
| *torch man* | safe-cracker |
| *cheeser* | safe that is easy to open |
| *finger man* | informer |
| *equaliser* | gun |

When I started writing books myself, my first, curiously, was a book about people in prison. As part of the research, I visited prisons throughout the UK and in countries as far apart as the United States and Russia. People in prisons around the world have their own vocabulary. Here are some words and phrases that you would come across in any prison in Britain today. I keep the list handy. After all, I used to be a Member of Parliament and now I work for the BBC, so most of my friends have been arrested.

| | |
|---|---|
| *bacon, bacon head* | a paedophile (rhyming slang: bonce (head) > nonce) |
| *bang-out* | to beat up |
| *bang-up* | to lock in a cell |
| *bare* | plenty, lots of, as in 'I have bare cigarettes' |
| *bird* | time in prison (rhyming slang: bird-lime) |
| *blag* | to rob |
| *carpet* | a sentence of three years |
| *cat* | a convict |
| *drum* | a house |
| *drum* | to burgle |
| *hench* | big, well-built |
| *jammer* | knife, usually a homemade one |
| *kanga* | prison officer (rhyming slang: 'kanga(roo)' to 'screw') |
| *nicker* | chaplain (rhyming slang: vicar) |
| *nonce* | paedophile |
| *raze-up* | cut with a razor, as in 'I'll raze you up' |
| *roasting* | hanging about, expecting something to happen |
| *salmon* | tobacco |
| *skins* | cigarette papers |
| *sweeper* | someone who collects cigarette butts |
| *vanilla* | a judge (rhyming slang: vanilla fudge) |
| *vera* | cigarette paper (rhyming slang: Vera Lynn = skin) |
| *winda warrior* | someone who shouts out of windows |

In 2014, the British prison drama *Starred Up* borrowed its title from an institutional term referring to a juvenile offender who is prematurely transferred to an adult jail. But that wasn't the only bit of jailhouse jargon used in the film, which premièred in New Orleans at the Zeitgeist Multi-Disciplinary Arts Center. The producers felt obliged to send out a glossary of jailhouse jargon to critics to help them understand what was going on. How would you have fared?

In prison:

1. What is a 'fraggle'?
   *A prisoner with a bad haircut*

*A vulnerable prisoner*
*A very far prisoner*

2. What does 'gwap' mean?
   *Drugs*
   *Sweets*
   *Money*

3. What is the slang word for a mobile phone in British prisons?
   *Tech*
   *Jelly-bone*
   *Dingle-dangle*

4. Which of the following does NOT mean 'kill'?
   *Off*
   *Top*
   *Semolina*

Answers: 1. A vulnerable prisoner. 2. Money. 3. Tech. 4. Semolina.

'Doing porridge' is slang for serving a prison sentence. Why? Because, once upon a time, a very thin porridge or gruel was the staple diet in British prisons.

. . . . . . . . . . . . . . . . . . . . . . . . . . . . . . . . . . . . . . . . . . . . .

## UNCLES AND AUNTS

It's a mistake to try to put on your uncles and aunts when you are already wearing your Oscar Hocks and your bottles of booze. Your trouble and strife will think you're elephant trunk again.

Rhyming slang, a jargon with an exhilarating, if limited, vocabulary, has been used in the English-speaking world for more than a hundred years – and not just in prisons. If you fancy adding some colour to your everyday language, you could try adopting a few of these memorable words and phrases.

| | | | |
|---|---|---|---|
| *apple pies* | eyes | *bacon and eggs* | legs |
| *big bloke* | coke (as in cocaine) | *bonny fair* | hair |
| *bottles of booze* | shoes | *bowl of chalk* | talk |
| *brothers and sisters* | whiskers | *by the peck* | neck |
| *Charlie Beck* | cheque | *Charlie Chalk* | talk |
| *Charlie Horner* | corner | *Charlie Rocks* | socks |
| *cocked hat* | rat (an informer) | *cracks-a-cry* | die |
| *daisy roots* | boots | *dig and dirt* | shirt |
| *elephant trunk* | drunk | *fiddle and flute* | suit |
| *fifteen and seven* | heaven (enjoyable) | *fine and dandy* | brandy |
| *fleas and ants* | pants | *frog a log* | dog |
| *garlic and glue* | stew | *ginger ale* | jail |
| *grocery store* | door | *hair and brain* | chain |
| *hairy float* | coat | *hard and flat* | hat |
| *heart and lung* | tongue | *heavenly bliss* | kiss |
| *here and there* | chair | *hook of mutton* | button |
| *I declare* | chair | *ivory float* | coat |
| *Jerry McGinn* | chin | *Jimmy Hope* | soap |
| *leg-rope* | hope | *mother and daughter* | water |
| *mumbly pegs* | legs | *ones and twos* | shoes |
| *Oscar Hocks* | socks | *Oscar toes* | joes |
| *pair of braces* | races | *peaches and pears* | stairs |
| *pot of jelly* | belly | *rattle and jar* | car |
| *raw and ripe* | pipe | *red steer* | beer |
| *rise and shine* | wine | *rocks and boulders* | shoulders |
| *roots* | boots | *roses red* | bed |
| *ruby rose* | nose | *rumble and shock* | knock (on the door) |
| *satin and silk* | milk | *scarlet pips* | lips |
| *sighs and tears* | ears | *slick and sleeth* | teeth |
| *smack in the eye* | pie | *smear and smudge* | judge |
| *strong and thin* | gin | *stump the chalk* | walk |
| *tar and feather* | weather | *tears and cheers* | ears |
| *thick and dense* | expense | *three or four* | door |
| *ting-a-ling* | ring | *tip and tap* | cap |

| | | | |
|---|---|---|---|
| *train wreck* | neck | *trouble and strife* | wife |
| *unders and beneath* | teeth | *very best* | chest |
| *wish me luck* | duck (dodge or escape) | *you know* | snow (cocaine) |

. . . . . . . . . . . . . . . . . . . . . . . . . . . . . . . . . . . . . . . . . . . . . . . . . .

## COCKNEY ALPHABET

In Britain, Cockney is the best-known form of rhyming slang and it comes with its own curious alphabet:

| *The alphabet* | *The derivation* |
|---|---|
| A for 'orses | 'ay for 'orses |
| B for mutton | beef or mutton |
| C for miles | see for miles |
| D for ential | differential |
| E for brick | 'eave a brick |
| F for vescence | effervescence |
| G for get it | gee! forget it! |
| H for bless you | aishfa (a sneeze) |
| I for the engine | Ivor the engine |
| J for oranges | Jaffa oranges |
| K for restaurant | café or restaurant |
| L for leather | 'ell for leather |
| M for sis | emphasis |
| N for lope | envelope |
| O for the wings of a dove | O, for the wings of a dove (song) |
| P for relief | self-explanatory |
| Q for the bus | queue for the bus |
| R for mo | 'alf a mo |
| S for you | [it']s for you |
| T for two | tea for two |
| U for me | you for me |
| V for la France | vive la France! |
| W for a bet | double you for a bet |
| X for breakfast | eggs for breakfast |

| Y for husband | wife or husband |
| Z for wind | zephyr wind |

# N

## is for

## NEVER SAY DIE

Never say *die* if you've got more than one of them. *Dice* is the plural of *die*.

The English language is rich in curious words that have even curiouser plurals. Here's an A to Z of a few. You will need a big dictionary to discover the meaning of some. I found them all in *Webster's Third New International Dictionary*:

| SINGULAR | PLURAL | SINGULAR | PLURAL |
|---|---|---|---|
| Adai | Adaize | brother | brethren |
| Chetty | Chettyars | Dukhobor | Dukhobortsky |
| englyn | englynion | Feis | Feiseanna |
| goosefoot | goosefoots | holluschick | holluschickie |
| iter | intinera | juger | jugera |
| Kuvasz | Kuvaszok | landsman | landsleit |
| mongoose | mongooses | never-was | never-weres |
| ornis | ornithes | paries | parietes |
| quadrans | quadrantes | rubai | rubaiyat |
| shtetl | shtetlach | tenderfoot | tenderfoots |
| ulcus | ulcera | vila | vily |
| wunderkind | wunderkinder | Xhosa | Amaxhosa |
| yad | yadayim | zecchino | zecchini |

Having given you twenty-six curious plurals each beginning with a different letter of the alphabet, let me give you another twenty-six, each *ending* with a different letter of the alphabet.

| SINGULAR | PLURAL | SINGULAR | PLURAL |
|---|---|---|---|
| vas | vasa | chub | chub |
| calpul | calpullec | squid | squid |
| bildungsroman | bildunsgromane | riff | riff |
| hog | hog | matzo | matzoth |
| jajman | jajmani | Bhumij | Bhumij |
| puli | pulik | court-martial | courts-martial |
| seraph | seraphim | torte | torten |
| buffalo | buffalo | sheep | sheep |
| Qaraqalpaq | Qaraqalpaq | krone | kroner |
| plural | plurals | matzo | matzot |
| ushabti | ushabtiu | Pshav | Pshav |
| mother-in-law | mothers-in-law | plateau | plateaux |
| pince-nez | pince-nez | | |

. . . . . . . . . . . . . . . . . . . . . . . . . . . . . . . . . . . . . . . . . . .

## SINGULAR PLURALS

Here are twenty-five everyday words with perplexing plurals.

| SINGULAR | PLURAL | SINGULAR | PLURAL |
|---|---|---|---|
| ox | oxen | son-in-law | sons-in-law |
| potato | potatoes | piccolo | piccolos |
| attorney general | attorneys general | lieutenant colonel | lieutenant colonels |
| opus | opera | index | indices |
| teaspoonful | teaspoonfuls | mister | messrs |
| man-of-war | men-of-war | manservant | menservants |
| oboe | oboes | cherub | cherubim or cherubin |
| crisis | crises | datum | data |
| cannon | cannon | addendum | addenda |

| SINGULAR | PLURAL | SINGULAR | PLURAL |
|---|---|---|---|
| agenda | agenda* | phenomenon | phenomena |
| madam | mesdames | pelvis | pelves |
| paymaster general | paymasters general | brigadier general | brigadier generals |

*Strictly speaking *agend* is the singular of *agenda* but nowadays *agenda* is often used as the singular, and *agenda* or *agendas* are both considered acceptable as plurals.

## is for

## MNEMONICS, DON'T FORGET

The mnemonic, named after Mnemosyne, the goddess of memory, is a system designed to help you remember things.

The first one that came into my life was SKILL. Designed to remind me of the excretory organs of the body (Skin, Kidneys, Intestines, Liver, Lungs), it is the only thing my biology teacher taught me that I haven't forgotten.

To bring the vertebral bones of the spinal column to mind (the cervical, dorsal, lumbar, sacrum and coccyx), this is your mnemonic:

*Cl*ever *D*ick *l*ooks *s*illy *c*lot.

The world of medicine offers us a plethora of mnemonics, many of which are acronyms:

| | |
|------|------------------------------------------|
| HOG  | Hepatic Output of Glucose |
| SCUM | Secondary Carcinoma of the Upper Mediastinum |
| IMP  | Idiopathic Myeloid Proliferation |
| DUMP | Diffuse Uncontrolled Monotal Peristalsis |

| PAL | Pyogenic Abscess of the Liver |
| CAD | Coronary Artery Disease |
| ALAS | Amino Levulose Acid Synthestase |

Don't worry. I am none the wiser, either. But this next one proved useful when I wanted to impress my son-in-law, who happens to be a vet. It will help you remember the names of a frog's arteries, in the order in which they branch off the main aorta:

*L*ittle *m*en *i*n *s*hort *b*lack *m*ackintoshes.

Lingula, mandibular, innominate, subclavian, brachial and musculocutaneous are the arteries you need to remember.

For the geological periods in descending order of age (Cambrian, Ordovician, Silurian, Devonian, Carboniferous, Permian, Triassic, Jurassic, Cretaceous, Eocene, Oligocene, Miocene, Pliocene, Pleistocene, Recent), try remembering this:

*C*amels *o*ften *s*it down *c*arefully. *P*erhaps *t*heir *j*oints *c*reak? *E*arly *o*iling *m*ight *p*revent *p*ermanent *r*heumatism.

Here is one that will help you get the order of battles of the Wars of the Roses:

*A* *b*oy *n*ow *w*ill *m*ention *a*ll *t*he *h*ot, *h*orrid *b*attles *t*ill *B*osworth.

And this is the order of the battles in longhand: St Albans, Blore Heath, Northampton, Wakefield, Mortimer's Cross, the Second Battle of St Albans, Towton, Hedgy Moor, Hexham, Barnet, Tewkesbury, Bosworth.

Here is one from all our childhoods that ought to be about history, but isn't:

*R*ichard *o*f *Y*ork *g*ave *b*attle *i*n *v*ain

That gives us the colours of the rainbow, of course: red, orange, yellow, green, blue, indigo and violet.

This one used to remind us of the order of the planets, until some wiseacre decided that Pluto is no longer officially a planet. (He has always been one of my favourite dogs.):

*My Very Easy Method: Just Set Up Nine Planets*

Mercury, Venus, Earth, Mars, Jupiter, Saturn, Uranus, Neptune, Pluto.

Most mnemonics are used as aids for students. This one is very different. It comes from another age and was known to our great-grandparents as Nanny's mnemonic:

*Hideous fools, morons, keep silent!*

Far from the phrase representing Nanny's attitude towards her employers, it reminds her of the items she should check when making sure her charges are presentable. Hair brushed? Face washed? Middle neat? Knees clean? Shoes brushed and tied?

Some mnemonics come in the form of rhymes. This is known as the drinking man's mnemonic:

*Beer on whisky very risky.*
*Whisky on beer never fear.*

As poetry it may not amount to much, but it should help you avoid a hangover.

And while we have our glasses at the ready, Judy Parkinson introduced me to this one, designed to jog the memory when it comes to the size and order of champagne bottles. Here they are in order:

12

| *Magnum* | equivalent of | 2 bottles |
| *Jeroboam* | equivalent of | 4 bottles |
| *Rehoboam* | equivalent of | 6 bottles |
| *Methuselah* | equivalent of | 8 bottles |
| *Salamanazar* | equivalent of | 12 bottles |
| *Balthazar* | equivalent of | 16 bottles |
| *Nebuchadnezzar* | equivalent of | 20 bottles |

And here is the mnemonic:

*M*y *J*oanna *R*eally *M*akes *S*plendid *B*urping *N*oises.

Another from Judy's collection is the one that helps you remember the order of precedence within the British peerage. In descending order it goes: duke, marquess, earl, viscount, baron – easily remembered with:

*D*id *M*ary *E*ver *V*isit *B*ognor?

I have kept the best to last. This mnemonic helps us remember the mathematical quantity *pi* and does so in a mathematical way. Learn the phrase:

How I wish I could calculate *pi*

The number of letters in each word gives you *pi* up to six places:

3.141592

Easy as *pi*, eh?

# L

## is for

## LETTERS PLAY

The weird and wonderful world of words is a world that depends for its existence entirely on the letters of the alphabet, each one of which happens to be a word in its own right.

Some letters even have several meanings. I have dug into a dozen dictionaries to come up with these twenty-six:

A      a major blood group

B      in men's pyjama sizes in some countries, medium

C      the cardinal number of the set of all real numbers

D      a proportional brassière cup size, smaller than DD and larger than C

E      a flag bearing the letter E, for 'efficiency', presented during the Second World War as an award by the army or navy to factories meeting or passing their production schedules of war materials

F      the medieval Roman numeral for 40

G      the fifth tone in the scale of C major, or the seventh tone in the relative minor scale, A minor

H      the horizontal component of the Earth's magnetic field

I      the imaginary number that is the square root of minus 1

J      the medieval Roman numeral for 1

K       in computer technology, the number 1,000 or 1,024
L       an extension at right angles to one end of a building
M       a printing unit
N       in optics, the index of refraction
O       the exclamation *oh*
P       in music, softly
Q       in biblical criticism, the symbol for material common to the Gospels of
        Matthew and Luke that was not derived from the Gospel of Mark
R       are (as in 'oysters R in season')
S       the energy state of an electron in an atom having an orbital angular
        momentum of zero
T       the relation between points and closed sets in topological space
U       a Burmese title of respect allied to a man
V       the symbol of Allied victory in the Second World War
W       the twenty-third in order
X       a film recommended for adults only
Y       in mathematics, the y-axis
Z       the medieval Roman numeral for 2,000

In *Word Play* I am taking you from A to Z and back again, so here are
twenty-six more one-letter words, this time running from Z to A.

Z       a buzzing sound
Y       a principal railway track and two diverging branches arranged like the letter Y
X       a mistake or error
W       a printer's type for producing the letter W
V       a V-shaped neck of a dress, sweater or blouse
U       characteristic of the upper classes
T       an offensive soccer formation
S       a grade assigned by a teacher rating a student's work as satisfactory
R       one of the three Rs (writing, reading and arithmetic)
Q       the ratio of the reactance of the resistance of an oscillatory circuit
P       the chemical symbol for phosphorus
O       zero
N       an indefinite number

M    an antigen of human blood that shares a common genetic locus with the N antigen

L    an elevated railway

K    in mathematics, a unit vector parallel to the z-axis

J    in mathematics, a unit vector parallel to the y-axis

I    an excessively egotistic person

H    something having the shape of the letter H

G    a sum of a thousand dollars

F    a grade assigned by a teacher rating a student's work as so inferior as to be failing

E    the second class Lloyd's rating for the quality of a merchant ship

D    a semi-circle on a pool table that is about twenty-two inches in diameter and is used especially in snooker games

C    a sum of 100 dollars

B    a motion picture produced on a small budget and usually shown as a supplement to the main features

A    a chiefly Scots form of all

• • • • • • • • • • • • • • • • • • • • • • • • • • • • • • • • • • • • • • • • • • • • • • • • • •

## TWO'S COMPANY

And if single-letter words leave you cold, don't worry. Most of the words in the book are a little longer – like these:

*aa*    a type of volcanic lava

*ag*    relating to agriculture

*ai*    a South American sloth

*bu*    a Japanese coin

*da*    a heavy Burmese knife

*dy*    a type of sediment deposited in some lakes

*ea*    a stream

*fu*    an administrative division of China and Japan

*fy*    an interjection

*gi*    a costume worn for judo and karate

*gu*    a kind of violin used in the Shetland islands

*ie*    a mat or basket made from a certain type of fibre

*io*    a large hawk from Hawaii

*ix*    the axle of a cart or wagon

*jo*    a sweetheart

*ka*    a personality double

*ki*    any of several Asian and Pacific trees

*li*    a Chinese unit of measure

*ob*    an objection

*od*    a force

*oe*    a whirlwind

*om*    a mantra

*oo*    an extinct Hawaiian bird

*ri*    a Japanese unit of measure

*sy*    a chiefly dialectical spelling of 'scythe'

*ug*    a feeling of disgust

*vi*    a Polynesian tree

*yi*    in Chinese philosophy, the faithful performance of one's
       specified duties to society

. . . . . . . . . . . . . . . . . . . . . . . . . . . . . . . . . . . . . . . . . . . .

## FROM ALOHA TO ZIZZ

These twenty-six words are longer still, and what's interesting about them is that each one begins and ends with the same letter:

| aloha | blob | cynic | dad | ewe |
|---|---|---|---|---|
| fluff | grinning | health | iambi | Jernej |
| kick | lull | mum | neon | octavo |
| pop | Qaraqalpaq | razor | syllables | tot |
| unau | valv | wow | Xerox | yolky |
| zizz | | | | |

Wow, eh?

*Aloha*, is a Hawaiian greeting, and *zizz* is a slang word for a sleep. *Iambi* is the plural of *iambus*, part of a line of poetry having two syllables; *Jernej* is a Yugoslavian forename; *Qaraqalpaq* is a Turkic people of Central Asia; *unau* is an animal, a type of sloth; and *valv* is a reformed spelling of valve.

. . . . . . . . . . . . . . . . . . . . . . . . . . . . . . . . . . . . . . . . . . . .

## ALPHABET WORD CHAIN

This is wordplay and now it's playtime. Think of a word beginning with *a* and ending with *b*. Then think of a word beginning with *b* and ending with *c*. Then think of a word beginning with *c* and ending with *d*. And go on, right through the alphabet. Any word will do to fill each gap. How far can you get before you run into trouble? (As far as *i* to *j* in my case.)

| | | | | |
|---|---|---|---|---|
| adverb | basic | cold | dove | elf |
| flag | girth | Hindi | i???j | junk |
| kill | loom | moon | nuncio | overlap |
| p???q | queer | rats | sit | tableau |
| u???v | vow | wax | xerography | yez |
| zebra | | | | |

I was left with three gaps: *i–j*, *p–q*, and *u–v*. These can all be filled by choosing uncommon proper names. For example, *Igej* is a town in Hungary and *Inathganj* is a place in Pakistan; *Pontacq* is a wine from the south of France; and *Ulanov* and *Ushpitov* are Russian towns.

*Yez*, by the way, is an Anglo-Irish pronoun meaning 'you' in the plural.

. . . . . . . . . . . . . . . . . . . . . . . . . . . . . . . . . . . . . . . . . . . .

## A TO Z IN THE MIDDLE

Here are three lists of words. In each list, the middle letters of the words run from A to Z. In the case of the seven-letter words, the first three letters and the last three letters also form words; in the case of the nine-letter words, the first four and the last four letters also form words; and in the case of the eleven-letter words, the first five letters and the last five letters form words. Unfortunately examples of nine- and eleven-letter words with *q* in the middle are missing. Yes, wordplay is like life itself. There are occasional disappointments.

| 7 LETTERS | 9 LETTERS | 11 LETTERS |
|---|---|---|
| carAvan | bungAlows | blockAdings |
| jawBone | rainBowed | underBought |
| teaCher | blueCoats | extraCtable |
| banDits | snowDrift | screwDriver |
| vetEran | bothEring | adultErated |
| warFare | goldFinch | satinFlower |
| bagGage | kiloGrams | underGround |
| witHout | brigHtens | unrigHtable |
| manIkin | handIwork | deterIorate |
| conJure | flapJacks | interJangle |
| weeKend | sparKling | underKeeled |
| lowLand | paneLwork | oversLoping |
| barMaid | clayMores | blackMailed |
| furNace | lameNtory | heaveNwards |
| bayOnet | bestOwing | trampOlines |
| ramPart | tramPling | enterPrises |
| ubiQuit | ???? | ???? |
| curRant | mayoRship | butteRflies |
| penSion | brimStone | sweepStakes |
| vanTage | sideTrack | forgeTtable |
| butUmen | consUlate | prestUdying |
| canVass | disaVowed | extraVagate |
| hogWash | bushWomen | lightWeight |
| manXman | trioXides | overXpress |
| copYcat | pansYlike | staphYlions |
| manZana | waltZlike | hydraZonium |

. . . . . . . . . . . . . . . . . . . . . . . . . . . . . . . . . . . . . . . .

## A WHAT?

In English, the two indefinite articles are *a* and *an*. When a word begins with a consonant, the indefinite article that goes before it is always *a* – for example:

a boy
a cow
a dog
a fish
a horse
a lumberjack
a mother
a noise
a raspberry
a strawberry
a xylophone

Given that's the case, you might expect every consonant to be preceded by the indefinite article *a* as well – but it isn't. Yes, we have a *b* and a *c* and a *d*, but then we have:

an F
an H
an L
an M
an N
an R
an S
an X

And the strangeness doesn't stop there. With words that begin with vowels, the indefinite article is always *an*:

an angel
an elephant
an igloo
an orange
an umbrella

And while we have an *a*, an *e*, an *i* and an *o*, when we get to *u*, for some reason it's: a *u*.

I am as bewildered as you are – but, wait, there's more.

If you spell out the *sound* of each letter of the alphabet, do they all begin with the letter they represent?

Some do, for example:

| | |
|---|---|
| Ay | A |
| Bee | B |
| Dee | D |
| Gee | G |
| Jay | J |
| Pee | P |
| Tee | T |
| Zed | Z |

But some don't:

| | |
|---|---|
| Eff | F |
| Aitch | H |
| Ell | L |
| Emm | M |
| Enn | N |
| Are | R |
| Ess | S |
| Doubleyou | W |

# K

## is for

## KUMMERSPECK

As I mentioned in the Introduction, I was born in Germany. Once upon a time I spoke German. Over the years I have forgotten most of it, but some words I do remember. *Kummerspeck* is one of them.

*Kummerspeck* translates as 'grief bacon' and is the German word used to describe the weight one puts on in times of trouble. It's a brilliant word, isn't it?

The Germans have a remarkable knack, unparalleled in any other language, for creating compound words – words that are made by putting other words together. Not only does this result in some pretty lengthy examples – *Schwarzwälderkirschtorte* is Black Forest cherry cake – but it allows the Germans encapsulate concepts for which there is no singular English word. For example, *Schadenfreude* (literal translation 'harm-joy') is the pleasure we derive from the harm that comes to others, a useful word for which we have no equivalent.

Here are a few more of my favourite German compound words – or *Lieblingsdeutscheverbindungwörter*, as I like to call them:

| | |
|---|---|
| *Freundschaftbezeigungen* | 'demonstrations of friendship' |
| *Sitzpinkler* | a man who urinates sitting down |
| *Lebensabschittgefährter* | used to mean 'lover' or 'partner' but actually translates as 'the person I am with today' |
| *Tintenfish* | 'ink fish' = squid |
| *Stachelschwein* | 'sting pig' = porcupine |
| *Glühbirne* | 'glowing pear' = lightbulb |
| *Handschuhschneeballwerfer* | 'a person who wears gloves to throw snowballs' |

Did you notice that the German word for gloves is **Handschuhe** which translates as 'handshoes'?

Ben Schott, the author of *Schott's Miscellany* published a whole book of the German compound words he made up himself, *Schottenfreude: German words for the human condition*. Here are two of my favourites to inspire you to come up with your own:

| | |
|---|---|
| *Schubladenbrief* | the letter you write but never send – translates as 'drawer letter' |
| *Zeitungsdunkel* | consternation that people read a newspaper you disapprove of; translates as 'newspaper arrogance' |

. . . . . . . . . . . . . . . . . . . . . . . . . . . . . . . . . . . . . . . . . . . . . . . .

## KARAT SOUP

Sometimes the English used by English-speaking people makes me despair. Then I go abroad and discover that the English used by non-English-speaking people is even worse. On my travels I have collected examples of 'foreigners' English' from all over the world. Here are the best – or worst, depending on how you look at it:

French widow in every bedroom.
*Advertisement for a French hotel*

Parsons are requested not to occupy seats in this café

without consummation.
*Notice in French café*

Please leave your values at the front desk.
*Sign in Paris hotel lift*

In case of fire please do your utmost to arm the hall porter.
*Notice in Austrian hotel*

Visitors are requested not to throw coffee or other matter into the basin. Why else it stuffs the place inconvenient for the other world.
*Notice in an Italian hotel*

WELCOME TO HOTEL COSY: Where no one's stranger.
*Notice in Indian hotel*

Teppanyaki – before your cooked right eyes.
*Notice in Japanese restaurant*

Look out our new baby is on our car!
*Baby on board sticker, Hong Kong*

. . . . . . . . . . . . . . . . . . . . . . . . . . . . . . . . . . . . . . . . . . . . . . . . .

## TRANSLATION PLEASE

Foreigners' English may be bad at times, but the way English-speaking people speak other languages is almost invariably worse. Here is a glossary of words and phrases in French, German, Arabic, Spanish, Italian and Latin, with a selection of translations supplied by English-speaking students:

*abito* a piece of

*à la russe* in a hurry
*apéritif* dentures
*bacchich* backache

*abhorros* four-legged animal used for racing

*Angebot* to wait, loiter
*arriba* large stream
*baroque* short of money

*à la carte* served from the trolley

*apenas* joy, pleasure
*Auspuff* cobweb duster
*Beau Geste* big joke

*bonis avibus* free ride on public transport

*château* French conversation

*damnosa* very inquisitive

*gendarme* strong arm of the law

*laissez-faire* idle woman

*n'importe* there is no port left

*pas de deux* father of twins

*son et lumière* your son is smoking

*terra incognita* fear of the unknown

*campagna* Italian girlfriend

*cortège* small house in the country

*déjeuner* travel

*grande dame* fat lady

*ma foi* my liver

*nouvelle vague* modern novel

*passé* father has spoken

*sotto voce* slurred speech

*ça ne fait rien* good weather

*crèche* sound of breaking crockery

*en ami* hostile person

*karat* vegetable

*maladie* madam

*par excellence* very good father

*presto* tight shoe

*terra cotta* fear of beds

* * * * * * * * * * * * * * * * * * * * * * * * * * * * * * * * * * * * *

# RESIDENT ALIENS

The English language owes so much to so many. Here are twenty-five 'English' words imported from other languages:

| ENGLISH WORD | LANGUAGE OF ORIGIN | ENGLISH WORD | LANGUAGE OF ORIGIN |
|---|---|---|---|
| *bamboo* | Malay | *chocolate* | Nahuati |
| *damask* | Hebrew | *Eskimo* | Cree |
| *fakir* | Arabic | *gingham* | Malay |
| *hammock* | Taino | *igloo* | Eskimo |
| *jaguar* | Guarani | *kowtow* | Mandarin Chinese |
| *lemon* | Arabic | *mattress* | Arabic |
| *nadir* | Arabic | *orangutan* | Malay |
| *pariah* | Tamil | *quinine* | Quechua |
| *raccoon* | Powhatan | *shawl* | Persian |
| *thug* | Hindi | *ukulele* | Hawaiian |

| ENGLISH WORD | LANGUAGE OF ORIGIN | ENGLISH WORD | LANGUAGE OF ORIGIN |
|---|---|---|---|
| *voodoo* | **Ewe** | *wadi* | **Arabic** |
| *X* | **Arabic** | *yogurt* | **Turkish** |
| *zebra* | **Kikongo** | | |

. . . . . . . . . . . . . . . . . . . . . . . . . . . . . . . . . . . . . . . . .

## HOBSON-JOBSON

I was born in Germany. My father was born in England. My mother was born in India. Her father was in the Indian Army and her mother was a missionary. I have inherited their copy of a remarkable book, first published in 1886. Edited by Henry Yule and Arthur C. Burnell, it is called *Hobson-Jobson: A Glossary of Colloquial Anglo-Indian Words and Phrases, and of Kindred Terms, Etymological, Historical, Geographical, and Discursive.*

A 'hobson-jobson' is a word or phrase that has been borrowed from another language and adapted to sound and look like a word in the borrowing language. There are more than two thousand words of Anglo-Indian origin in *Hobson-Jobson*. Here's a selection:

| | | | |
|---|---|---|---|
| *kedgeree* | *loot* | *pundit* | *swastika* |
| *bandanna* | *dungarees* | *Blighty* | *shampoo* |
| *bangle* | *indigo* | *cot* | *thug* |
| *bungalow* | *musk* | *cushy* | *veranda* |
| *cash* | *pyjamas* | *jodhpurs* | *cashmere* |
| *chutney* | *polo* | *jungle* | *hullabaloo* |
| *cummerbund* | *sarong* | *shawl* | *khaki* |

My mother's favourite curry was a vindaloo. 'Vindaloo' is a word that has come to us from India, but its etymology is from the Portuguese: ***vin d'halo***, 'wine with garlic'.

. . . . . . . . . . . . . . . . . . . . . . . . . . . . . . . . . . . . . . . . . . . . . .

## BON MOT

I think the last word on the subject belongs to Goethe:

*Wer fremde Sprachen nicht kennt, weiss nichts von seiner eigenen.*

I'm not going to argue with that.

# J

**is for**

**JARGON**

The cognitive continuum is concerned with objectives related to knowledge and the intellectual abilities and skills, rising from comprehension to evaluation. The effective continuum covers the range of behavioural responses, from passive acceptance of stimuli to the organisation of an individual.

In the second place there are grounds for thinking that the availability of analytical assessments of jobs would facilitate the preparation of grade-descriptions for a new structure in a situation in which the allocation of jobs to grades at the stages of implementing and maintaining that structure would be undertaken by whole job procedures.

I didn't make it up. Those two paragraphs were written for real. The world of work is now awash with jargon. Here are some everyday words and phrases that you can hear in any office on any day of the year. Do they get on your wick as much as they get on mine? (I haven't offered definitions because, as we all know, business jargon is completely meaningless.)

*Helicopter view*          *Run it up the flagpole*     *Ideas shower*

| | | |
|---|---|---|
| *Going forward* | *Let's action that* | *Empower* |
| *Take it to the next level* | *Circle back* | *Staff engagement* |
| *Square the circle* | *Reach out* | *Put a record on and see who dances* |
| *Low-hanging fruit* | *Get all your ducks in a row* | *Intrepreneurs* |
| *Leverage* | *Synergy* | *I'm thinking in real time* |
| *Execute* | *The next lever drill down* | *Let's take this off line* |
| *Let's start cascading relevant information* | | |

Those clichés are pretty meaningless. With the business jargon that follows, interpretation can be helpful:

| | |
|---|---|
| *activate, to* | to send another email and cc in more names |
| *advanced design* | beyond the comprehension of the ad agency's copywriters |
| *all new* | parts not interchangeable with existing models |
| *automatic* | that which you can't repair yourself |
| *channels* | the trails left by interoffice emails |
| *clarify, to* | to fill in the background with so many details that the foreground goes underground |
| *conference* | a day out |
| *confidential email* | one in which people have been bcced into rather than cced |
| *co-ordinator* | the person who has a desk between two expediters (see expedite) |
| *developed after years of extensive research* | discovered by accident |
| *expedite* | to confound confusion with commotion |
| *forwarded for your consideration* | you hold the bag for a while |
| *give someone the picture* | make a long, confused and inaccurate statement to a newcomer |

| | |
|---|---|
| *in conference* | nobody can find him/her |
| *in due course* | never |
| *infrastructure* | (1) the structure within an infra, (2) the structure outside the infra, (3) a building with built-in infras |
| *it's in the process* | never |
| *let's get together on this* | I'm assuming you're as confused on this as I am |
| *policy* | we can hide behind this |
| *see me* | come down to my office, I'm lonely |
| *sources* | *reliable source* – the person you just met; *informed source* – the person who told the person you just met; *unimpeachable source* – the person who started the rumour originally |
| *top priority* | it may be idiotic, but the boss wants it |
| *under active consideration* | we're looking in the files for it |
| *we will look into it* | by the time the wheel makes a full turn, we assume you will have forgotten about it too |

These eight gems require proper translation. The first six are for real, the last two just for fun.

There is a degree of preoccupation in the atmosphere.
Translation: *it's raining*

There is an obligation to work with unusually distant time horizons.
Translation: *plan ahead*

Basically, we are endeavouring to review the validity of the schedules.
Translation: *we're trying to keep the schedules up to date*

On initial arrival relevant information was laid before us indicative of the conversion not being of limited duration equipment-wise.
Translation: *when we arrived we found it wouldn't take long to convert the equipment*

A set of arrangements for producing and rearing children, the viability of which is not predicated on the consistent presence in the household of an adult male acting in the role of husband and father.
Translation: *Dad isn't home much*

Experiments are described which demonstrate that in normal individuals the lowest concentration in which the sucrose can be detected by means of gustation differs from the lowest concentration in which sucrose has to be ingested in order to produce a demonstrable decrease in olfactory acuity and a noteworthy conversion of sensations interpreted as a desire for food into sensations interpreted as a satiety associated ingestion of food.
Translation: *experiments show that a normal person can taste sugar in water in quantities not strong enough to interfere with his sense of smell or take away his appetite*

A slight inclination of the cranium is as adequate as a spasmodic movement of one optic to an equine quadruped utterly devoid of any visionary capacity.
Translation: *a nod is as good as a wink to a blind horse*

Such are the vicissitudes of this our sublunary experience.
Translation: *such is life*

. . . . . . . . . . . . . . . . . . . . . . . . . . . . . . . . . . . . . . . . . . . . . . . .

## PLAIN TALK

Plain talk has become so rare that there is money to be made out of it. Alan Siegel, a Miami-based communications and design consultant, has made hundreds of thousands of dollars translating the incomprehensible English of government departments, banks and insurance companies into English that ordinary people can understand.

The problem has been escalating. In the 1970s, President Carter insisted that every government department engage 'a simple-writing expert'.

As the White House lawyer said, when Carter protested about an incomprehensible piece of legalese, 'I see your point, Mr President. I had better laymanise the whole thing.'

'Laymanise' is gobbledygook. Using a grandiose word when a simpler one is available is not a good thing. Here are my top twenty gobbledygook words to avoid:

| GOBBLEDYGOOK | PLAIN TALK |
| --- | --- |
| subsequent to | after |
| prior to, antecedent to | before |
| rationale | reason |
| conjecture, speculate | guess |
| converse | talk |
| interrogate | question |
| hypothesise | suppose, let's say |
| in the vicinity of | near |
| approximately | about, around |
| audible | aloud, out loud |
| perceptible, visible | in sight, noticeable |
| negligent | careless |
| preponderance | greater weight |
| acquiesce, concur | agree |
| emphasise | stress |
| substantially contemporaneous | at about the same time |
| equitable | fair |
| aggregate of, totality of | all |
| totality of circumstances | whole picture |
| earned compensation | pay |
| supersede | replace |

. . . . . . . . . . . . . . . . . . . . . . . . . . . . . . . . . . . . . . . . . . . . . . . .

# GOBBLEDYGOOK GENERATOR

If, on the other hand, you do not wish to have the stupidity of your remarks made obvious, the *Word Play* Gobbledygook Generator™ is your kind of toy. To invest your every utterance with a modern-as-tomorrow ring of decisive knowledgeable authority, pick one word from each of the three columns and string the three words chosen together. You will never be short of something to say because the Generator can provide you with 140,608 three-word combinations, whether it's *inherent coincidental interference* or simple *distributive exponential feasibility* you're after.

| | | |
|---|---|---|
| inherent | coincidental | interference |
| emancipative | exemplificatory | efficiency |
| substantial | preventive | interdependence |
| ambivalent | expansive | projection |
| reversible | participatory | motivation |
| permanent | degenerative | eventuality |
| gradual | aggregating | diffusion |
| partial | universal | mobility |
| societal | falsificatory | vacancy |
| adequate | evolutionary | flexibility |
| global | appropriative | finality |
| responsive | prior | phase |
| traditional | illusory | transparency |
| dialectical | concordant | adaptation |
| fictitious | allocated | factionalism |
| defunctionalised | frustrated | extension |
| existential | restrictive | periodicity |
| positivistic | accidental | denudation |
| elitist | fluctuating | affinity |
| predicative | simulated | transcendence |
| ultimative | digital | specification |
| temporal | convergent | psychosis |
| intransigent | totemic | competence |
| obsolete | elongating | structure |
| antiauthoritarian | innovative | disparity |
| flanking | homogeneous | escalation |
| multilateral | identifying | synthesis |
| bilateral | transfigurative | consistency |
| representative | discrepant | motivation |

quantitative
concentrated
ameliorating
divergent
indicative
immanent
synchronous
contradictory
differentiated
systematised
inductive
structural
integrated
determinative
coincidental
nonfragmenting
interfractional
descriptive
coherent
fortuitous
proliferative
compatible
distributive

culminating
diversifying
alliterative
usurpative
erupting
deteriorative
obstructive
decentralised
imitative
co-operative
conglomerate
progressive
recessive
programmed
eliminative
differential
complementary
dynamic
substantive
contributory
component
uniform
exponential

mobility
cancellation
sufficiency
equivalence
turbulence
discontinuity
potency
expectancy
accumulation
plasticity
stagflation
permanence
epigenesis
solidification
application
implication
deterioration
constructivism
polarity
classification
deformation
extrapolation
feasibility

# I

**is for**

## INSTANT SUNSHINE

What's the word you most like the sound of? The word that brings you instant sunshine?

For the Scottish novelist Alexander McCall Smith it's 'fantoosh'.

'Fantoosh' is a word used mainly by Scottish people to show extreme pleasure, but it's the sound rather than the meaning that counts here. Ann Widdecombe, former MP, says this is her favourite-sounding word: 'rodomontade'.

'Rodomontade' is boastful behaviour. We all know what English novelist Jeffrey Archer's favourite-sounding word means. The word is: 'energy'.

The late Spike Milligan's favourite was: 'fish'.

What's yours?

When Cambridge Dictionaries conducted a survey to find the nation's favourite-sounding words, these emerged as the Top Twenty. I particularly like 1, 4, 7, 10 and 20.

| 1. Nincompoop | 2. Love | 3. Mum | 4. Discombobulated |
|---|---|---|---|
| 5. Excellent | 6. Happy | 7. Squishy | 8. Fabulous |
| 9. Cool | 10. Onomatopoeia | 11. Weekend | 12. Incandescent |
| 13. Wicked | 14. Lovely | 15. Lush | 16. Peace |
| 17. Cosy | 18. Bed | 19. Freedom | 20. Kiss |

According to another survey, these are words we least like the sound of:

| 1. Moist | 2. Panties | 3. Phlegm | 4. Smear |
|---|---|---|---|
| 5. Pustule | 6. Croak | 7. Mucus | 8. Congeal |
| 9. Dangle | 10. Chunk | | |

And in 2015, apparently, these are the words and phrases that *irritated* us most:

| 1. Chillax | 2. Work hard, play hard | 3. With all due respect | 4. At the end of the day |
|---|---|---|---|
| 5. Honestly… | 6. To be frank | 7. Everything happens for a reason | 8. Literally |
| 9. Hard-working families | | | |

. . . . . . . . . . . . . . . . . . . . . . . . . . . . . . . . . . . . . . . . . . .

## AS ITHERS SEE US

In 1786 the great Scottish poet Robert Burns wrote one of his best-loved poems: 'To a louse: on seeing one on a lady's bonnet at church'. It contains some famous lines:

> *O wad some Powr the giftie gie us*
> *To see oursels as ithers see us!*

Which can be translated simply as:

> *And would some Power the small gift give us*

*To see ourselves as others see us!*

This is how the compilers of a leading American dictionary see us. The team at the *Merriam-Webster Dictionary* recently chose their top ten uniquely 'British' words. These were they:

| | | | |
|---|---|---|---|
| 1. prat | 2. whinge | 3. knackered | 4. jiggery-pokery |
| 5. plonk (as in cheap wine) | 6. chunter | 7. twee | 8. gormless |
| 9. boffin | 10. pukka | | |

. . . . . . . . . . . . . . . . . . . . . . . . . . . . . . . . . . . . . . . . . . . . .

# THINKING POSITIVELY

I like to think that mine's a sunny disposition, but I realise that much of the language I use is oddly disobliging.

When was the last time you felt 'consolate' or 'gruntled' because the weather was 'clement', giving you a feeling of 'gust'?

If your answer is a little time in coming, I am not surprised. 'Consolate', 'gruntled', 'clement' and 'gust' are all legitimate words, but we are more familiar with them in their negative sense; their positive forms are seldom, if ever, used.

Here are some more words that we are unaccustomed to seeing in their positive light:

| | |
|---|---|
| antibiotic | biotic (relating to life) |
| deodorant | odorant (something odorous) |
| disinfectant | infectant (something that infects) |
| feckless | feckful (efficient, powerful) |
| illicit | licit (legal, allowable) |
| impeccable | peccable (inclined to sin) |

| | |
|---|---|
| impervious | pervious (something capable of being penetrated) |
| indelible | delible (able to be deleted) |
| indomitable | domitable (capable of being tamed) |
| ineffable | effable (able to be uttered or expressed) |
| inevitable | evitable (avoidable) |
| innocuous | nocuous (harmful) |
| insipid | sipid (tasty, full of flavour) |
| ruthless | ruth (an archaic term for pity or compassion) |
| uncanny | canny (familiar, without mystery) |
| unconscionable | conscionable (scrupulous, conscientious) |
| uncouth | couth (polished, polite) |
| unkempt | kempt (tidy, trim) |
| unspeakable | speakable (capable of being spoken) |
| unwieldy | wieldy (manageable) |

# H

**is for**

**HEAR EAR 'ERE HERE!**

The English language is full of surprises. What you see (or hear) isn't always what you get. Or expect.

A bully has nothing to do with a bull: it comes from the Dutch word for lover, ***boel***.

Humble pie has nothing to do with humility: cheap cuts of meat were once known as ***umbles***.

Titmice have no connection with what you might think: ***tit*** used to mean small and ***mase*** once meant a kind of bird.

Nitwits may be witless, but the word comes from the Dutch ***niet wit***, meaning 'I don't know'.

The big cheese comes not from cheese, but from ***chiz***, the Hindu for 'thing'.

Guinea pigs aren't pigs and don't come from Guinea. India ink comes from China. Turkeys come from North America, not Turkey. And blindworms aren't blind: they are legless lizards that can see.

Words aren't always what you might expect them to be. They aren't always what they sound like – or look like. You might think that a *barguest* is a guest in a bar, but, oh, no, it's not. It's a ghost or a goblin, often shaped like a large dog.

Here is more proof that, with words, what you see is not always what you get:

*Bedrape* is not rape occurring in a bed but is an intensive form of the verb *drape*.

*Bedrug* is not a bedspread but an intensive form of the verb *drug*.

*Deadlily* is not a dead lily but is an adverb meaning 'in a deadly manner'.

*Forestation* is not a station or outpost at a frontier but is the establishment of a forest.

*Forestress* is not a female forester but a verb meaning 'to place stress on the first part of the word'.

*Interminable* is not an adjective meaning 'to penetrate with mines', but an adjective meaning long-lasting.

*Intermine* is not a verb meaning 'to last for a long time', but is a verb meaning 'to penetrate with mines'.

*Nunlet* is not a small nun but is a small South American bird.

*Racemate* is not a member of the relay team but is an adjective meaning 'unable to rest'.

*Redial* is not a verb meaning 'to dial again', but is an adjective meaning 'relating to redia, a type of larva'.

*Restable* is not a verb meaning 'to stable again', but is an adjective meaning 'able to rest'.

*Townsite* is not a mineral named after someone named Towns, but is the site of a town.

*Wellsite* is not at the site of a well, but is a mineral named after someone called Wells.

. . . . . . . . . . . . . . . . . . . . . . . . . . . . . . . . . . . . . . . . . . . . . . . . .

## WHAT DID YOU SAY?

Sometimes what you see is deceptive. Sometimes what you hear isn't what you are supposed to hear. Oronyms are words and phrases that sound the same but aren't: *iced ink* and *I stink* are nice examples. Here are some more of my favourites:

The stuffy nose can lead to problems
The stuff he knows can lead to problems

Are you aware of the words you have just uttered?
Are you aware of the words you have just stuttered?

He would kill *Hamlet* for that reason
He would kill *Hamlet* for that treason

Some others I've seen ...
Some mothers I've seen ...

The secretariat's sphere of competence
The secretariat's fear of competence

Reading in the library is sometimes allowed
Reading in the library is sometimes aloud

. . . . . . . . . . . . . . . . . . . . . . . . . . . . . . . . . . . . . . . . . . . . . . . .

## HERE HEAR!

Homonyms are two words hidden in one sound. A homonym is a pair of words that are pronounced the same but spelt differently. *Right* and *write* are homonyms and so are *feet* and *feat*, and *meet* and *meat*.

With just a hint from me, can you find ten homonyms that are linked in some way to the animal kingdom:

1. husky:
2. long thin candle:
3. exist:

4. make a hole:

5. second person:

6. slang for money:

7. fly away:

8. rotate slowly:

9. child's cry:

10. parts of a chain:

Now find ten more with a plant connection:

1. give up:

2. punish by blows:

3. escaping of water:

4. put underground:

5. existed:

6. flowing onward motion:

7. shore of the sea:

8. objects placed in straight lines:

9. duration:

10. military officer:

## ANSWERS

Homonyms with an animal connection:

1. husky: *hoarse, horse*

2. long thin candle: *taper, tapir*

3. exist: *be, bee*

4. make a hole: *bore, boar*

5. second person: *you, ewe*

6. slang for money: *dough, doe*

7. fly away: *flee, flea*

8. rotate slowly: *turn, tern*

9. child's cry: *mewl, mule*

10. parts of a chain: *links, lynx*

Homonyms with a plant connection:

1. give up: *cede, seed*
2. punish by blows: *beat, beet*
3. escaping of water: *leak, leek*
4. put underground: *bury, berry*
5. existed: *been, bean*
6. flowing onward motion: *current, currant*
7. shore of the sea: *beach, beech*
8. objects placed in straight lines: *rows, rose*
9. duration: *time, thyme*
10. military officer: *colonel, kernel*

. . . . . . . . . . . . . . . . . . . . . . . . . . . . . . . . . . . . . . . . . . .

## DAFFYNITIONS

Daffynitions appear in fictionaries, not dictionaries, and make you realise there might be more to a word than you thought. Sometimes they involve homonyms. Sometimes they don't.

**acorn**
an oak in a nutshell

**afford**
a car some people drive

**announce**
one-sixteenth of a pound

**appear**
something you fish off

**arrest**
what to take when you're tired

**attack**
a small nail

**auctioneer**
a man who looks forbidding

**avoidable**
what a bullfighter tries to do

**bacteria**
the rear of a cafeteria

**barber shop**
a clip joint

**carbuncle**
an automobile collision

**chair**
headquarters for hindquarters

**conceit**
I-strain.

**crowbar**
a bird's drinking place

**cube root**
diced carrots

**denial**
where Cleopatra lived

**eclipse**
what a barber does for a living

**fastidious**
someone who is quick and ugly

**gossip**
letting the chat out of the bag

**hogwash**
pig's laundry

**information**
how air-force planes fly

**knob**
a thing to adore

**mummy**
an Egyptian pressed for time

**paradox**
two doctors

**quadruplets**
four crying out loud

**rhubarb**
bloodshot celery

**rubberneck**
what you do to help her relax

**snoring**
sheet music

**dentist**
someone who looks down in the mouth

**egomania**
a passion for omelettes

**flood**
a river that's too big for its bridges

**hay**
grass *à la mode*

**ice**
skid stuff

**kindred**
a fear of relatives coming

**melancholy**
a dog that likes watermelons

**obesity**
surplus gone to waist

**parole**
a cell-out

**raisin**
a worried grape

**ringleader**
first one in the bathtub

**shotgun**
a worn-out gun

**tears**
glum drops

**drill sergeant**
an army dentist

**extinct**
dead skunk

**goblet**
a small turkey

**heroes**
what a guy in a boat does

**illegal**
a sick bird

**khaki**
what you have to use before you can start your vehicle

**motel**
William Tell's sister

**out-of-bounds**
a tired kangaroo

**propaganda**
a socially correct goose

**rebate**
putting another worm on the hook

**romance**
ants in Rome

**sleeping bag**
a nap sack

**unabridged**
a river you have to swim across

**vitamin**
what you do when someone
comes to the house

**walkie-talkie**
a grounded parrot

**wind**
air in a hurry

**woe**
opposite of giddy-up

**yellow**
what you do when you
stub your toe

**zinc**
where you wash the
zaucepans

# G

## is for

## GEOGRAPHY LESSON

The longest place name in Britain is:

*Llanfairpwllgwyngyllgogerychwyrndrobwllllantysiliogogogoch*

It's a village in Wales.

The country with the longest name in the world?

*The United Kingdom of Great Britain and Northern Ireland*

That was a surprise, wasn't it?

And abbreviated to *UK* it becomes the country with the shortest name, too.

Strictly speaking, in full the United Kingdom's name is the longest country name in *English*: some countries have names that, when given in Arabic, are a little longer. And even in English, the UK's sovereign position is not totally secure. *The Economist* reported recently that in order to get into the World Trade Organization, without disturbing the sensibilities of the People's Republic of China, Taiwan had to agree to be known as

'The Separate Customs Territory of Taiwan, Penghu, Kinmen, and Matsu (Chinese Taipei)'.

. . . . . . . . . . . . . . . . . . . . . . . . . . . . . . . . . . . . . . . . . . . . . . . . . .

## SENSE OF PLACE

Lots of things have been named after places and lots of places have names that mean something. How long a list of place names with double meanings can you conjure up? Here's mine:

*berlin*
a type of carriage

*china*
fine porcelain

*etna*
a container for heating liquids

*fulham*
a loaded die

*geneva*
a liquor

*guernsey*
a woollen jumper

*harrow*
to break up and level soil

*holland*
a cotton fabric

*japan*
to coat with glossy black lacquer

*jersey*
a knitted jumper

*kent*
knew

*lima*
a bean

*limerick*
a humorous verse

*morocco*
a soft leather

*pacific*
peaceful

*scotia*
a concave moulding

*surrey*
a light carriage

*tripoli*
a soft, friable rock

*ulster*
a long, loose overcoat

Perhaps it's no surprise that this phenomenon can be found to excess in the land of excess. Look at all the states in America that are doing double duty:

*Alabama*
a genus of moths

*Alaska*
a mixed yarn

*Arkansas*
a type of apple

*Delaware*
one of a breed of fowls

*Florida*
a large yellow peach

*Georgia*
a feminine proper name

*Idaho*
a potato

*Indiana*
a vivid red colour

*Kansas*
an adjective used to refer
to the second glacial stage
during the glacial epoch
in North America

*Maine*
to lower a sail

*Maryland*
tobacco

*Michigan*
a card game

*Minnesota*
a breed of swine

*Mississippi*
a game resembling
bagatelle

*Montana*
a sheep

*Nevada*
pseudonymous surname
of Emma Wixom, an
American singer

*New Hampshire*
a fowl

*Oklahoma*
a form of gin rummy

*Oregon*
a ship

*Texas*
the narrow topmost
storey of a grain elevator

And it's not just the states but the towns in them too:

*Amarillo*
a Venezuelan tree

*Atlanta*
a genus of molluscs

*Austin*
relating to St Augustus

*Baltimore*
a butterfly

*Boston*
a waltz

*Buffalo*
to bewilder

*Charlotte*
a dessert

*Cincinnati*
a wild-card poker game

*Dearborn*
a light four-wheeled
carriage

*Denver*
battleship grey, a colour

*Fresno*
a modified drag scraper,
an earth-digging device

*Long Beach*
a light yellowish-brown
colour

*Milwaukee*
a variety of apple

*Montgomery*
an Asian Indian breed of
dairy cattle

*Phoenix*
a mythical bird

*Springfield*
a US army rifle

*Toledo*
a sword

*Wichita*
an Indian people

*Worcester*
a type of china or
porcelain

*Yonkers*
young men

. . . . . . . . . . . . . . . . . . . . . . . . . . . . . . . . . . . . . . . . . .

## DING DONG IN TEXAS, BEER IN DEVON

The United States boasts some remarkable place names. I have made a list of my favourites and I want to visit them all one day. As names they may seem incredible, but I promise you will find every one of them on a map.

| | | |
|---|---|---|
| Bad Axe, Michigan | Bald Knob, Arkansas | Cut and Shoot, Texas |
| Ding Dong, Texas | Eek, Alaska | Eighty Eight, Kentucky |
| Embarrass, Wisconsin | Horse Thief, Montana | Intercourse, Pennsylvania |
| Jackass Flats, Nevada | King of Prussia, Pennsylvania | Left Hand, West Virginia |
| Marrowbone, Kentucky | Nameless, Kentucky | Plain Dealing, Louisiana |
| Slap Out, Illinois | Social Circle, Georgia | Sweet Gum Head, Louisiana |
| Tobacco, Kentucky | Truth or Consequences, New Mexico | What Cheer, Iowa |
| Why, Arizona | Whynot, Mississippi | Yum Yum, Tennessee |

Happily, the Americans don't have a monopoly on peculiar place names. In the United Kingdom, we have some wonderfully named places as well:

| | | |
|---|---|---|
| Pratt's Bottom, Kent | Ugley, Essex | Lost, Aberdeenshire |
| Thong, Kent | North Piddle, Worcestershire | Golden Balls, Oxfordshire |
| Beer, Devon | Great Snoring, Norfolk | Westward Ho!, Devon |
| Pity me, County Durham | Ham and Sandwich, Kent | Land of Nod, Yorkshire |

. . . . . . . . . . . . . . . . . . . . . . . . . . . . . . . . . . . . . . . . . .

## HIDE AND SEEK

Hiding the names of countries inside sentences, then asking someone else to find them has long been a popular word game in our family. Trust me:

as games go, it's more challenging and entertaining than it sounds.

Here's how it works. You are looking for two countries – in this sentence:

Have you heard an animal talk in dialect?

Have you spotted the countries yet? Look again:

Have you heard an animal talk in dialect?

The countries are Malta and India. Does that help?

Have you heard an ani*mal ta*lk *in dia*lect?

It's fun devising sentences of your own, but to get you started take a look at these. There are two countries hidden in each line:

Such a display could be either grand or rather vulgar.
In December mud and slush surround the fine palace.
Children put on galoshes to go out in the rain.
Give a dog a bone and give him a little water.
If your exhaust pipe rusts you just have to shrug and accept it.
Interpol and the FBI discover hidden marksmen.
Evening classes may help an amateur to improve his painting.

*Answers*

Su*ch a d*isplay could be either gr*and or ra*ther vulgar.
In Decem*ber mud a*nd slush surround the fi*ne pal*ace.
Children pu*t on ga*loshes *to go* out in the rain.
Give a do*g a bon*e and give him *a li*ttle water.
If your exhaust pi*pe ru*sts you just have to shr*ug and a*ccept it.
Inter*pol and* the FBI discover hid*den mark*smen.
Evening classes may hel*p an ama*teur to improve his *pain*ting.

. . . . . . . . . . . . . . . . . . . . . . . . . . . . . . . . . . . . . . . . . . . . . . . . . .

## TEN TIMES FOUR

There are twelve countries in the world whose names contain just four letters. You know all but one of them, I'm sure. What are they?

The answer?

*Eire, Chad, Cuba, Fiji, Iran, Iraq, Laos, Mali, Oman, Peru, Togo*

They are the eleven you have heard of. Here is the twelfth: 2,400 kilometres north-east of New Zealand, it's one of the smallest countries on earth and, by all accounts, it is an island paradise:

*Niue*

. . . . . . . . . . . . . . . . . . . . . . . . . . . . . . . . . . . . . . . . . . . . . . . . . .

## HAVANA GOOD TIME

To people of a certain generation, this line:

*My wife's gone to the West Indies*

prompts this question:

*Jamaica?*

which is followed up immediately with this response:

*No, she went of her own accord!*

When you hit the road, wherever you're going, be sure to pack a pun:

*In Kenya*: How are you enjoying your holiday? Safari, so good.

*In Athens*: Even if the Greeks invented the deep frieze, they didn't think it was worth Parthenon.

*In Moscow*: It must have been the vodka Russian to my head that made me see red.

*In La Paz*: I'll take your word for it, but will the police Bolivia?

*In Santiago*: I wouldn't mention human rights unless you want a Chile reception.

*In the Middle East*: The situation in the Gulf isn't improving – things are going from Iraq to ruin.
At least no one will go hungry in Dubai because of all the sand which is there.

*In America*: Following a major earthquake in California, a group of citizens set up the San Andreas Fund, which just goes to prove what they say about some Californians being generous to a fault.
You can always tell a baby from Alabama by its Southern drool.
Meet the man from Miami. If you think his jacket is florid, you should see his wife's: it's even Florida!

# F

**is for**

## FOOD, GLORIOUS FOOD

Gazing at the computer screen in moments of desperation, I console myself with three thoughts: a cheese straw at six, dinner at eight, and to be immortal you've got to be dead.

Food and words – they're the stuff of life. And in the matter of food, as with everything else, I'm a very lucky individual. I live with one of the world's great cooks. I feast like a king – quite literally, at times, since my wife has made a speciality of the favourite dishes of English monarchs since the Norman Conquest. She has published a book on the subject, *Eating Like A King*, and it is a tradition my eldest daughter, Saethryd, is continuing, appearing at the Chalk Valley History Festival and the 100 Minories Symposium, cooking up a royal storm.

Here is my favourite right royal dish. It's called 'Quyncys in Compost': once tried, it is never forgotten. And it is a pudding that has stood the test of time: Henry VI (aged eight) had it at his coronation banquet in 1422.

You will need:

   2½ ounces whole stem ginger
   3 fluid ounces sherry wine

4 quinces or large firm pears
8 ounces caster sugar
22 fluid ounces red wine
8 ounces stoned dates
2 level teaspoons ground cinnamon
1 level teaspoon ground ginger
a pinch of salt

Cut the ginger into thin slices and leave to soak in the sherry in a covered jar for three days. Peel the quinces or pears and slice into rounds about a quarter of an inch thick. Remove the core from each piece of fruit. Dissolve the sugar gently in the wine and heat until the syrup starts to thicken (about 15 minutes). Add the fruit to the wine syrup and simmer gently until cooked but still firm (about 10 minutes). Add the dates, spices and salt. Continue heating without boiling until the flavours are thoroughly blended. Taste, and add more sugar if necessary. The wine should have syrupy consistency and the fruit should be firm. Leave to cool. Strain the ginger, reserving a tablespoon of the liquid. Stir the reserved liquid and the ginger into the wine syrup. Serve well chilled.

Serves 6

The food of kings (and queens) has made its contribution to the world of words. The Victoria Sponge (another of my favourites) was Queen Victoria's favourite cake, and the Battenberg was made to celebrate her daughter Princess Victoria's wedding to Prince Louis of Battenberg.

When it comes to eating and drinking, all too often we're gobbling and sluicing without knowing to whom we are indebted.

## BÉCHAMEL SAUCE

Béchamel sauce is a white sauce made with flour, butter and milk. It forms the basis of many a dish today. The sauce's origins are probably Italian but its name is seventeenth-century French and comes from a steward of Louis XIV – another Louis, Louis de Béchamel – for whom the sauce was first created.

## COCKTAIL

We all love a cocktail, so much so that there are many stories that claim the etymology of the word. My favourite is that the cocktail, which means a mixed drink, was named after an Aztec goddess, Xochitl, who created such a libation to give to her lover. For me, that's more appetising than the other more widely accepted etymology, which is that cocktails are named after mixed-breed horses that were docked and therefore known as *cock-tails*.

## EPICURE

An epicure is a person devoted to sensual enjoyment. Epicurus was a Greek philosopher (341–270 BC), whose school of thought was that one should weigh up each activity in terms of how much pleasure it would give you. Contrary to popular belief, the Epicureans led relatively austere lives: when weighing up whether the pleasure of drinking heavily was worth the hangover, they decided it was not.

## GARIBALDI

Giuseppe Garibaldi (1807–82) was an Italian general of great import. The garibaldi biscuit is a biscuit of great import in my house, where it is thoroughly enjoyed. Similar to an Eccles cake, it consists of currants squashed between two layers of biscuit. It was named after Giuseppe, who was said to have a particular fondness for pastry with raisins in it.

## GRAND MARNIER

The drink was invented by Louis Alexandre Marnier-Lapostelle in 1870. The name? Well, that was the invention of César Ritz, who was manager of the Savoy at the time. When asked by his good friend what he should call this new orange liqueur, César suggested 'Grand Marnier', partly as a perverse nod to the trend in Paris at the time of christening everything '*petit*' and partly as a well-meaning dig at his friend, who was not blessed in the height department.

## GROG

Nowadays 'grog' is a collective term for all types of alcohol; it originally referred to cheap liquor. The term came about when Admiral Sir Edward

Vernon sought to ration the rum being drunk on his ships by watering it
down. The admiral's nickname was 'Old Grog' because of a waterproof
cloak he wore made of grosgrain. (Incidentally, after the battle of Trafalgar
in 1805, rum became known as 'Nelson's blood' because his body was
placed in a barrel of it to preserve it on its journey home.)

## KIT KAT
The Kit Kat, the world's best-selling chocolate biscuit (I have been to the
factory in York where they produce a billion of them each year), is named
after the Kit Kat Club, a late seventeenth-century political and literary
club, which met in a London pie shop owned by pastry chef Christopher
Catling. The club took its name from an abbreviated version of Catling's.

## LUSH
'Lush' is a slang term for a drunkard. The origins of the word are to
be found in an eighteenth-century drinking club called the City of
Lushington. Stories as to whom the club was named after vary. Some
claim it was after a brewer who has never been traced, others that it was
named after Dr Thomas Lushington, a chaplain who was famously fond of
a tipple.

## MARMALADE
Marmalade was originally made from quinces rather than oranges.
Etymologists believe the English word probably evolved from the
Portuguese *marmelo*, meaning 'quince'. I prefer the story that when Mary,
Queen of Scots, was poorly all she could stomach was this quince preserve,
earning it the nickname *Marie Malade,* sick Mary.

## MARZIPAN
Marzipan was traditionally eaten on St Mark's Day, 25 April. It comes
from the Latin *marci panis*, meaning Mark's bread.

## OMELETTE ARNOLD BENNETT
'Good taste is better than bad taste,' wrote Arnold Bennett (1867–1931),
'but bad taste is better than no taste at all.'

I would argue that *The Old Wives' Tale* is the finest novel written by an Englishman in the twentieth century. If you haven't yet read it, do. You won't be disappointed.

And if you haven't yet tasted an Omelette Arnold Bennett, let me tell you: your tastebuds haven't lived.

The story goes that Bennett, for a while the highest-earning author in the world, when writing his novel *The Imperial Palace*, stayed at London's Savoy Hotel where the chefs created this perfect omelette in his honour. The dish is still on the menu at the Savoy today. There are many versions in circulation, from the rudimentary to those involving bells and whistles and Béchamel sauce. Here is mine. I like to keep things simple:

smoked haddock
fish stock or milk
a good grating of Parmesan cheese
salt and pepper
3 eggs
butter
1 tablespoon double cream

Poach the fish, in fish stock or milk, for around 7 minutes. Remove the fish from the liquid and allow to cool, then flake it. Mix with the Parmesan and season to your taste.

Lightly beat the eggs. Melt the butter in an omelette pan. Pour in the beaten eggs and swirl to coat the pan. As the eggs start to set, top with the fish and cheese mixture. After a minute or so, pour over the cream. Transfer under the grill to brown the top. Sprinkle with a little extra cheese at this point, if you like. Once the top is looking lovely and golden, remove. *Voila!* Omelette Arnold Bennett *à la* Brandreth. **PAVLOVA** Anna Pavlova (1881–1931) was a world-famous Russian ballet dancer. This tasty dessert of meringue, fruit and cream was invented by a New Zealand chef to celebrate her tour of Australia and New Zealand in the 1920s.

## PEACH MELBA

Another dessert named after a great artist, the peach melba, predates the pavlova by about thirty years. It was created by the famous chef Georges Auguste Escoffier (1846–1935) to honour soprano Dame Nellie Melba's performance in Wagner's *Lohengrin* at Covent Garden in 1892. It is a delicious mixture of peaches, ice cream and raspberry sauce. Dame Nellie's name has its own story. Nellie Melba (1861–1931) was born Helen Mitchell and chose her stage name as a tribute to her place of birth, Melbourne.

## SANDWICH

One of the best-known eponyms in the language, the sandwich was named after John Montagu, 4th Earl of Sandwich (1718–92). A notorious gambler, the story goes that, in 1762, he spent twenty-four hours at the card table without leaving his chair. He demanded his cook bring him a constant supply of food that would not interfere with his game. He was delivered serving after serving of roast beef between two slices of bread and thus the 'sandwich' was born.

## SOLE VÉRONIQUE

I have come across several stories about the origin of this classic dish of poached fish with a white wine cream sauce and grapes. Most credit it to Escoffier and say it was created to celebrate the 1903 London opening of the opera *Véronique*. Although I haven't been able to trace its source, I prefer the story given by Rosie Boycott, in her book of eponyms, *Batty, Bloomers and Boycott*. She writes that the dish was invented by a Monsieur Malley, *saucier* at the Ritz, who gave instructions for the creation of the new dish to an under-chef and told him to prepare it for that evening's party. When the great man returned, he found his young colleague brimming with excitement and asked why. The under-chef replied that his wife had just given birth to their first child, a daughter, Véronique. '*Alors,*' Malley declared, 'we will call this new dish *filet de sole de Véronique*'.

## TOM COLLINS

A Tom Collins is a drink made with gin, lemon juice, sugar and water. Some say its name is a bastardised version of that of its creator, John

Collins, a nineteenth-century London bartender, who worked at Limmer's Old House. The recipe was first put down in writing in 1876 by the American 'mixologist' Jerry Thomas. He called it a Tom Collins because of the notorious 'Tom Collins Hoax' of 1874. The hoax was a practical joke that, apparently, was all the rage in New York at the time. The prank went like this:

CHAP ONE: *Have you seen Tom Collins?*

CHAP TWO: *No, who the deuce is Tom Collins?*

CHAP ONE: *Well I don't know much about him, but he says he knows all about you, and he is telling terrible lies about you.*

CHAP TWO: *Where can I find the scoundrel?*

CHAP ONE: *He generally hangs out at so-and-so's saloon.*

And off the prankee would run to the named bar to avenge his honour, while the prankster chuckled at his mischief-making.

New York bartenders got so used to the prank being played that, when an angry chap stormed into their saloon demanding to see a 'Mr Collins', they put their own spin on the joke. They would mix up the gin drink and bellow back 'Here's your Mr Collins!' and the rest of the punters would fall about laughing to see another hapless fellow falling victim to the prank.

# E

**is for**

**ENIGMA VARIATIONS**

'Enigma' was the name given to the encryption machine used by German cryptographers during the Second World War. British intelligence used the world's first programmable electronic digital computer named Colossus to decode Enigma encryptions. Colossus was able to sift through thousands of code permutations that Enigma apparently generated at random. By this means it was able to crack German coded messages far faster than human code breakers. If you have seen the 2014 film *The Imitation Game*, starring Benedict Cumberbatch, you will know all this.

Understanding a few principles about the relative frequencies in a language can be an invaluable tool in deciphering a secret message. In English:

The letters of highest frequency in descending order are: *e, t, a, o, n, i, r, s, h*. These account for 70 per cent of any English text.
The letters of median frequency in descending order are: *d, l, u, c, m*.
The letters of low frequency in descending order are: *p, f, y, w, g, b, v*.
The letters of lowest frequency, in descending order are: *k, x, q, j, z*.
Vowels account for about 40 per cent of the letters in a given text.
Half of all words in English begin with: *a, o, s, t, w*.
Half of all words in English end with: *d, e, s, t*.

In English the most frequently used double letters are: *ee, ff, oo, ss, tt.*
Other common doubles are: *cc, mm, nn, pp, rr.*

Using a basis of 10,000 word-counts, the ten commonest words in
English, arranged by letter totals, are, in order of frequency:

Two-letter: OF, TO, IN, IT, IS, BE, AS, AT, SO, WE
Three-letter: THE, AND, FOR, ARE, BUT, NOT YOU, ALL,
ANY, CAN
Four-letter: THAT, WITH, HAVE, THIS, WILL, YOUR, FROM,
THEY, KNOW, WANT

. . . . . . . . . . . . . . . . . . . . . . . . . . . . . . . . . . . . . . . . . . . . . . . . . . .

## COUNT ON ME

Having journeyed with me this far into the world of wordplay, you will
have discovered that words are seldom as simple as at first they seem.
They are wily little fellas and often lead double lives. The words that are
numbers are no exception.

For example, a 'forty-nine' is a customer in an American diner who leaves
without paying, 'sixty-six' is a two-handed card game and 'seventy-four' is
a type of South African fish.

To give you a flavour of what the world of numbers can do for your
vocabulary, here are twenty-five words you can do more than count on:

| *Zero* | *one* | *two* |
|---|---|---|
| a place in Lauderdale County, Mississippi | the ultimate being | a two-dollar bill |
| *three* | *four* | *five* |
| a rugby three-quarter | a type of racing boat | a basketball team |
| *six* | *seven* | *eight* |
| a high-scoring shot in cricket | the rower sitting behind the stroke in an . . . | the racing boat in which they row |

*nine*
a baseball team

*ten*
a measure of coal

*eleven*
a football or cricket team

*twelve*
a shilling

*thirteen*
an Irish term for an
English shilling

*fourteen*
a special order

*fifteen*
a rugby union team

*Sixteen*
a place in Meagher
County, Montana

*seventeen*
a corpse

*eighteen*
the size of a piece of
paper cut eighteen from
a sheet

*nineteen*
the score of zero in
cribbage

*twenty*
a twenty-dollar bill

*twenty-one*
a limeade

*twenty-two*
a rifle or pistol with a
.22 calibre

*twenty-three*
the end

*twenty-four*
a day

*twenty-five*
a variation of the card
game, spoil-five

. . . . . . . . . . . . . . . . . . . . . . . . . . . . . . . . . . . . . . . . . . . .

## COUNT UP: EON, TOW, THERE

If, like me, you enjoy the Channel 4 TV show *Countdown*, you will enjoy
games that involve numbers, letters and anagrams. Here I am going to
combine all three, taking the letters in the numbers from one to twenty
and seeing what anagrams can be made out of them. After one, two, three,
without digging deep into the dictionary, it's not easy.

*one*
eon

*two*
tow

*three*
there

*four*
rouf (obsolete form of
'roof' and 'rough')

*five*
veif (Old Norse for
something flapping and
waving)

*six*
xis (plural of xi, the
fourteenth letter of the
Greek alphabet)

**seven**
evens

**eight**
teigh (obsolete form of the past tense of 'tee', meaning to draw)

**nine**
nein ('nine' in the fourteenth century and the German for 'no')

**ten**
net

**eleven**
Leven (surname of, among others, pioneering biochemist Aaron Theodore Leven, whose achievements included some preliminary work on the identification of DNA)

**twelve**
velvet ('velvet' in the fifteenth and sixteenth centuries)

**thirteen**
threiten (Scots form of threaten)

**fourteen**
neetrouf (slang form of 'fourteen') – *really?*

**fifteen**
fiftene (medieval spelling of 'fifteen')

**sixteen**
sextine (a type of poem)

**eighteen**
teeheeing (present participle of 'teehee' meaning 'to titter')

**nineteen**
ninetene (fourteenth-century spelling of 'nineteen')

**twenty**
twynte ('twynt', an obsolete noun meaning a jot or participle)

If you spell out the numbers one, two, three, four, five, six, and so on, you will notice that they contain the vowels *e*, *i*, *o* and *u*, but not *a*. What is the first number that has an *a* in it when spelt as a word?

The answer is a long time coming: it's one hundred and one.

. . . . . . . . . . . . . . . . . . . . . . . . . . . . . . . . . . . . . . . . . . . . . . . . . . .

# CRYPTARITHMETIC

When is a letter of the alphabet not a letter? The answer is: when it's a number.

In these puzzles each letter represents a different digit. See if you can work out which letter represents which digit.

```
    E
    E
    E +
   ME
```

(E = 5, M = 1)

```
     O
    NO +
    ON
```

(O = 9, N = 8)

```
    SEND
    MORE +
   MONEY
```

(S = 9, E = 5, N = 6, D = 7, M = 1, O = 0, R = 8, Y = 2)

```
    TEN
    TEN
   FORTY +
   SIXTY
```

(T = 8, E = 5, N = 0, F = 2, O = 9, R = 7, Y = 6, S=3, I = 1, X = 4)

```
    TWO
    THREE
    SEVEN +
    TWELVE
```

(T = 1, W = 0, O = 6, H = 9, R = 7, E = 2, S = 8, V = 5, N = 4, L = 5)

· · · · · · · · · · · · · · · · · · · · · · · · · · · · · · · · · · · · · · · · · · · · · · · · · · · · ·

## SCIENTIFIC WORDS

Science has contributed thousands of new words to the language over
hundreds of years:

| | | |
|---|---|---|
| **magnetism (1616)** | **telescope (1619)** | **gravity (1642)** |
| **electricity (1646)** | **microscope (1656)** | **botany (1696)** |
| **zoology (1726)** | **oxygen (1789)** | **atom (1801)** |
| **evolution (1832)** | **bacterium (1847)** | **pasteurise (1881)** |
| **hormone (1904)** | **vitamin (1905)** | **penicillin (1928)** |

In fact, of the estimated million and more words currently in the language,
more than half are reckoned to be scientific terms.

· · · · · · · · · · · · · · · · · · · · · · · · · · · · · · · · · · · · · · · · · · · · · · · · · · · · ·

## MEASURING UP

I am with the guy who said, 'If God had meant us to go metric, how come
he gave Jesus twelve disciples?'

When it comes to using and understanding measurements most of us
get by with an everyday mix of units: metres, yards, kilometres, miles,
litres, pints, ounces, degrees Celsius and Fahrenheit, volts and watts.
For the specialists in different fields of scientific work and commerce,
the vocabulary of metrology is richer and more varied. See how your
friends measure up in terms of scientific savvy by giving them the units of
measurement in the left-hand column and asking them if they know what
they are or what they measure.

| | | |
|---|---|---|
| *anagastrom* | *becquerel* | *cable* |
| one hundred-millionth of a centimetre | measuring radiation activity | 240 yards |

*hertz*
frequency

*joule*
measuring work, energy,
quantity of heat

*kelvin*
measuring
thermodynamic
temperature

*link*
7.92 inches

*newton*
measuring force

*ohm*
measuring electric
resistance

*pascal*
measuring pressure, stress

*peck*
two gallons or a quarter
of a bushel

*quire*
24 sheets of paper

*radian*
plane angle between two
radii of a circle

*siemens*
measuring electric
conductance

*tesla*
measuring magnetic flux
density

*tun*
216 gallons

# D

### is for

## DOROTHY AND FRIENDS

'A friend of Dorothy' is a phrase for describing someone who is gay, and most authorities date the phrase to 1939 and the popularity of the film *The Wizard of Oz*, in which Judy Garland played the heroine, Dorothy Gale.

I love *The Wizard of Oz*, too, and have even played Dorothy on stage, but my favourite Dorothy is not the fictional Dorothy Gale but the all-too-real Dorothy Parker (1893–1967), poet, short-story writer, critic, wit.

Few played with words quite like Dorothy:

> The first thing I do in the morning is brush my teeth and sharpen my tongue.
> The cure for boredom is curiosity. There is no cure for curiosity.
> Beauty is only skin deep, but ugly goes clean to the bone.
> If you want to know what God thinks of money, just look at the people He gave it to.
> This is not a novel to be tossed aside lightly. It should be thrown with great force.
> I don't know much about being a millionaire, but I'll bet I'd be darling at it.
> Don't look at me in that tone of voice.

You can lead a horticulture, but you can't make her think.

Brevity is the soul of lingerie.

This wasn't just plain terrible, this was fancy terrible. This was terrible with raisins in it.

That woman speaks eighteen languages, and can't say, 'No,' in any of them.

Dorothy Parker was wonderfully witty, but awfully vulnerable:

> *Four be the things I'd have been better without:*
> *love, curiosity, freckles and doubt.*

And she had a problem:

> *I like to have a martini,*
> *Two at the very most.*
> *After three I'm under the table,*
> *After four I'm under my host.*

When it comes to witty wordmeisters, who else deserves a place in the *Word Play* Hall of Fame? I will give you an Englishman, an Irishman and two Americans, one male, one female – and five lines from each.

## NOËL COWARD (1899–1973)

> *I like long walks, especially when they are taken by people who annoy me.*
> *Television is for appearing on – not looking at.*
> *You ask my advice on acting? Speak clearly, don't bump into the furniture, and if you must have motivation, think of your pay packet on Friday.*
> *Work is more fun than fun.*
> *People are wrong when they say opera is not what it used to be. It is what it used to be. That is what's wrong with it.*

## OSCAR WILDE (1854–1900)

> *The world is a stage but the play is badly cast.*

*Always forgive your enemies, nothing annoys them more.*
*It is absurd to divide people into good and bad. People are either charming*
  *or tedious.*
*Some cause happiness wherever they go, some whenever they go.*
*I like men who have a future and women who have a past.*

## WOODY ALLEN (1935– )

*Eighty per cent of success is showing up.*
*When I was kidnapped my parents snapped into action: they rented out my*
  *room.*
*I'm not afraid of death – I just don't want to be there when it happens.*
*Life doesn't imitate art, it imitates bad television.*
*Not only is there no God, but try finding a plumber on a Sunday.*

## JOAN RIVERS (1933–2014)

*I don't exercise. If God wanted me to bend over he'd have put diamonds on*
  *the floor.*
*The first time I see a jogger smiling, I'll consider it.*
*I hate housework. You make the bed, you do the dishes and six months later*
  *you have to start all over again.*
*I told my mother-in-law that my house was her house, and she said, 'Get*
  *the hell off my property.'*
*Never floss with a stranger.*

. . . . . . . . . . . . . . . . . . . . . . . . . . . . . . . . . . . . . . . . . . . . . . . . .

## REPARTEE

'You can stroke people with words,' said F. Scott Fitzgerald, and when it
came to stroking people, he knew a thing or two.

You can choke people with words as well, and there must be a cruel
streak in me somewhere because I think I get more of a buzz from the
choking than the stroking words. Here comes a small collection of classic

epee-grams: sharp and witty ripostes that give delight and once hurt a little. Who knows whether the individual to whom I have attributed the lines actually originated them? You'll recall the famous story of how Oscar Wilde admired one of the witticisms of James Neil Whistler:

'I wish I'd said that,' said Wilde.

'You will, Oscar, you will,' Whistler replied.

Many of the best jests attributed to Oscar Wilde in Britain are attributed to Mark Twain in the United States (and vice versa) and some of the most memorable of the Algonquips were going the rounds in Britain and America when Parker, Kaufman, Benchley and the rest were still in short pants. Who actually said what, where and when hardly matters. What counts is the quality of the quips.

Dorothy Parker was discussing with another woman a man whom they both knew. 'You must admit,' said the friend, 'that he is always courteous to his inferiors.'
'Where does he find them?' asked Miss Parker.

Dorothy Parker and a young actress were both about to pass through the same doorway when the actress drew back with the words, 'Age before beauty.'
'Yes, my dear,' replied Miss Parker, 'and pearls before swine.'

Hotel receptionist (on telephone): 'I beg your pardon, Miss Ferber, but is there a gentleman in your room?'
Edna Ferber: 'I don't know. Wait a minute and I'll ask him.'

The dancer Isadora Duncan suggested to the playwright Bernard Shaw that they should have a child together. 'Imagine,' she said, 'a child with my body and your brain!'
'Yes,' replied Shaw, 'but suppose it had my body and your brain.'

A reporter once asked the great Italian composer Giuseppe Verdi for his full address. 'I think,' said Verdi, 'that Italy will be sufficient.'

At an ambassadorial banquet, after everyone was seated, one of the lady guests complained a little too loudly that, according to the official order of precedence, she ought to be seated next to the ambassador. She was found to be right and several of the guests had to get up and move down to make room for her. Feeling somewhat conscience-stricken at the fuss she had made, the lady said to the ambassador: 'You and your wife must find these questions of precedence extremely troublesome.' 'Not really,' was the reply. 'We have found by experience that the people who matter don't mind and the people who mind don't matter.'

A young man sitting next to a very attractive woman at dinner found himself at a loss for conversation and said, merely for the sake of saying something: 'I hate that man sitting opposite us.'
'You mean the man with the moustache?' asked the young woman. 'That's my brother.'
'No, no,' stammered the young man, hastily. 'I mean the one without the moustache.'
'That's my husband.'
'I know,' replied the young man. 'That's why I hate him.'

Zsa Zsa Gabor, when asked how many husbands she had had, replied, 'You mean apart from my own?'

Mahatma Gandhi was asked what he thought about Western civilisation. 'I think,' he said, 'that it would be a very good idea.'

The essence of repartee is that it should be spontaneous. Most of us, however, don't think of a deft and devastating retort until after the time for using it has passed. The French have a neat phrase to describe these 'wish words': *l'esprit d'escalier* – the witty remarks you think of while going down the stairs from a party. It's all too easy to be after-witted and come up with a post-riposte, but repartee that's actually departee is useless.

Friend: 'Isn't that dress a little young for you, dear?'
Dorothy Parker: 'Do you think so, dear? I think yours suits you perfectly. It always has.'

Barber: 'How would you like your hair cut, sir?'
George S. Kaufman: 'In silence.'

Reporter: 'Can you play the violin?'
George Burns: 'I don't know. I never tried.'

Nancy Astor: 'If you were my husband, I'd poison your coffee.'
Winston Churchill: 'If I were your husband, I'd drink it.'

Lewis Morris: 'There's a conspiracy of silence against me. What should I do, Oscar?'
Oscar Wilde: 'Join it.'

Notorious bore: 'I passed your house yesterday.'
Oscar Wilde: 'Thank you.'

Reporter: 'Do you know what an extravaganza is?'
Groucho Marx: 'I ought to. I married one.'

If you feel you simply haven't been blessed with rapier like wit, don't worry. As G. K. Chesterton said: 'Silence is the unbearable repartee.'

. . . . . . . . . . . . . . . . . . . . . . . . . . . . . . . . . . . . . . . . . . . . . . . . .

## WORDS ABOUT WORDS

*Man does not live by words alone, despite the fact that he sometimes has to eat them.*

Adlai Stevenson

*Some words teem with hidden meaning – like Basingstoke.*

W. S. Gilbert

*The trouble with words is that you never know whose mouth they've been in.*

Dennis Potter

*He writes so well he makes me feel like putting my quill back in my goose.*

Fred Allen

*Authors with a mortgage never get writer's block.*

Mavis Cheek

*A good novel tells us the truth about its hero; but a bad novel tells us the truth about its author.*

G. K. Chesterton

*'The cat sat on the mat' is not a story; 'the cat sat on the dog's mat' is a story.*

John le Carré

*The four most beautiful words in our common language: I told you so.*

Gore Vidal

*Good intentions are invariably ungrammatical.*

Oscar Wilde

*It usually takes more than three weeks to prepare a good impromptu speech.*

Mark Twain

*The trouble with the dictionary is that you have to know how a word is spelt before you can look it up to see how it is spelt.*

Will Cuppy

*The art of conversation is the art of hearing as well as of being heard.*

William Hazlitt

*Short words are best and the old words when short are the best of all.*

Winston Churchill

*Talkers are not good doers.*

William Shakespeare

Finally, don't forget:

*A fine quotation is a diamond on the finger of a man of wit, and a pebble in the hand of a fool.*

Joseph Roux

# C

## is for

## CROSSWORDS

In 2000, the actor Sir John Gielgud died, aged ninety-seven, with a completed crossword at his bedside. He attributed his longevity to his passion for crosswords. 'Completing the crossword is the only exercise I take,' he used to say. 'I smoke non-stop and solving the crossword clears the fumes.'

Gielgud filled every idle minute with his beloved crossword. Once, on a film set, another actor looked over Gielgud's shoulder when the great man had just completed his puzzle.

'Sir John, ten across? What on earth is DIDDYBUMS?'

'I don't know,' answered Gielgud airily, 'but it does fit frightfully well.'

2013 marked the centenary of the crossword puzzle and people around the globe, in their millions, are still hooked on this classic word game. It appeals to all sorts and has done from the start. In 1925 Buckingham Palace released an official statement declaring Queen Mary an enthusiast; in 1954 her granddaughter, Princess Margaret, went one better, entering the crossword competition in *Good Housekeeping* and winning first prize.

The Queen enjoys a crossword (the *Daily Telegraph*'s, I'm told), and so do some of those banged up at Her Majesty's pleasure. Dedication to completing the crossword has been given more than once as an excuse for missing a court appearance and, in the 1920s, one lag expressed delight at his incarceration as it would give him time to finish his puzzle without distraction.

What is it about this enigmatic grid of black and white squares that holds such universal appeal?

Crosswords exercise our little grey cells, of course; and they test our vocabulary and general knowledge. But the urge to solve a crossword is about more than mental gymnastics. Humans are by nature problem solvers. The impulse that led us to the wheel also brought us the crossword. And we love the crossword because, unlike so many things in our complicated lives, the puzzle is solvable and finite: there is a right answer. The crossword allows us to bring order to chaos. It challenges, absorbs, comforts and distracts us. As Martha Petheridge, the first female crossword-puzzle editor, said at the height of the Great Depression, 'Who can worry about the rent when you are trying to solve twenty-five down?'

The crossword was a Christmas gift to us all from a man named Arthur Wynne. Originally from Merseyside, Wynne was the son of the editor of the *Liverpool Mercury*. He moved to New York in 1905 and pursued his own career in newspapers. In 1913 he was working at the *New York World* as editor of the 'Fun' section. Wanting something a little bit special for that year's seasonal supplement, he came up with the 'Word-Cross'. Derived from the ancient game of acrostics and the Victorian pastime of word squares, Wynne's first puzzle was diamond-shaped. It was published on Sunday, 21 December 1913, with thirty-one simple clues, no black squares and very little fanfare.

The story might have ended there, but a few readers wrote in expressing their enthusiasm for the new brain-teaser and, much to the chagrin of the typesetters, it was back the following week. With a catchy new name, the 'Crossword' spent the next ten years at the *World*, building a loyal but limited following. It hit the big-time in 1924, when a pair of Harvard graduates, Dick Simon and Max Schuster, decided to go into publishing. The young bucks had set up a company, found offices and employed a secretary – but one thing was missing: an idea.

Enter Dick's aunt Wixie. One afternoon, over tea, she asked her nephew if he knew where she could buy a book of crossword puzzles, like the ones in her favourite newspaper. Dick and Max hotfooted it down to the offices of the *World* and came away with an agreement to publish the first-ever book of crosswords. Twelve months later 400,000 copies had been sold, a worldwide phenomenon launched and a publishing empire born.

America went crossword crazy. Everywhere you looked people were hunched over their puzzle books. There were crosswords on dresses and crosswords in church – displayed beneath the pulpit, with answers relating to the sermon of the day. Theatre skits were performed about the craze, with puzzles featuring in the printed programmes. Couples announced their engagement by crossword. Fifteen thousand people fought their way into the Chicago public library on a single day to find the solution to a particularly fiendish clue; the Baltimore and Ohio Railroad put dictionaries in every carriage of every train and one unfortunate Brooklyn housewife was shot dead when she refused to help her husband solve his puzzle.

The first crossword published in the United Kingdom appeared in the *Sunday Express* on 2 November 1924. After initial scepticism, including an article in *The Times* branding the crossword a menace that had 'enslaved America', we succumbed to the puzzle's allure; but, being the intellectual powerhouses we are, the challenge of the straightforward 'definitional' crossword soon began to pall. A new, distinctly British, style of crossword began to emerge: the cryptic.

The literary critic Edward Powys Mathers began setting crosswords in the *Observer* in 1926. He used the pseudonym Torquemada, after the notorious Spanish inquisitor. His work as a critic and translator had given him a love for, and skill with, language. His clues contained puns, anagrams and large dollops of wit. During the late 1920s and 1930s

Mathers, along with Adrian Bell at *The Times* and Afrit at the *Listener*, pioneered and developed the cryptic crossword.

The cryptic was the complicated, intellectually brooding cousin of the definitional – it had mystique and depth; it played hard to get with a capricious, whimsical air. When the solution was 'water', the clue was no longer 'a chemical compound containing two molecules of hydrogen and one of oxygen' but the elliptical 'HIJKLMNO'. An 'apex' wasn't the highest point but 'a kiss from a monkey' and, on the mat, 'roast mules went topsy-turvy'.

It was through the cryptic that the special 'language' of the crossword developed. 'We hear' indicates a pun; 'strangely', 'unusual' or 'in a muddle' point towards an anagram; 'returning', a word reversal. But be wary: 'upset' could indicate a reversal or an anagram, and 'about' an anagram or an envelopment. Like any language, there are nuances and subtleties, and the more crosswords one completes the more fluent one becomes. (Here's a quick beginner's tip: the definition of the word is always contained in the clue – either at the beginning or at the end; separate it out and you will be on your way.)

Such is the mystique of the cryptic that it was even suspected of being involved in espionage. In the run-up to the D Day landings in 1944, Allied commanders became alarmed. Morning after morning the *Daily Telegraph* crossword appeared with yet another clue that led to a codeword for the operation – OVERLORD, NEPTUNE, MULBERRY. Nearly a dozen appeared in total. The clues had been set by one man, Leonard Dawe, the chief crossword setter at the paper for nearly twenty years. MI5 descended on his home in Surrey. Dawe managed to convince them that it was nothing more than the most incredible of coincidences.

Over the last century the crossword has entered the history books, the record books – the world's biggest crossword had 3,149 clues across and 3,185 clues down – and our hearts. There have been many imitators – and, in recent years, a numerical challenge in the form of the mathematical teaser, Sudoku – yet the appeal of the classic crossword remains undimmed.

. . . . . . . . . . . . . . . . . . . . . . . . . . . . . . . . . . . . . . . . . . . . . . . . . . . .

# BRANDRETH'S FIVE FAVOURITE CRYPTIC CLUES

1. An early gem from Torquemada: 'The artist has been cooked about with herbs' (5)
2. A clue from Ximenes, considered by many to be the master setter: 'Excitement – it will interrupt the end of term' (8)
3. The two millionth clue set by the *Telegraph*'s (and the world's) most prolific setter, Roger Squires: 'Two girls, one on each knee' (7)
4. 'A jammed cylinder' (5,4)
5. 'A stiff examination' (4, 6)

## *SOLUTIONS*

1. Saged
2. Hilarity
3. Patella
4. Swiss roll
5. Post mortem

# B

**is for**

**BREVITY**

This won't take long.

Calvin Coolidge (1872–1933), thirtieth president of the United States, was noted for his taciturnity. Once, at a dinner at the White House, an attractive young lady turned to him and said, 'Mr President, I've got a bet that I can get at least three words out of you tonight.'

Coolidge looked at her and smiled. 'You lose.'

I have held the record for making the longest-ever after-dinner speech. Until recently I believed I also held the record for writing the shortest poem. It seems not. The poet and philosopher Eli Siegel (1902–78) wrote a poem that he called 'One Question' and in it he manages to encapsulate in just four letters the essence of mankind's quest for self-understanding:

*I*
*Why?*

In the history of letters, the briefest romantic correspondence has to be the exchange between the Prince de Joinville (1818–1900) and the actress

Rachel Félix (1821–58). In 1840, seeing her on stage one evening, the prince sent his card to her dressing room with the words, 'Where? When? How much?'

Rachel replied: 'Your place. Tonight. Free.'

Even briefer, unbeatably so, was the correspondence that took place in 1862 between the French novelist Victor Hugo and his publisher. The author was on holiday and, anxious to know how his new novel, *Les Misérables*, was selling, wrote to the publisher: '?'

The reply came: '!'

# A

**is for**

## ALL'S WELL THAT ENDS WELL

. . . . . . . . . . . . . . . . . . . . . . . . . . . . . . . . . . . . . . . . . . . .

### BEFORE I GO

Towards the end of their lives most people make a will. In his, the German poet Heinrich Heine stipulated that in order to inherit his fortune his wife must remarry 'so that there will be at least one man to regret my death'.

Where there's a will there's often an insight into the life and character of the person whose will it is:

From the Last Will and Testament of Napoleon Bonaparte, signed at St Helena on 15 April 1821:

1. *I die in the apostolical Roman religion, in the bosom of which I was born, more than fifty years since.*
2. *It is my wish that my ashes may repose on the banks of the Seine, in the midst of the French people, whom I have loved so well.*

3. *I have always had reason to be pleased with my dearest wife, Marie Louise. I retain for her my last moment, the most tender sentiments – I beseech her to watch, in order to preserve my son from the snares which yet environ his infancy.*

4. *I recommend to my son, never to forget that he was born a French prince, and never to allow himself to become an instrument in the hands of the triumvirs who oppress the nations of Europe; he ought never to fight against France, or to injure her in any manner; he ought to adopt my motto – 'Everything for the French people.'*

5. *I die prematurely, assassinated by the English oligarchy . . . the French nation will not be slow in avenging me.*

From the Last Will and Testament of Alfred Bernhard Nobel, signed in Paris on 27 November 1895:

*The whole of my remaining estate shall be dealt with in the following way: The capital shall be invested by my executors in safe securities and shall constitute a fund, the interest on which shall be annually distributed in the form of prizes to those who, during the preceding year, shall have conferred the greatest benefit on mankind. The said interest shall be divided into five parts, which shall be apportioned as follows: one part to the person who shall have made the most important discovery or inventions within the field of physics; one part to the person who shall have made the most important chemical discovery or improvement; one part to the person who shall have made the most important discovery within the domain of physiology or medicine; one part to the person who shall have produced in the field of literature the most outstanding work of an idealistic tendency; and one part to the person who shall have done the most or the best work for fraternity among nations, and for the abolition or reduction of standing armies and for the holding and promotion of peace congresses. It is my express wish that in awarding the prizes no consideration whatever shall be given to the nationality of the candidate, so that the most worthy shall receive the prize where he be Scandinavian or not.*

The Will of a Philadelphia industrialist who died in 1947:

*To my wife I leave her lover, and the knowledge that I wasn't the fool she thought I was.*

*To my son I leave the pleasure of earning a living. For twenty-five years he thought the pleasure was mine. He was mistaken.*

*To my daughter I leave $100,000. She will need it. The only business her husband ever did was to marry her.*

*To my valet, I leave the clothes he has been stealing from me for ten years. Also, the fur coat he wore last winter while I was in Palm Beach.*

*To my chauffeur, I leave my cars. He almost ruined them and I want him to have the satisfaction of finishing the job.*

*To my partner, I leave the suggestion that he take some clever man in with him at once if he expects to do any business.*

. . . . . . . . . . . . . . . . . . . . . . . . . . . . . . . . . . . . . . . .

## AFTER I'M GONE

After you've gone, what's left in terms of words, other than your will? Just your epitaph, I suppose – if you are fortunate enough to get one. John Gay (1685–1732), poet and playwright, wrote his own:

*Life is a jest; and all things show it.*
*I thought so once; but now I know it.*

Call mine a grave sense of humour, but one of the word games I like to play involves drafting my own epitaph. For inspiration I use these, classics of the genre. Here are three of my favourites:

Epitaph on a man called Longbottom who died young:

*Ars longa, vita brevis*

Epitaph on a pioneer aviator:

*There was an old man who averred*
*He had learnt how to fly like a bird.*

*Cheered by thousands of people*
*He leapt from the steeple.*
*This tomb states the date it occurred.*

Epitaph in Enosburg, Vermont:

*Here lies the body of our Anna*
*Done to death by a banana,*
*It wasn't the fruit that laid her low*
*But the skin of the thing that made her go.*

Those three are supposed to be genuine, but I think they are too good to be true. I know the ones that follow are authentic:

Epitaph in Burlington, New Jersey, 1798:

*Here lies the body of Sudan Lowder*
*Who burst while drinking a Seidlitz powder.*
*Called from this world to her Heavenly Rest*
*She should have waited till it effervesced.*

Epitaph in Tombstone, Arizona, 1958:

*Here lies*
*Les Moore*
*Four slugs*
*From a 44*
*No Les*
*No More*

Epitaph on a drunkard:

*He had his beer*
*From year to year,*
*And then his bier had him*

Epitaph on Martha Snell:

> *Poor Martha Snell, she's gone away,*
> *She would if she could but she could not stay;*
> *She'd two bad legs and baddish cough*
> *But her legs it was that carried her off.*

Epitaph on Ann Mann:

> *Here lies the body of Ann Mann,*
> *Who lived an old woman*
> *And died an old Mann.*

The Tired Woman's Epitaph:

> *Here lies a poor woman who always was tired,*
> *She lived in a house where help was not hired;*
> *Her last words on earth were: 'Dear Friends, I am going*
> *Where washing ain't done, nor sweeping, nor sewing;*
> *But everything there is exact to my wishes;*
> *For where they don't eat there's no washing of dishes.*
> *I'll be where loud anthems will always be ringing,*
> *But, having no voice, I'll be clear of the singing.*
> *Don't mourn for me now; don't mourn for me never –*
> *I'm going to do nothing for ever and ever.'*

Epitaph from Aberdeen, Scotland:

> *Here lie the bones of Elizabeth Charlotte,*
> *Born a virgin, died a harlot;*
> *She was aye virgin at 17,*
> *A remarkable thing in Aberdeen.*

Epitaph at Great Torrington, Devon:

> *Here lies a man who was killed by lightning;*

*He died when his prospects seemed to be brightening.*
*He might have cut a flash in this world of trouble,*
*But the flash cut him, and he lies in the stubble.*

Epitaph from Australia:

*God took our flower – our little Nell:*
*he thought he too would like a smell.*

Epitaph on Arabella Young:

*Beneath this stone*
*A lump of clay*
*lies Arabella Young*
*Who on the 21st May*
*1771*
*Began to hold her tongue.*

John Dryden's epitaph for his wife:

*Here lies my wife.*
*Here let her lie!*
*Now she's at rest*
*And so am I.*

Epitaph on John Wood:

*Here lies John Bun,*
*He was killed by a gun;*
*His name was not Bun, but Wood;*
*but Wood would not rhyme with Gun,*
*but Bun would.*

Epitaph on a dentist:

*Stranger! Approach this spot with gravity!*

*John Brown is filling his last cavity.*

Epitaph on a child of seven months:

> *If I am so quickly done for,*
> *what on earth was I begun for?*

Epitaph on a wife:

> *The children of Israel wanted bread*
> *The Lord he sent them manna;*
> *But this good man he want a wife*
> *And the devil sent him Anna.*

· · · · · · · · · · · · · · · · · · · · · · · · · · · · · · · · · · · · · · · · · · · · · · ·

## LAST WORDS

*Zynder*, meaning *cinder*, is the last word in the last volume of the world's largest dictionary. The compilers could hardly have thought of a more appropriate last word. Ashes to ashes, dust to dust, zynders to zynders: even those who protest that they never go to funerals have to in the end.

Even if we don't want to, we all die. And even if we don't mean to, we all utter last words. If we are famous or infamous someone may be on hand to record our last words – or to improve on them if they don't seem up to scratch.

Deciding your last words is a great game to play when you're young, and at any age you can enjoy inventing apt last words for others:

> *The atheist*: 'I was kidding all along.'
> *The lift operator*: 'Going up?'
> *The judge*: 'I have no precedent for this.'
> *The bridge player*: 'I pass.'
> *The train driver*: 'End of the line.'

*The gossip*: 'I'm dying to tell someone.'
*The fatted calf in the parable of the prodigal son*: 'I hear the young
master has returned.'

Few could – or would want to – rival the famous last words of General
Sedgwick who, in 1864, during the American Civil War, peered over the
parapet at the Battle of Spotsylvania and remarked, 'They couldn't hit an
elephant at this dis – '

And I believe that these are authentic, too:

*Dylan Thomas, poet*: 'I have had eighteen straight whiskies. I think
that is the record.'
*Lord Palmerston, prime minister*: 'Die, my dear doctor, that's the last
thing I shall do!'
*Edmund Kean, actor*: 'Dying is easy. Comedy is hard.'
*Lytton Strachey, writer*: 'If this is dying then I don't think much of it.'
*Elvis Presley, singer*: 'I'm going to the bathroom to read.'

According to Steve Jobs's sister, the Apple founder's last words were: 'Oh,
wow. Oh, wow. Oh, wow.'

*Raphael, painter*: 'Happy.'
*Frank Sinatra, singer*: 'I'm losing it.'

Marie Antoinette stepped on her executioner's foot on her way to the
guillotine. Her last words: '*Pardonnez-moi, Monsieur.*'

*Sir Isaac Newton*: 'I don't know what I may seem to the world. But
as to myself I seem to have been only like a boy playing on the
seashore and diverting myself now and then in finding a smoother
pebble or a prettier shell than the ordinary, whilst the great ocean of
truth lay all undiscovered before me.'
*Leonardo da Vinci*: 'I have offended God and mankind because my
work did not reach the quality it should have.'

Murderer James W. Rodgers was put in front of a firing squad in Utah and asked if he had a last request. He replied: 'Bring me a bullet-proof vest.'

*John Wayne, actor, to his wife*: 'Of course I know who you are. You're my girl. I love you.'

Playwright Eugene O'Neill was born in a room at the Broadway Hotel in New York and died, age sixty-five, in a Boston hotel: 'I knew it! I knew it! Born in a hotel room and, goddamn it, dying in a hotel room.'

*Groucho Marx*: 'This is no way to live.'
*Emily Dickinson, poet*: 'I must go in, for the fog is rising.'
*Cecil Rhodes, empire builder*: 'So little done, so much to do.'
*William Hazlitt, essayist*: 'Well, I've had a happy life.'
*Heinrich Heine, poet*: 'God will forgive me. It's his profession.'

And to end with? I have found three that feel particularly fitting as we bring *Word Play* to a close.

The last words of Dominique Bonhours, Jesuit priest and grammarian:

*I am about to – or I am going to – die; either expression is used.*

Joseph Henry Green, surgeon, was checking his own pulse as he lay dying. His last word:

*Stopped.*

And finally? The last words of the poet Matthew Prior:

*The end*

# Acknowledgements

I have been collecting words about words for more than half a century. Those to whom I know I am indebted for their contributions to this book include Geoffrey Chaucer, William Shakespeare, Samuel Johnson, P G Wodehouse, Charles and Alice Brandreth (my parents), Harold Gardiner (my old English teacher) and an assortment of friends, colleagues and word-meisters, among them: Dave Crosland, Michael Curl, Clive Dickinson, Darryl Francis, Alan F G Lewis, Peter Newby and Paul Williams. I am especially indebted to my daughter, Saethryd Brandreth, for her editorial contribution, and to my publisher, Mark Booth, and to the team at Coronet who have helped bring *Word Play* into being, notably Fiona Rose, Kerry Hood, Hazel Orme and Linda Crosby.

Thirty-five years ago, when I wrote *The Joy of Lex* and *More Joy of Lex*, the precursors to this book, I was inspired by the work of the great Willard Espy, especially his *Almanac of Words at Play*, and by two endlessly instructive and entertaining journals: A Ross Eckler's *Word Ways* and Laurence Urdang's *Verbatim*. More recently, as Patron of The Queen's English Society, I have been enjoying the QES journal, *Quest*. Once upon a time, when working on a book like this, you did your research in the pages of learned journals and in the library. Now you do much of it on the internet. In some ways it's easier: you don't have to leave the house. In other ways it's more challenging: how relia-ble are your sources? I am hoping that what I have shared with you in *Word Play* is both interesting and accurate. That said, if you know I have got something wrong do let me know so that I can put it right. One of the advantages of the e-age is that you can contact me directly. You will find me on Twitter: @GylesB1.

In preparing *Word Play* I have consulted dozens of dictionaries, from *The English Dialect Dictionary* (1905) to *The Handbook of American Indians North of Mexico* (also 1905). I have relied most, however, on *The Oxford English Dictionary* and its assorted supplements and offshoots, and *Webster's New International Dictionary*. In the 1970s, I first met Dr Robert Burchfield, then editor of the *OED*, and Dr Frederick C Mish, editorial director of G and C Merriam, publishers of the Merriam-Webster Dictionaries. I am greatly indebted to them and to their colleagues and successors for their guidance and encouragement. I am especially grateful, of course, to my friend Susie Dent, *OED* alumna and doyenne of *Countdown*'s Dictionary Corner, for her years of friendship and inspiration.

From *Batty, Bloomers and Boycott* by Rosie Boycott to *Letters Play!* by my friend Richard Whiteley, I have been reading books about words since I first dipped into my father's collection of books by Ivor Brown and Ernest Gowers in the 1950s. If, inadvertently, I have stolen other people's flowers to arrange in my wordaholic's vase without proper acknowledgement, do please let me know and I will endeavour to put matters right in future editions.

Immediately I am grateful to the following authors and copyright holders for permission to reproduce their material here: palindromes from *Language on Vacation* by Dmitri A Borgmann; *Tom Swifties* by Roy Bongartz; rejection letters from *Dear Sir, Drop Dead* by Donald Carrol; Franglais from *Let's Parler Franglais* by Alan Coren; Xeme from *Word Power* by Hunter Diack; Authorisms and Lifelaws from *The Official Rules* by Paul Dickson; Winifred's Bloomers from *Noel Coward* by Cole Lesley; Quoting Shakespeare by Bernard Levin; superpuns from Marcus Brigstocke, Milton Jones and Tim Vine, and Violinists are Unstrung from *A Pun My Soul* by Alan F G Lewis; wills from *Where There's a Will* by Robert S Menchin; predictive text typos from *Just My Typo* by Drummond Moir; Dorothy Parker's review of Lay Sermons from *The Portable Dorothy Parker*; From Acclumsid to Zuche from *Poplollies and Bellibones* by Susan Kelz Sperling; Bushisms from *The Bush Tragedy* by Jacob Weinsberg; *Ma Crepe Suzette* by Kenneth Williams.

A final word of thanks must go to my brilliant friend Ray Ward. He read *Word Play* in hardback and sent me an array of corrections and improvements that I have included in this paperback edition where I could. I have learnt much from Ray, including the fact that 'buffalo' is an uncommon but legitimate verb meaning to bully, intimidate or baffle, so that 'Buffalo buffalo Buffalo buffalo buffalo buffalo Buffalo buffalo' is a grammatically correct sentence, meaning 'Buffalo (bison) from Buffalo (the city) buffalo (bully or baffle) other buffalo (bison) from Buffalo (the city), who themselves buffalo (bully or baffle) other buffalo (bison) from Buffalo (the city).'